Decolonial Marxism

Decolonial Marxism

Essays from the Pan-African Revolution

Walter Rodney

Edited by
Asha Rodney, Patricia Rodney,
Ben Mabie and Jesse Benjamin

VERSO
London • New York

First published by Verso 2022

1 3 5 7 9 10 8 6 4 2

Verso
UK: 6 Meard Street, London W1F 0EG
US: 388 Atlantic Avenue, Brooklyn, NY 11217
versobooks.com

Verso is the imprint of New Left Books

ISBN-13: 978-1-83976-411-0
ISBN-13: 978-1-83976-414-1 (US EBK)
ISBN-13: 978-1-83976-413-4 (UK EBK)

British Library Cataloguing in Publication Data
A catalogue record for this book is available from the British Library

Library of Congress Cataloging-in-Publication Data
A catalog record for this book is available from the Library of Congress

Typeset in Sabon by MJ & N Gavan, Truro, Cornwall
Printed and bound by CPI Group (UK) Ltd, Croydon, CR0 4YY

Contents

IV: Building Socialism

Foreword

Walter Rodney Completes Marx

Ngũgĩ wa Thiong'o

Colonization with all its interlinked economic, political, cultural and even psychic dimensions, has been central to the making of capitalist modernity. It was the new colonies in the West that fuelled Atlantic slave trade with the African body as commodity, and slavery, with the African body providing unpaid labor for the colonial plantations, and racism, with all its dehumanization of the African body and mind. Negation of the African humanity. All these fueled the development of Europe and the West. The major cities of Europe were built by riches from slave trade, slavery and colonialism. Three of the major nuclear powers today – the USA, Britain and France – were also major players in enslavement and colonization. Western Modernity is rooted in the looting of a continent.

But one of the most frequently propagated colonial mythologies is that of Europe and the West having developed Africa. All the major thinkers of the European enlightenment from Hume to Kant and Hegel advanced the same thesis also embodied in Missionary and Explorer narratives about the continent. The myth continues today with the West seen as donor to Africa.

It was Walter Rodney who best articulated a refutation of that mythology in his now universally acclaimed classic: *How Europe Underdeveloped Africa*. This and Fanon's *The*

Wretched of the Earth are really the basic material for helping make sense of the contradictions which still haunt Africa and all the formerly colonized of Asia and South America. The African post-colonial elite is very protective of their phony identities; Francophone, Anglophone and Lusophone. But they are never protective of the resources of the conntinent. Ninety per cent of these resources, including diamonds, gold, oil, copper, cobalt, uranium are still owned by Western corporations. Africa, the biggest continent in the world, continues to be the main donor to Europe and the West.

See the contradiction. Europe gave Africa the resources of their accents, the basis of those phony identities. Africa gave Europe access to the resources of the continent. Accents for Access: that is really the story of Africa's underdevelopment by Europe, well captured and analyzed by Walter Rodney.

Rodney was able to do this because of his Marxian approaches to history which enabled him to see clearly the intertwinmen of economics, politics, culture and values, which, under capitalism rests on the primary contradiction between labor and capital. But he was able to add the racial and colonial dimension to this. Race, gender and colonialism were integral to development of capitalism to its current stage of global imperialism.

Colonization is colonizer and colonized. So decolonization at the economic, political, cultural and psychic levels has to involve both the colonizer and the colonized. Even our methodologies need to be decolonized from their Eurocentric basis. Marxist class analysis needs the dimensions of race and colony and gender to complete it.

These essays, *Decolonial Marxism,* will be an important companion to our continued learning from the same Pan-African mind that showed us clearly how Europe underdeveloped the continent. With the dimesnions of race and colony added to class analysis, Rodney completes Marx.

I

Marxist Theory
and Mass Action

1

A Brief Tribute to Amilcar Cabral

In Amilcar Cabral, Africa had a giant who bridged the gap between theory and practice, and hence represented the embodiment of revolutionary *praxis*. Cabral was a theoretician of the highest calibre – but only because he was involved in changing the ugly realities of colonized African society. He supervised a People's War of Liberation with great distinction – but only because of the soundness of his scientific worldview and his capacity to apply it penetratingly to the social relations of Guinea-Bissau.

The few pages which Cabral devoted to an analysis of the African societies of Guinea-Bissau are of extraordinary perceptiveness and authenticity. This is understandable, since the accuracy of the interpretation was literally a matter of life and death. The massive task of political mobilization that the African Party for the Independence of Guinea and Cape Verde (Partido Africano da Independência da Guiné e Cabo Verde – PAIGC) so strikingly achieved was based on a correct appreciation of such niceties as the relations between youth and elders among the Balanta people; or ties between a quasi-feudal Fula lord and his aliens, or the role of the itinerant Manding trader within the colonial economy. Based on this political mobilization, the military conflict has in turn been decidedly resolved in favour of the PAIGC in most parts of Guinea-Bissau.

It is the element of commitment which sets Cabral apart from the common run of intellectuals who boast of being 'neutral' and 'un-biased', thereby passively accepting the perpetuation of the colonial status quo. At the same time,

Cabral's work as a revolutionary African intellectual also contrasts sharply with the purpose of the early European anthropologists who openly oriented their study towards the maintenance of colonial rule, by writing 'intelligence reports' for the occupying power. Cabral was serving as an intelligence officer of the army of liberation, when he unravelled the intricacies of segmentary lineage groups and the stratified social formations which exist in Guinea-Bissau. The fact that the Portuguese colonial regime has virtually fallen apart in contrast to the surging growth in the area of liberated Guinea is the ultimate proof of the reactionary nature of the colonial relationship and the progressive character of the intellectual work carried out by Cabral and his colleagues.

Paradoxical as it may seem, Cabral (leader of a nationalist movement) was constantly playing down the importance of mere nationalism. He did so through perceiving the difference between a political outlook limited to nationalism and one which encompassed a revolutionary transformation of the people's lives along Socialist lines. It is this revolutionary transformation that was the supreme objective in Cabral's eyes. This he stressed on the innumerable occasions when he stood before the villagers of Guinea-Bissau. He put it to them that:

> Independence is not just a simple matter of expelling the Portuguese, of having a flag and a national anthem. The people must be secure in the knowledge that no one is going to steal their labour, that the wealth of the country is not going into somebody else's pocket. Even today the Guinean people stand naked and are still afraid of the river, the rain and the forest. We tell the Guinean people that by their work the river will be tamed, and the rain will be put to good use.

Here was the straightforward language meant to fortify against further manifestations of neo-colonialism, the growth of a national bourgeoisie, and the perpetuation of ignorance and fear among the masses.

4

Cabral saw that the nationalist struggle chronologically preceded the Socialist revolution, but that it was imperative to prepare for the subsequent Socialist revolution from the onset of the national phase. Armed struggle was the unavoidable path to the liberation of Guinea. Yet, politics has remained in command throughout. The PAIGC has constantly involved itself in the cadre formation, mass mobilization and the creation of democratic Socialist structures and attitudes. All of these programmes benefited from the long-term vision of Amilcar Cabral, leader of the PAIGC since its inception in September 1956.

For those of us who aspire towards a deeper appreciation of historical dialectics, Cabral's analyses are models for study; one doubts whether even the sceptic can remain unimpressed by the strength and flexibility of his arguments concerning the role of respective strata and classes within the Guinean revolution. Cabral broke away from a rigid categorization of this or that class as 'reactionary' or 'revolutionary'. Instead, he was concerned with the dual revolutionary/reactionary potential of most of the elements involved in the nationalist struggle. He examined the specifics of Guinean society and pinpointed the methods by which revolutionary potential could be realized under the guidance of the PAIGC.

Franz Fanon, perhaps more than anyone else, is responsible for popularizing the notion of the revolutionary nature of the African peasantry. Speaking at the Franz Fanon Centre in Milan, Cabral found it necessary to caution that while the peasantry had the greatest objective interest in the struggle, the peasantry was not a revolutionary force – rather it constituted the principal physical force available to the armed struggle.

The contradiction between himself and Fanon is more apparent than real. What Cabral is warning against is the facile conclusion drawn by some that the peasants will be *spontaneously* revolutionary. Bitter experience has shown that this is not true even for the industrial working class, in spite of the highly socialized nature of industrial production. Cabral was in effect renewing the battle against the concept of revolutionary spontaneity and restating the case for painstaking mobilization by the most conscious elements. Then, and only then, would the peasantry become a revolutionary force.

Great political leaders derive their stature from their relationship to a given social class, usually when that class is on the ascendant. In this instance, Cabral's greatness is tied into the forward movement of the labouring population of the Guinea-Bissau, Africa and the Third World. Not only is he a product and spokesman for that movement, but he has been an active agent in moulding the force of change in an anti-imperialist direction. Indeed, one can say that Amilcar Cabral still remains an active agent working against imperialism, both through the legacy of his thought and in the structures he left behind. It would be idle and dangerous to deny that the enemy still has the capacity to sow divisions and cause confusion within the Guinean liberation movement. Cabral's own assassination is testimony to this effect. But at a certain point, a movement becomes irreversible, and all the efforts of the enemy smack of desperation and insanity, as we have seen in the last days before the Vietnamese people achieved their historic victory over US imperialism. Victory in Guinea Bissau, for the popular forces, in Angola and in Mozambique, is the only justification that Cabral would require, and on all fronts that victory is in the making.

2

Masses in Action

Over the past decade, Guyana has been stirred into a state of constant self-examination. The results, however, have been meagre and disappointing, largely because the discussion has been confined to the period after 1953, and to the personalities, failures and recriminations of that era.[1] There is a tacit assumption that only in 1953 did mass involvement in Guyanese political affairs begin, national political leaders arise, and racial suspicion and strife find expression. Guyanese history began a long time ago. Even the beginning of the twentieth century is an arbitrary and not entirely satisfactory point at which to take up the story of the Guyanese masses; but it does allow some scope for at least an interim examination of the Guyanese past in terms which are relevant to the working class.

By the end of the nineteenth century the net result of nearly three centuries of varied activity by external forces on the Guyana mainland was the creation of a small society limited to the coastlands, to the production of sugar and to all that went with sugar in terms of class stratification and foreign exploitation. Today, the fundamentals of the situation remain unaltered, with sugar accounting for more than 40 per cent of national revenues. Yet the old colonial system had its critics; the most serious of all possible critics – the working masses. It is the contention here that both the marginal modification of an entirely sugar-bound society and the hostility evoked by that society are to be traced to the years after 1900, and in particular to the period of the First World War.

Bauxite

In the economic sphere the principal supplement to sugar in Guyana today is bauxite. At the outbreak of the First World War a number of mining concessions were issued when geological evidence indicated that extensive deposits of bauxite were likely to be encountered in Guyana. The largest concession was held by the Demerara Bauxite Company, which was registered locally in 1916, backed by American and Canadian financial interests. The Demerara Bauxite Company built the town of Mackenzie before the end of the war; and early in November 1919 there was a *Chronicle* report that the company had just exported 1,500 tons of bauxite – its fourth shipment.[2]

All Guyanese welcomed the discovery of bauxite, but there was a revealing debate about the role of American capital, when it was ascertained that the Northern Alumina Company of Toronto, of which the Demerara Bauxite Company was a subsidiary, was merely a facade for US capitalists. Primarily, the question was posed in terms of British imperial interests versus those of the United States; and in fact the British government suspended the granting of mineral concessions in Guyana during the latter stages of the war, with the hope that British capital would give a better account of itself after the struggle in Europe had ended. But there was also the underlying assumption in the Guyanese press that local interests could well have been jeopardized by US capital, and local entrepreneurs demanded the opportunity to be allowed to raise capital and take the initiative in the bauxite industry. As it turned out, the North American financiers and industrialists had the field to themselves. The Demerara Bauxite Company quickly joined forces with and took partial control of Sprostons, the most important engineering and shipping firm in Guyana at that time; and together they came to dominate the Demerara river and with it a significant section of the economy.

Growth of US Imperialism in Latin America

Stimulated by wartime conditions, trade between Guyana and the United States was on the increase, and imports from the US were rapidly outstripping imports from Britain. Guyana was but a small part of a process of development taking place in the whole Latin American and Caribbean area. In Jamaica, the US had gone further towards capturing the local market than in any other British West Indian territory; while in Surinam it was also US capital which had started the bauxite industry. This new US offensive was a further stage in the decline of European influence in the southern Americas, a process which started with the Haitian revolution.

The nineteenth century had already shown that European decline meant replacement by US domination. This situation was being seriously discussed in the Caribbean and Latin America at the end of the First World War. The *Argosy* gave prominence to a discourse by an Argentine intellectual on the dangers that were imminent because of US imperialism. All the British West Indian islands were particularly concerned that the British were planning to relinquish their Caribbean possessions to the United States. The answer to this new threat, they felt, was a federation; though curiously enough, this too was envisaged in broad hemispheric terms to include Canada. Subsequently, the hopes of federation were dashed, while the fears that the British would relinquish their possessions to the US were fully justified in every respect except that of international law.

Simultaneously with bauxite, the more glamorous attraction of diamonds was presented. By 1922 the diamond industry was flourishing, accounted in value for one quarter of the exports of Guyana. Since gold had been discovered in 1882, with rubber and balata providing further incentives, and with bauxite and diamonds in the offing too, it is not surprising that the 'bush' acquired a new meaning for Guyanese and the habit of looking inland was probably enhanced by the partial breakdown of the traditional relations with Europe, which the war effected. During the war, people keenly debated the feasibility of such schemes as a road to link up with the main Pan-American highway, and a railway deep into the hinterland, while an economic survey of the Rupununi region was proposed.

The parallel with Guyana of 1966 is striking. The interior can be seen to represent in the consciousness of the Guyanese an escape from the insular and colonial relations of the narrow coastal strip and, incidentally, it is clear that the masses are taking the initiative in the matter. This consciousness, for obvious geographical reasons, is absent from the islands of the Caribbean, but it is not unique so far as the mainland territories are concerned. A modern historian sees the most characteristic element of Latin American history as being its 'El Dorado Spirit';[3] and that spirit was perfectly exemplified by the Guyanese 'Pork-Knocker', as well as being shared by those who remained behind.

Precious little emerged out of the hope that the interior offered Guyana a brighter future. All that came of the scheme of communication with the hinterland was the Rupununi cattle tract, which was opened in 1917. The gold rush of the 1880s had declined considerably in the early years of the twentieth century. Mushroom companies had collapsed as yields proved unremunerative, and the diamond industry was to follow a similar pattern. Both minerals continued to produce regular revenue, but the scale of operations was small. At a glance, it seems that the Guyanese had overestimated their resources; but it was those who believed that the country had only minor alluvial deposits of gold and diamonds – but no supplies at great depth – who were living in a world of fancy. The woeful ignorance and apathy of the colonial regime militated against the rational utilization of Guyana's resources.

Indentured Immigration

The conception of change which the Guyanese workers entertained during the war was by no means restricted to the exploration of the interior. On a number of vital fronts, they were prepared to wage a struggle against the forces of oppression. One of their most crucial battles was for an end to indentured immigration, and subsequently for the prevention of exploitation of the same ilk.

There were veiled indications in the Guyanese press that when McNeil and Chiman Lal, the two commissioners from India, visited Guyana in 1916 to investigate the indenture system, they were carefully guided to their sources of information; and there were strong assertions on the part of the Indian and Negro workers that they had struggled uncompromisingly against the system of indenture. The commissioners' report was not decisively condemnatory, but in any event 18 April 1917 saw the arrival of the last ship bringing indentured immigrants from India. By the time that the last indentured contracts were served, all sectors of the society became nominally free.

Indenture, unlike slavery, was constantly producing free citizens in large numbers, some of whom were repatriated at the expiry of their contract. Indeed, the rate of repatriation was quite high. In the twenty years between 1891 and 1911 a total of 36,016 Indian immigrants returned home, compared with the 65,764 who arrived during the same period. Many of the Indians who remained in Guyana, like the freed Negroes, moved away from the sugar estates and attempted to set themselves up as an independent peasantry. In 1890, 30 per cent of the East Indians earned their living outside of the sugar estates; while by 1911 less than half of those labourers brought to Guyana in the interest of the sugar industry were still to be found on the sugar estates. The population of Guyana in December 1917 was 314,000, out of whom

137,000 were Indians, and only 62,000 of them were labouring on the sugar estates.

Rice

Rice provided the basis for the East Indian withdrawal from the sugar plantations. Some African slaves and their descendants had planted rice in Guyana and elsewhere, but it was not a crop that was widespread in West Africa, in contrast to India, from where the indentured immigrants brought techniques of irrigated rice farming. As early as 1905, Guyanese rice imports began to drop, and shortly afterwards the local rice industry was not only taking care of the domestic consumption but was also exporting. Under wartime conditions, the rice industry was able to set its sights clearly on exports, because it was easy to capture the West Indian market which was starved of food imports. In Guyana itself there were food shortages, making it necessary for an embargo to be placed on the export of rice in 1917. However, in March 1919, permits were once more issued for the export of rice to the West Indian islands, so that the rice industry emerged from the crucible of the war as Guyana's second agricultural activity.

Naturally enough the East Indian peasants wanted land. The planter and government attitude towards the settlement of indentured immigrants on small holdings was not initially favourable, but both in Trinidad and Guyana they were prepared to grant small amounts of land if this would keep labour from returning to India. Besides, the land had to be properly drained and irrigated for rice farming, and the crop needed to be financed and marketed. All these problems have only been successfully tackled in the last few years, so that for decades the rice farmers waged a constant struggle against drought and flood, and against the voraciousness of the Georgetown merchants who advanced credits and then bought the paddy or rice at ridiculously low prices. Yet, for all this, the East Indian peasant, like the ex-slaves who had managed to set up free villages in Guyana, had to some extent escaped the toils of the plantation system, and it is probably significant that, according to Chandra Jayawardena, 'the Indians of the rice-growing villages consider the Indian plantation labourers to be disorderly and immoral'.[4] Throughout the Caribbean, the heritage of sugar is one of degradation.

Indian 'Middle Class'

While the mass of the East Indian population was either labouring on the sugar estates or in the rice fields, there were also small numbers of merchants and professional men of the race already prominent by 1917, precisely because indenture had long been producing free citizens. Clearly such individuals had already acquired interests quite different from the East Indian workers and peasants. It was an East Indian landowner and rice miller, Gayadeen, who was a principal opponent to the scheme of setting up a cooperative rice mill, when this was proposed late in 1918. His intention was that the peasants should be entirely dependent on him, and he issued a thinly veiled threat to increase the rent of the ground and the houses of the East Indian peasants over whom he held the whip hand. Veeraswamy, a Georgetown lawyer, was accused of hypocritical posturing when he called upon the East Indian workers of Guyana to fight for king and country, while allowing himself to be persuaded that he was too valuable an asset to Guyana to risk enlistment. However, it was the small East Indian section of the 'middle class' to whom the indentured and ex-indentured immigrants looked for guidance and leadership, and in turn the lawyers and merchants sought to articulate the interests of the East Indian community as a whole.[5] For instance, when there was a serious disagreement on a sugar estate, the labourers would trek to Georgetown and seek the assistance of prominent individuals like Luckhoo and Veeraswamy.

Racial Consciousness

It appears that by the 1890s the East Indians had begun to consolidate some sort of community life. By 1917 there were forty-six mosques and forty-three temples, while only two temples had been seen by a royal commission in 1870.[6] The end of indenture, though not as decisive as the end of slavery, produced a new wave of communal feeling among the East Indians of Guyana, one of the products of which was the British Guiana East Indian Association. The idea was put into practice on the initiative of Mr Mudhoo Lall Bhose, and the other signatories of the first circular calling for the formation of the association were J. Viapree, Rampersaud Sawh, E. Kawall, J.D. Rohee, M. Ishmael, A.S. Ruhoman and Peter Ruhoman. On 13 February 1919 the association came into being with Mr J. Luckhoo as the first president.[7] The aims and objects of the British Guiana East Indian Association were the social, intellectual and moral improvement of its members by means of debates, lectures, writing of essays, and the provision of library and recreational facilities. After some disagreement, it was decided that the Association should also indulge in political activities. The Association also published *Indian Opinion* as its official organ, championing the cause of the East Indians in Guyana. In addition, there was a keen interest in the affairs of the Indian subcontinent. The editorial of an early issue of *Indian Opinion* published in May 1919 dealt with the recent disturbances in India and the affairs of the Indian National Congress.

There was a simultaneous resurgence of Negro racial consciousness. It was also linked to the end of indenture, since discussions of the role and status of the East Indians in Guyana inevitably involved comparisons with the Negroes. But even more decisive was the impact of the American Negro struggle. The government twice attempted to pass legislation (in 1918 and 1919) against the importation of American Negro literature, which was widely read among the Guyanese Negro masses. The end of the war saw the attempts of the Pan-African movement to lobby the Peace Conference in France. Meetings were held in various places, notably in the town halls of Georgetown and New Amsterdam, to discuss the question of sending a delegate to Versailles. Letters to the press, lectures and sermons on the problems of the Negro were all common, drawing frequently on examples from the US.

By 1923, the Negro masses had formed organizations such as the Georgetown branch of the Universal Negro Improvement Association (Marcus Garvey's), the African Communities League and the Negro Progress Convention. The relatively small Portuguese community also sought to organize itself around the Portuguese Benevolent Society. There was much talk among them of their 'Portuguese patrimony', of the need to preserve the Portuguese language in Guyana, and of the desirability of a Portuguese political party.

The Class Struggle

Co-existing with the emphasis on racial identity was a powerful upsurge of class consciousness. The Rev. M.A. Cossou, speaking at McKenzie in February 1919, remarked that 'if, as President Wilson has said, the world must be safe for democracy, the relations between capital and labour must be of the best'. Three months later, the preamble to a resolution of workers in Georgetown proceeded as follows: 'That this meeting of the working classes in the City of Georgetown and delegates from various associations of the working classes in the electorate of the counties of Demerara, Essequibo, Berbice and the Town of New Amsterdam, expresses ... etc.' These were typical expressions of the awareness of the fundamental class contradictions in the society.

Rising Prices

During the war, prices had rocketed. A commission appointed to prepare a report on the salaries of civil servants found that on average the cost of living had increased 150 per cent by 1918. What improvement would the end of the war bring? This was the principal question posed by Guyanese as the conflict in Europe neared an end. In December 1918, shortly after the Armistice of the previous November, Rev. R.T. Frank, a great champion of the workers, warned them not to expect too much. In particular, he was gloomy but realistic in his assessment that the cost of living would not fall. He urged the formation of labour unions, and it was precisely the high prices of goods during and after the war that forced the workers to organize themselves.

Dockers' Agitation

As early as 1905, H.N. Critchlow, then eighteen years old and a dock labourer, conceived with some other waterfront workers the idea of going on strike for higher wages. It was put into practice that very year, precipitating widespread rioting which was answered by the guns of the police. When another attempt at strike action was made the following year, Critchlow, as the spokesman of the dock workers, was brought before the city magistrate on a charge of 'preventing a labourer named Abraham Richie from earning an honest living'. The charge was dropped but so was the scheme for striking. It was not until 1916 that a new move was made. The hours of work for waterfront labourers at that time were 6.30 a.m. to 6.00 p.m., with an interval of one hour for breakfast. The dockers determined that the hours should be reduced and that the wages of 64 cents per day should be increased to 84 cents. With the help of J. Sydney McArthur, a Georgetown barrister, and Nelson Cannon, a member of the Court of Policy, they prepared a petition to the government. When this failed, militant strike action gained the workers their demands.

The first success of the waterfront workers in 1916 was an empty one, since prices continued to spiral, and in September 1918, they returned to the attack. Led once more by Critchlow, they demanded increases for both casual and full-time workers, a different system of payment and a reduction of hours. The dockers bargained astutely, drawing up a detailed cost of living index showing the increases in the prices of foodstuffs and other essentials. Working a full six-day week of sixty-nine hours, regular employees could earn a maximum of only four dollars and eighty cents per week, which was manifestly inadequate when placed against the cost of living index. The Chamber of Commerce, which handled the negotiations for Bookers and other Water Street firms, claimed that they were not responsible for the rise in the prices of basic foodstuffs, and they were at first prepared to grant an increase of no more than one shilling per week. The dockers were adamant and won their point. In a final letter conceding victory to the workers, the Chamber of Commerce added ominously that 'the Council hopes that this will place a period on recurring demands'.

The length of the dockers' working day then stood at nine hours. The 'Eight-Hour Day' became the next rallying cry of these workers, and claims for this were pressed on the Chamber of Commerce early in December 1918. The Chamber had already hinted that they intended to call a halt to any further improvements in the lot of the dockers; and they now expressed 'extreme regret and surprise that the labourers, within six weeks of a generous and liberal concession of all the terms demanded in their petition dated 16th September, 1918, should again approach the Chamber for further concessions'. The merchants claimed that since the beginning of the war, the scale of payment had risen by nearly 100 per cent, and, to knock off one hour from the nine-hour day would mean in effect another increase of 10 per cent. The Chamber's continued rejection of the dockers' claim for the eight-hour day was categorical, leaving no room for bargaining. Thus, in January 1919, militant strike action was decided upon, leading directly to the formation of the British Guiana Labour Union.

The British Guiana Labour Union (BGLU)

The BGLU celebrates its anniversary on 11 January, but the organization which was in existence on 11 January 1919 seems to have been no more than a 'Porters Union', an unofficial entity called into being by the waterfront strike. It was on 6 April that a meeting was held at the Unique Friendly Society in Regent Street at which Critchlow proposed a resolution for the establishment of a labour union, and this was carried. Two representatives of Bookers were also invited, and from them came the suggestion for the formation of an Industrial Council for settling disputes between the dockers and the Water Street employers. The three-man council met shortly afterwards and recommended the eight-hour day and certain wage increases.

Out of the agitation of the dockers arose an organization which transcended their own struggle. As one correspondent to the *Argosy* pointed out, the tense post-war labour situation in the world at large which was regularly treated in the Guyanese press could not help but influence the Guyanese proletariat. It was a testimony to the revolutionary mood of labour throughout the land that requests started pouring in for membership of the BGLU from various parts of the country.

In April a meeting at Victoria (East Coast Demerara) decided in favour of a labour union branch for the area. The following month the workers of Bagotville (West Coast Demerara) followed suit; these were typical examples of the movement that led to the rapid establishment of a countrywide workers organization. All sectors of labour were involved, including tradesmen. The first president, M. Hosanah, was a tailor; and there were even jibes that residents of the Alms House or Old People's Home were allowed to join the union. This came about because the union was also a Friendly and Burial Society, thus grafting itself on to one of the oldest forms of social organization that the masses of Guyana had experienced.

The BGLU had a wide base of direct industrial action. The latter portion of 1919 and most of 1920 witnessed a succession of disputes and strikes involving, among others, the railways, the electric company, the sawmills, sugar estates, the *Argosy* and the docks. The pressure of this agitation, carried on by manual workers, was sufficient to gain advantages even for the Water Street clerks, though it was not surprising that these white-collar workers never showed real loyalty to the workers' movement.

The first annual general meeting in 1920 was something of a fiasco, and the union nearly disintegrated. Membership fell from a peak of 13,000 to a few hundred, but the union continued to function as a pressure group. By 1923, the delegates to the general conference could look back on a few years of solid achievement. One union campaign had led to the passage early in 1922 of a Rent Restriction Bill. There was a rumour in January 1923 that the Rent Act was about to be repealed, and the workers prepared to resume the fight if necessary. This was one of several ways in which the workers indicated that they would use the union to undertake tasks other than wage negotiations.

One resolution of the 1923 conference aimed at the establishment of a voluntary organization to provide advice which would prevent the masses from indulging in petty litigation in cases which could be settled out of court. Another principal concern was with unemployment, against which a petition was organized. Perhaps the most ambitious of the moves taken by the BGLU was its attempt to convene the first ever West Indian Conference in 1920. Unfortunately, only the Trinidad Working Men's Association was able to send delegates – the remaining territories expressing willingness but inability to attend. The chance to develop a common West Indian perspective for the labour movement was therefore lost, though workers' struggles in Trinidad were closely watched in Guyana.

Rural Revolution

It is necessary to stress that the awakening among the Guyanese masses was countrywide, and not simply confined to the activities of the urban workers in Georgetown. The BGLU took an interest in plantation labourers also, though its activities on the plantations were severely limited by the managers' opposition to their labourers joining the union. East Indian labourers for the most part continued to use Crosby[8] and the Immigration Department to voice their problems, asking prominent Indian lawyers to intercede on their behalf. This was by no means a passive arrangement. Both the Crosby and the Indian lawyers had to meet huge deputations who arrived in Georgetown from the particular plantation or area where the grievances were felt.

Often the whole plantation staff left en masse as happened in 1917 and again in 1924 with labour from Ruimveldt. On the latter occasion there was an encouraging unity between rural and urban effort. Four thousand Indians and Negroes started to march on Georgetown with flags, sticks and their tools – some to meet Critchlow at the BGLU office and others to the Immigration Department to complain about irregular wages. Apart from the formation of the labour union, the initiative on the issues concerning the wellbeing of the masses came from the rural peasantry. The chairman of the Victoria Institute remarked in April 1919 that 'Georgetown looks to the East Coast to decide its political matters', and the facts did bear out this situation. The weapons which the rural proletariat and peasantry fashioned for their struggle included credit banks and agricultural societies, while the village councils and the village chairmen's conferences provided forums for the expression of the will of the rural masses and their determination to confront the planter class. In February 1919, the attorney general accused A.A. Thorne, a workers' representative in the Combined Court, of wanting to see a set of Bolsheviks in some village led by the village chairman. In reply the chairman of the West Bank Agricultural Society noted that 'the Attorney General has brought in the ominous Russian term ... The question was one of capital and labour. Labour was represented by the Farmers' Conference and the Village Chairman's Conference.'

Cane Farming

One of the most significant trends during the war era was the development of a system of cane growing on a peasant farming basis. In 1897 a royal commission had recommended grants-in-aid to cane farmers. Very little was done by the government to implement the report, but farmers and sugar planters worked out private arrangements on some estates. The farmers faced considerable difficulties, such as the transportation of their cane to the factories and its unloading, but they organized themselves to overcome these problems and to win higher rewards from the sugar estates that purchased their product. In March 1919 the Cane Farming Movement proposed legislation to regularize the relationship between the small cane farmer and the estate that bought and milled his cane. They pointed to Trinidad where there was a small amount of legislation passed on the subject in 1902, though what the Guyanese farmers would have preferred was an extensive code such as that which was in existence in Queensland, Australia.

Co-operative Credit Banks

Alongside the cane farming system there sprung up the Co-operative Credit Bank movement, since loans over the period from sowing to crop time were essential. In fact, credit facilities played an ever-greater role in the young rice industry. A number of Co-operative Credit Banks were established early in the century, but they became really important as the cane farming movement intensified, as the rice industry grew, and when the popularly influenced Local Government Board took over the scheme in 1916. At the end of 1915, only three banks were registered; by the end of 1916 they had increased to 18; and by 1918 there were 26 Co-operative Credit Banks in existence. The numbers of shareholders increased from 220 in 1915 to 5,815 in 1918; and in the same period the working capital had risen from 611 dollars to 28,020 dollars.

The operations of the Ann's Grove-Clonbrook Co-operative Credit Bank can be taken as a typical example. During the year 1918 it issued loans to 156 shareholders amounting to 2,508 dollars. These extended over periods of from one to twelve months and involved sums of from five to twenty dollars. Clients were chiefly paddy growers, along with provision and cane farmers, hucksters, coconut-oil makers and small businesses. Their efforts were obviously small, since there were narrow limits to what could be wrung from the colonial regime.

The Reaction of the Plantocracy

Every one of the tendencies so far pinpointed represented a direct or potential threat to the old colonial system. The opening up of the interior, the end of Indian indenture, the rise of cane farming and the organization of the proletariat were all seen by the plantocracy as undermining the structure of the sugar society.

In the 1890s, when the gold fields were opened, the sugar planters found great difficulty in maintaining a steady supply of labour at the wages they offered and this was the situation which gave rise to the royal commission in 1896. But the recommendation of the commission that Crown Lands should be opened up to peasants was anathema to the planters. According to J. Eleasar, a Georgetown solicitor, 'the Crown Lands were locked up and kept from the people's reach for many, many years because it was thought by the planters that anything done to settle the people on the land would tend to take away labour from the sugar estates.' That was common knowledge among the masses. By the end of the war the planters were more anxious than ever, because bauxite, balata, rice, gold, diamonds, cane farming and irrigation schemes offered alternative employment to Guyanese workers formerly bound to the sugar estates. The planters therefore embarked on a counter-revolutionary offensive.

After the 1896 commission, the proprietors of Vryheid's Lust (Berbice river) encouraged the cultivation of canes on their estates by farmers, the lands being given free of rent. This practice was adopted by a number of other estates. In

December 1918 the cane farmers were suddenly told that they would have to pay nine and twelve dollars per acre. No notice was given, neither was there any increase offered to the farmers for their canes. La Bonne Mere was the only estate which did not pursue this reactionary policy. In vain did the farmers propose alternative schemes for the continuation of the cultivation of estate lands. What the planters wanted was an excuse to introduce legislation for further immigration, the only method which they knew to maintain the hierarchal plantation system. They took land out of production which the cane farmers were eager to work; and within a short period, in Berbice alone, the estates of Adelphi, Canefield, Bath, La Retraite, Highbury, Goldstone Hall and Everton were closed – ostensibly because of a shortage of labour, when in fact there were many people willing to work if only the starvation wages were increased.

The Colonization Scheme

Early in 1919, the chairman of the Planters' Association approached the attorney general claiming that there had been a reduction of 6,000 acres in the cane industry, and that there was a prospect of greater reduction if planters did not get new supplies of labour. Out of this request was born the Colonization Bill, which aimed at introducing into Guyana another influx of cheap labour, preferably from India.

The planters introduced the measure at a time when wartime Defence of the Colony Regulations were still in force. Thorne complained that 'it was manifestly unfair that when the labourers who were interested in the matter were told they were not to deal with the matter as a result of the times in which they lived, that on the other hand the capitalists could meet together and formulate a scheme'. However, the workers refused to be gagged. They recognized the Colonization Scheme for what it was – an attempt to undercut local labour and keep them in a position of subjection. They campaigned vigorously against the proposal when it came before the Combined Court, and warned the elected representatives that they should express popular opposition to the bill. A *Chronicle* editorial countered by saying that 'the elective members would be very foolish to be terrorised by agitators, who warn them not to vote for these proposals at the peril of their seats.' It hinted darkly that such action would supply the strongest arguments for the creation of Crown Colony Government. Such threats did not stop the workers all over the country from making their position plain. Every one of the anti-colonization meetings held all over the country was a success, while the pro-colonization faction found that their meetings were invariably fiascos.

Although the Combined Court did send a mission to England and India, nothing came of the Colonization Scheme. Nevertheless, it was the most important issue of public debate in Guyana at the end of the First World War, and it showed decisively how keenly the masses were assessing their colonial situation and how determined they were to put an end to it. In the mood they were in, nothing escaped the vigilance of the masses. When the government introduced legislation to ban the import of Negro American literature, the workers fought this on two occasions; when a reactionary Jury Bill was brought forward, the workers again fought bitterly, though without success; and on yet another occasion, popular opposition nipped in the bud a proposal of the governor's that a vagrancy law should be passed to coerce labourers to work on public works at ridiculous wages.

The Constitution

A reminder of the type of political system existing in Guyana is necessary at this juncture. In 1891, the Court of Policy, which was until then a purely nominated body, was reformed to allow the election of fourteen members along with the eight members nominated by the governor, who together sat in the Combined Court. There were also two elected financial representatives, though the power over finance was constantly in dispute, because it introduced a clash with the executive authority of the governor. In any event, it took some time before the governing body reflected the change in the Constitution, the nature of that change being to give some representation to the coloured and Portuguese 'middle class'.

Given the very narrow and restricted franchise, it is obvious that the new representatives in the Combined Court after 1891 were not elected by the workers, and did not represent the workers. But some benefits were derived by having in the centre of local political power a group of individuals who were opposed to the planter class and to many aspects of the old colonial system. For instance, as Raymond Smith noted, it is probably significant that the rice industry started at a time when the sugar industry was depressed, and when the new 'middle class' were coming into power after the constitutional reforms of 1891. Besides, the 'middle class' themselves were not satisfied. They clamoured for more control over the affairs of the country, especially in the financial sphere; and as so often happens, they encouraged the workers to shout along with them to make as great a noise as possible.

The year 1916 appears to have been decisive. A Recall Movement was launched against the then governor, Egerton, who had become unpopular with the Georgetown merchants because he interfered with their unwholesome speculation in rice exports. However, the 'middle class' played to a public gallery which had its own reason for abhorring the colonial system and its representative, the governor. The workers, too, began to take up the cry for a more democratic Constitution and for a political programme for their own betterment. As one correspondent of the *Chronicle* wrote in October 1918,

'It is a common thought among the poorer peoples of this colony that places under British rule do not make rapid progress ... Until the policy of the country gets into the hands of the people through their representatives, it is bound to make slow progress.'

By the end of the war, the electorate was faced with a 'Progressive Party', which was not an organizational unit, but an alliance of politicians, that had emerged out of the Recall Movement with the intention of capturing all fourteen of the seats which were to be filled by election. Again, they identified themselves with the masses, and this itself was to provide grounds for disillusionment when they were successfully elected.

Political Influence of the Masses

The influence which the workers wielded under the limited franchise of the pre-adult suffrage era is usually underestimated. The physical unrest of the masses was a factor which had always to be taken into account. During the first three decades of this century, disturbances and riots erupted with great frequency. Known as 'bread riots', one could not ask for more blatant examples of people asking for bread and being given bullets. The breathless haste with which the colonial regime read the Riot Act was a testimony to their deep-rooted fear of mass action that they had inherited from the sugar planters and slave owners.

Quite apart from the threat of violence, the workers made an impact through public meetings. Georgetown workers met under the auspices of the BGLU to discuss the relative merits of Percy Wight and P.N. Cannon, concluding that the latter was an enemy of the working class; workers in New Amsterdam met and demanded that Eustace Woolford should return to the constituency and give an account of his stewardship in the

Combined Court, and especially to explain his ambivalence on the Colonization Bill which the workers had denounced; while peasant farmers of the East Coast Demerara met at Victoria Village, condemned the government in power, and agreed to form a 'Political Association', embracing members from Anne's Grove and Bachelor's Adventure. All this was in the period after the Recall Movement and the formation of the 'Progressive Party', and it may appear futile because the workers had no vote.

Yet the popular clamour had its effect on those who held the vote and those who appeared as representatives of the people. By 1923, for example, Cannon had lost the Georgetown mayoralty, and while he himself retained a seat in the Combined Court the candidates whom he supported were all unsuccessful. Proof of the impact of popular agitation against the Colonization Bill came when the government itself decided to hold a number of public meetings to win support for the measure. The workers simply invaded those meetings, held in 1919, and passed resolutions of their own calling for improvements in sanitation, drainage and irrigation and wages before they would consent to a further influx of immigrant.

The Suspension of the Constitution in 1928

Everyone felt that the Constitution of 1891 had outlived its usefulness. The 'middle class' wanted more power, especially over the finances and the executive; while the planter class, having already ceded some of their authority to the 'middle class', and seeing the spectre of mass power if more liberal reforms were granted, were willing to let the British crown take direct responsibility for the colony of British Guiana. Dissatisfaction with constitutional forms was in fact general in the British West Indies after the war, and resulted in the appointment of a royal commission, which visited the area and reported in 1922. The Wood Commission, as it was called, rejected the demands of the Guyanese planter class to take a step backward, but neither did it allow the presence of elected members on the executive as the 'Progressive Party' requested. No important changes were made, so the elections of 1926 were held under the Constitution of 1891.

A.R. Webber, one of Guyana's few historians, and an individual who was himself personally involved in the politics of the period, wrote that the elections of October 1926 were 'fought with unexampled ferocity', and that 'the declaration at the polls showed a sweeping victory for the Popular Party; and a complete and devastating rout of their opponents, who were well possessed of this world's goods'.[9] But practically every seat was judicially challenged, and eventually five members of the Court of Policy were unseated on legal technicalities. No doubt the Colonial Office was being informed of these developments, as well as receiving advice from the planter group to put an end to the Constitution which gave power to the upstart 'middle class' and encouraged the workers to dabble in politics.

As mentioned before, as early as 1919, there were dark hints that if the elected members allowed themselves to be influenced by popular agitators this would 'supply the strongest arguments for the creation of a Crown Colony government'. Again in 1925, this idea was publicly voiced by the governor of British Guiana when he returned to England; and in 1927 it was decided to put it into practice.

No one quite knew what was the purpose of the commissioners who visited Guyana in 1927 – at least not until the following year when it became clear that they had been seeking excuses to suspend the Constitution. At any rate, the Constitution of 1891 was so radically changed that the effect was to remove all power from the elected representatives. It is clear that even the small measure of representation under the Constitution of 1891 was seen by the colonial regime as a threat. Thus in 1928, not for the first time nor for the last, a constitutional coup d'état was effected to break local resistance to the British imperial system.

Race and Class

In so far as reflection on the period under discussion is understandably influenced by the present conjuncture of circumstances in Guyana, it is obvious that the question of the inter-relation between race and class consciousness is of the utmost importance. In the decade after 1955, these two factors proved antagonistic, and consequently the anti-colonialist struggle of the Guyanese masses received a serious setback. However, between 1900 and 1928 the situation was entirely different. Then, it was the awareness among both Indians and Negroes of the peculiar disadvantages under which their own race laboured that precipitated an attack on the colonial society.

Racial consciousness was mobilized when a group felt it laboured under special disadvantages. *Indian Opinion* launched an attack on the government for keeping the East Indian masses in a state of illiteracy. It pointed out that of 20,000 children of East Indian parentage of school-going age, only 6,000 were attending school. This was branded as 'a neglect not only inexcusable, but culpable'. On an issue such as this communal anger was jointly directed against the colonial regime, because the Negro masses were at that very moment waging a struggle to lay the foundations of a more democratic educational system, rejecting the 'Payment by Results' and other limitations which were in vogue since the Elementary Education Ordinance of 1876. Incidentally, the struggle of the teachers not only on their own behalf, but for a system of education which would benefit their pupils and the country, is undoubtedly one of the most magnificent in the annals of the history of the Guyanese working class.

Apart from the demands for more education, there was also some consideration given to the curricula, and one of the suggestions of the East Indian community was that Indian languages should be taught. One striking feature of the debate on the issue by the Teachers' Association was the position taken by R. French, who argued that unless they took steps to teach the Indian languages, the latter would disappear, as the African languages of the slaves had disappeared, and the community would be the poorer. This, and many other views on related topics, indicated that the racial groups in Guyana were seriously addressing themselves to an examination of where they stood, of what they possessed of value, and of what changes were desirable. At every juncture, they were unmasking the colonial society as the enemy.

When in 1917 the East Indians succeeded in having marriage ceremonies by Moulvis and Pandits recognized, they had gained a victory over the white-Christian-capitalist conception of the society,[10] and it was against this that the Negro masses too were directing their fire. They joined in the refrain of the Negroes of the United States that blacks had fought side by side with whites during the war, and now they should be given new opportunities. It is extremely significant that the colonial administration saw the associations such as the Negro Progress Convention not as racist groups but as class formations. The literature from the United States was anathema because it was being widely read by 'the poorer classes of society'; and it was suggested that the local branch of Garvey's movement should be banned because it was 'Bolshevik'.

The Rev. Frank wrote in January 1919 of the Negro masses of Guyana: 'the possibilities wrapped up in them and the powers within them are immense.' This applied equally to the East Indian masses; but for the release of the energies of all concerned, there was necessarily a process of self-realization, which was taking place in a framework of racial groupings rather than in the context of 'nation'. That process of communal self-realization did not inevitably bring the races into conflict, nor retard the formation of organizations along class lines, nor weaken the struggle against colonialism.

What occurred in the period after 1955 was that communal awareness was for various reasons turned inwards to exacerbate racial contradictions among the Guyanese workers and peasants. I say 'exacerbate' because racial conflict in Guyana was an inevitable concomitant of the fact that indentured labour (East Indian, Chinese and Portuguese) was conceived specifically to break the back of Negro opposition to the planter class. Throughout the decades after Indian immigration began in 1838, there were differences over wages between racial groups on the sugar estates, brought about by the deliberate policy of the planters of playing one group off against another. No doubt, racial conflict fed racialism, and vice versa; and indeed, there are a host of other such interconnections that one could make. What is certain is that simple and definitive explanations must give way to a more sober analysis of the complexities of the development of the Guyanese mass movement – of the relationship between racial consciousness and racial prejudice, between economic competition and racial conflict, between communal identification and class objectives.

3

Marxism and African Liberation

First of all, we must understand the background for this kind of debate. When one is asked to speak on the relevance of Marxism to Africa at this particular time, one is being asked to involve oneself in an historical debate – an ongoing debate in this country, particularly among the black population. It is a debate which has heightened over the last year, and from my own observations, it is being waged in a large number of places across this country.

Sometimes it appears in the guise of the so-called Nationalist versus the Marxist; sometimes it appears in the guise of those who claim to espouse a class position as opposed to those who claim to espouse a race position. Thus, it would not be possible for us in a single session to enter into all the ramifications of that debate, but it does form the background for our discussion.

It is an important debate. It is an important fact that such issues are being debated in this country today, just as they're being debated in Africa, in Asia, in Latin America and in many parts of the metropolitan world in Western Europe and in Japan. Because the widespread nature of the debate and its intensity at this time is a reflection of the crisis in the capitalist-imperialist mode of production. Ideas and discussion do not just drop from the sky. There is not simply a plot on the part of certain individuals to engage others in a meaningless debate.

Whatever the outcome of the debate, whatever the posture the different participants adopt, the very fact of the debate is representative of the crisis in capitalism and imperialism today; and as the crisis deepens, people find it more and more difficult to accept the old modes of thought that rationalize the system which is collapsing. Hence the need to search for new directions, and quite clearly, Marxism, Scientific Socialism poses itself as one of the most obvious of the available options.

The question is not new to Africa or to the black people as a whole – that is perhaps essential to understand. Many of us have raised before the question of the relevance of Marxism to this or that. Its relevance to Europe; many European intellectuals debated its relevance to their own society. Its relevance to Asia was debated by Asians. Its relevance to Latin America was debated by Latin Americans. Individuals have long debated the relevance of Marxism to their own time. Was it relevant to the nineteenth century? If so, was it still relevant to the twentieth century? One can debate its relevance to a given facet of the culture of society or to the society's law or culture as a whole.

These are all issues that have been debated before and we should have some sense of history when we approach this question today, because with that sense of history we can ask: why is it that the question of the relevance of Marxism to society always crops up? And, in a very brief answer, I would suggest that what is common to the application of the question is, first of all, a condition of struggle, a condition in which people are dissatisfied with the dominant mode of perceiving reality.

At that point they ask about the relevance of Marxism.

More than that, the second condition is that people ask the question because of their own bourgeois framework. One starts out located within the dominant mode of reasoning, which is the mode of reasoning that supports capitalism and which we will call a bourgeois framework of perception. And because one starts out that way, it becomes necessary to raise the question about the relevance of Marxism.

After one is advanced, it is probably more accurate to raise the question of the relevance of bourgeois thought, because the shoe would be on the other foot!

But initially, it is true that however much the bourgeoisie disagree, there is one common uniting strand to all bourgeois thought: they make common cause in questioning the relevance, the logic, and so on, of Marxist thought. And therefore, in a sense, when we ask that question, we are unfortunately also fitting into that framework and pattern. We are also, in some way, still embedded to a greater or lesser extent in the framework of bourgeois thought, and from that framework we ask with a great degree of hesitancy and uncertainty – what is the relevance of Marxism?

It is particularly true in our part of the world – that is, the English-speaking part of the world – because the Anglo-American tradition is one of intense hostility, philosophically speaking, towards Marxism; a hostility that manifests itself in a peculiar way. It manifests itself by trying to dissociate itself even from the study of Marxism. If you were to check on the continental tradition in Europe, you would find it is not the same. French, German and Belgian intellectuals, whatever their perspective, understand the importance of Marxism. They study it, they relate to it, they understand the body of thought that is called Marxism and they take a position vis-à-vis that body of thought.

In the English tradition, which was also handed down to this part of the world, to the Caribbean, to many parts of Africa, it is fashionable to disavow any knowledge of Marxism. It is fashionable to glory in one's ignorance, to say that we are against Marxism. When pressed about it one responds – but why bother to read it? It is obviously absurd.

So, one knows it is absurd without reading it and one doesn't read it because one knows it is absurd, and therefore one glories in one's ignorance of the position.

It is rather difficult to seriously address the question of the

35

relevance of Marxism unless one does the basic minimum of accepting that one should attempt to enter into this full body of thought, because it is a tremendous body of literature and analysis, and from the outside as it were, it is extremely difficult.

Indeed, I would say it is pointless, strictly from the outside, without ever having moved towards trying to grapple with what it is, to ask what is its relevance? It is almost an unanswerable question; and I think in all modesty, that for those of us who came from a certain background (and we all come from that background), one of the first things we have to do is establish a basis of familiarity with the different intellectual traditions, and as we become familiar with them we can then be in a better position to evaluate Marxism's relevance or irrelevance, as the case might be.

I will proceed on the assumption that what we are trying to discern in this discussion is whether the variants of time and place are relevant; or, let me put it another way, whether the variants of time and place make a difference to whether Marxism is relevant or not. In a sense we would almost have to assume its validity for the place in which it originated, Western Europe. We don't have the time to deal with that in detail. But we can then ask, assuming that Marxism has a relevance, has a meaning, has an applicability to Western Europe, or had in the nineteenth century, to what extent does its validity extend geographically? To what extent does its validity extend across time?

These are the two variables of time and place. They can be translated to mean historical circumstances: time; and culture: place – and what social and cultural conditions exist in each particular place. For us, to make it more precise, black people – no doubt well-meaning black people – ask the question whether an ideology which was historically generated within the culture of Western Europe in the nineteenth century is, today, in the third quarter of the twentieth century, still valid for another part of the world – namely Africa, or the Caribbean, or black people in this country; whether it is valid to other societies at other times. And this is the kind of formulation which I wish to present for discussion.

The Methodology of Marxism

I would suggest two basic reasons why I believe that Marxist thought, Scientific Socialist thought, would exist at different levels, at different times, in different places, and retain its potential as a tool, as a set of conceptions that people should grasp.

The first is to look at Marxism, as a methodology, because a methodology would, virtually by definition, be independent of time and place. You will use the methodology at any given time, at any given place. You may get different results, of course, but the methodology itself would be independent of time and place.

And essentially, to engage in a rather truncated presentation of Marxism, inevitably oversimplifying, but nevertheless necessary in the context of limited time I would suggest that, one of the real bases of Marxist thought is that it starts from a perspective of man's relationship to the material world; and that Marxism, when it arose historically, consciously dissociated itself from and pitted itself against all other modes of perception which started with ideas, with concepts and with words; and rooted itself in the material conditions and in the social relations in society.

This is the difference with which I will start. A methodology that begins its analysis of any society, of any situation, by seeking the relations that arise in production between men. There are a whole variety of things which flow from that: man's consciousness is formed in the intervention in nature; nature itself is humanized through its interaction with man's labour; and man's labour produces a constant stream of technology that in turn creates other social changes.

So, this is the crux of the Scientific Socialist perception. A methodology that addresses itself to man's relationship in the process of production on the assumption, which I think is a valid assumption, that production is not merely the basis of man's existence, but the basis for defining man as a special kind of being with a certain consciousness.

It is only through production that the human race differentiates itself from the rest of the primates and the rest of life.

What does Marxism pose itself against? It poses itself against a number of hypotheses, a number of views of the world which start with words and concepts. For those who are familiar with Marx's own evolution, it is well known that he started by looking first at Hegel – a very plausible and perceptive analyst of the nineteenth century who was guilty, in Marx's own estimation, of putting forward an entirely idealist position, one that placed ideas in the centre of the universe and saw the 'material' world as virtually deriving from those ideas.

In thinking about this, I felt that I wouldn't go into Hegel. I would go further than Hegel for a classic exposition of the idealist worldview. I take it from the New Testament, the Book of John, where he stated: 'In the beginning was the Word, and the Word was with God. And the Word was God.' That is the classic exposition of the idealist position. You take every other thing from there: the Word was God!

But we are suggesting that the word is itself an emanation from people's activity as they attempt to communicate with each other, as they develop social relations out of production, and that we shouldn't be mystified with words. Oh, naturally enough we will have to deal with concepts and with the force of consciousness, which is a very powerful force and one that even some Marxists have been tempted to underestimate.

Now, Marx, taking that broad framework of methodology, tried to apply it to Western Europe. He applied it to a range of societies in different places and at different times; but he concentrated his attention on Western Europe. If you examine the body of literature produced by Marx and Engels, you will find that they speak about slavery, about communal society, about feudalism; but, by and large, they concentrated on capitalism. They hardly even talk about socialism.

Marx's great contribution was his fantastic critique of an existing society, capitalist society. How did it come into being in a particular part of the world? The vast majority of their literature concerns this question.

But, as I said when I referred to pre-capitalist society, especially feudalism, they talked about some other parts of the world. Occasionally Marx mentions the Asiatic mode of production. Occasionally he came across to look at the data concerning the United States. So, he had something of a geographical span and a long time span.

It was so minimal, however, in comparison with the bulk of his work that it is true that a lot of people have taken Marx's method and his conclusions and have seen them as one and the same thing – that Marxism is not merely a certain methodology applied to Western Europe but is itself an ideology about Western Europe, about capitalism in the nineteenth century, and cannot transcend those boundaries, when clearly Marx was doing the job he had to do. He was looking at his own society, he was doing it under some of the most adverse conditions, he was doing it by mastering bourgeois knowledge and putting it to the service of change and revolution.

I would suggest, then, that the method was independent of time and place. It is implicit in Marx, and it becomes explicit in post-Marxian development – using Marxian in the literal sense of the life of Marx himself. After Marx's death you will get the evolution or the development of scientific socialist thought with other individuals recognizing that the methodology can be applied, must be applied to different times to different places.

Again, presenting our history in a very abbreviated form, we can look at Lenin, at his application of Marxist theory to Russian society. That is one of his principal contributions. The first major thesis of the young Lenin was *The Development of Capitalism in Russia*. He had to deal with his own society. He had to take those formulations out of the specific cultural and historical context of Western Europe and look at Eastern Europe, at Russia, which was evolving differently, and apply them to his own society. This he did.

He had at the same time to consider the time dimension that in the nineteenth century Marx was writing about what has now come to be called the classic period of capitalism, the entrepreneurial version of capitalism, and by the later nineteenth century this had given way to monopoly capitalism. It has given way to imperialism. So, Lenin had to deal with that method by applying it to a new dimension in time; so he wrote about capitalism in its imperialist stage.

So those are the two variants operating: first, the ideology; and second, the methodology of it being applied to different societies at different times (we'll stick to the methodology for the time being). Having made the point for Lenin, I hope it becomes clear for a number of people: Mao Zedong, for instance, applying it to Chinese society, which was a different society from Russian society; understanding the inner dynamics of Chinese society, relating to the question of the peasantry in a different and more profound way than any previous writer because that was the nature of Chinese society, and Mao had addressed himself to that.

And finally for our purposes, the most important example: the example of Amilcar Cabral, because he was dealing with Africa. Cabral, in one of his most important essays – the one titled 'The Weapon of Theory', if I recall correctly – began by making clear that the best he could do was to return to the basic methodology of Marx and Engels. But it was not possible for Cabral to begin the analysis of the history of

Guinea-Bissau by saying, 'I am going to look for classes', for example. He said, 'if I say this I will be denying that my people have any history because I do not perceive classes for a long period in the genesis of my own people.'

Then he referred back to Marx and Engels's classic statement that 'the history of all existing societies is the history of class struggle', to which Engels had appended a note saying that by 'all history', we mean 'all previously recorded history'. It so happens that the history of the people of Guinea-Bissau hasn't been recorded, and Cabral says, 'I want to record that history. We will use the Marxian method. We will not be tied by the concept which arose historically in Western Europe when Marx was studying that society.'

Marx uses the method, and he discerned the evolution of classes and of the phenomenon of classes itself as being a major determinant, the major determinant in Western European history at a particular point in time. Cabral says we will begin at the beginning. We will not even concern ourselves initially with classes. We will simply look at men in the process of production. We will look at modes of production in the history of Guinea, and we will see how our society evolved. So, without much of a fanfare he was showing the relevance of that methodology to African society.

If, and when, in the history of Guinea-Bissau, the aspect of class appears to have historical importance, then Cabral dealt with it. Until such time, he simply stuck to the basis of Marxian methodology which was to look at Guinean people in the process of production, at the various modes of production, social formations, cultural formations which arose historically and the direction in which the society was tending.

In many respects, when we ask the question today about the relevance of Marxism to black people, we have already reached a minority position, as it were. Many of those engaged in the debate present the debate as though Marxism is a European phenomenon and black people responding to it must of necessity be alienated because the alienation of race must enter into the discussion.

They seem not to take into account that already that methodology and that ideology have been utilized, internalized, domesticated in large parts of the world that are not European. That it is already the ideology of eight hundred million Chinese people; that it is already the ideology which guided the Vietnamese people to successful struggle and to the defeat of imperialism. That it is already the ideology which allows North Korea to transform itself from a backward, quasi-feudal, quasi-colonial terrain into an independent, industrial power. That it is already the ideology which has been adopted on the Latin American continent and that serves as the basis for development in the Republic of Cuba. That it is already the ideology that was used by Cabral, that was used by Samora Machel, which is in use on the African continent itself to underline and underscore struggle and the construction of a new society.

It cannot therefore be termed a European phenomenon; and the onus will certainly be on those who argue that this phenomenon, which was already universalized itself, is somehow inapplicable to some black people. The onus will be on those individuals, I suggest, to show some reason, perhaps genetic, why the genes of black people reject this ideological position.

When we investigate and try to centralize or keep central the concept of relevance, we must ask ourselves questions about the present. What kind of society, do we live in today? What kind of societies do black people live in today in different parts of the world? And while, of course, we as black people in this country, in the Caribbean and in different parts of Africa have our own independent historical experience, one of the central facts is that we are all in one way or another, located within the capitalist system of production.

The society about which Marx wrote, through a process of outgrowth, dominated Africa and the Americas in the era of mercantilism, which was the period that capitalism was growing to maturity. It dominated these parts of the world. It created slave society in the Americas.

Subsequent to the slave era, capitalism, even more powerful, was able to incorporate the whole world into a global network of production that derived from Western Europe and North America, a system which had a metropolitan centre or set of metropolitan centres, and a separate set of peripheries, colonies and semi-colonies.

So that we have all, historically, been incorporated within the capitalist system of production, and that is another dimension of the relevance of Marxism.

Even without the translation in terms of time and place, it seems to me that if we have become part of the capitalist-imperialist world, then we owe it to ourselves to relate to, to follow, to understand, and to hopefully adopt and adapt a critique of that capitalist system because that is essentially what Marx's writing is about. He was critiquing that capitalist system. He did so more effectively than any bourgeois writer, and if we want to understand the world in which we live, which is the world dominated by capitalism, then we must understand the centre of that system, the motor within that system, the types of exploitation which are to be found within the capitalist mode of production. So that is yet another factor.

Marxism as Revolutionary Ideology

My second consideration after methodology is to look at Marxism as a revolutionary ideology and as a class ideology.

In class societies, all ideologies are class ideologies. All ideologies derive from and support some particular class. So, for all practical purposes we have grown up in capitalist society, and bourgeois ideology is dominant in our society. These institutions in which we function were created to serve the creation of ideas as commodities, ideas which will buttress the capitalist system.

Now, I would suggest, historically, as Marx suggested himself, that the set of ideas we call Scientific Socialism arose within capitalist society to speak to the interest of the producers in that society, to speak to the interest of those who are exploited and expropriated, to speak to the interest of the oppressed, of the culturally alienated; and we must understand that of the two major sets of ideas before us, idealism and materialism, bourgeois philosophy and Marxist philosophy, that each of the two is representative of a particular class.

I don't have the time to go into all the historical roots of the formation of socialism, but briefly, in the nineteenth century it was in the rise of capitalist society that conditions were created for the development of socialist ideas. Out of the diverse and unsystematized socialist ideas, Marx was able to formulate a clear and systematic theory – Scientific Socialism. It had a particular class base and because it had this particular class base, it was revolutionary. It sought to transform and upend the relations in society.

Bourgeois ideology is of necessity status quo preserving. It seeks to conserve, it seeks to buttress the given system of production, the relations which flow, the relations which flow from a certain system of production.

A Scientific Socialist position is and remains revolutionary, because it aims, consciously aims, at undermining that system of production and the political relations which flow from it. This is what I mean by revolutionary.

From time to time there are Marxists who have arisen, who have attempted to deny or denude Marxism of its revolutionary content. That is true. There are Marxists who have become legal or armchair Marxists, who would like to see Marxism as merely another variant of philosophy and who treat it in a very eclectic fashion, as though one is free to draw from Marxism as one draws from Greek thought and its equivalent, without looking at the class base and without looking at whether an ideology is supportive of the status quo or not.

Nevertheless, by and large, we can see Marxism and Scientific Socialism as subversive of and antithetical to the maintenance of the system of production in which we live. Because ideas, let me repeat, do not float in the sky, they do not float in the atmosphere, they are related to concrete relations of production. Bourgeois ideas derive from bourgeois relations of production. They are intended to conserve and maintain those relations of production. Socialist ideas derive from the same production, but they derive from a different class interest and their aim is to overthrow that system of production.

Africa and Scientific Socialism

There again I will suggest that African people, like other Third World people, have virtually a vested interest in Scientific Socialism, because it offers itself to them as a weapon of theory. It offers itself to them as that tool, at the level of ideas, which will be utilized for dismantling the capitalist imperialist structure. This is its concern.

What I will attempt to deal with as best I can, are certain questions arising from individuals who might say yes to most of what I've said and then will ask the question, 'Is there no other alternative? Is there no other ideological system which is neither capitalist nor socialist, but is anti-capitalist, but addresses itself more humanely, if you like, to the interest of African people wherever they are?'

These questions are worth looking into because there are black people asking these questions, and we have to try and resolve them. My own formulation will be to suggest that we look at concrete examples of African or black people who have attempted to devise systems which they consider to be non-capitalist and non-socialist, systems they consider valid alternatives to Scientific Socialism for the emancipation of African people.

In this regard, we have a number of pan-Africanists, a number of African nationalists in Africa, in the Caribbean and in this country, who have taken that road. George Padmore did this at the end of his life and made a distinction between Scientific Socialism and pan-Africanism. He said this is the road we will follow: pan-Africanism. We do not want to follow that road which is capitalist, we do not want to go down the socialist road; we will derive for ourselves something that is pan-African.

In a sense, Nkrumah followed up on this; and although at one time he called himself a Marxist, he always was careful to qualify this by saying that he was also a Protestant. He believed in Protestantism, at the same time. So, he was trying to straddle two worlds simultaneously – the world which says in the beginning was matter, and the world which says in the beginning there was the word.

And inevitably he fell between these two. It's impossible to straddle these two. But there he was, and we must grant his honesty and we must grant the honesty of many people who have attempted to do this impossible task and follow them to find out why they failed.

They failed because their conception of what was a variant different from bourgeois thought and different from socialist thought inevitably turned out to be merely another branch of bourgeois thought.

And this was the problem, that bourgeois thought, and indeed socialist thought, when we get down to it, can have a variety of developments or roads and aspects or paths. With bourgeois thought, because of its whimsical nature, and because of the way in which it prompts eccentrics, you can have any road, because, after all, when you are not going any place, you can choose any road!

So, it was possible for these individuals to make what I consider to be a genuine attempt to break with the dominance of bourgeois thought and yet find, in the final analysis, that they had merely embraced another manifestation of that which they themselves had suggested they were confronting at the outset. There are a number of examples, some more apt than others. Some of the examples are Africans who I think were blatantly dishonest from the beginning. I do think that most of the ideologues of African socialism claiming to find a third path are actually just cheap tricksters; tricksters who are attempting to hoodwink the majority of the population. I don't think they're out to develop socialism. I don't think they're out to develop anything that addresses itself to the interest of the African people. But, nevertheless, it is part of the necessity of our times that our people no longer are willing to accept anything that is not put to them in the guise of socialism.

And, therefore, I shan't in fact go on to African socialism. What I'll do is take examples of those who were, in my opinion, being serious, being honest. And certainly Kwame Nkrumah was one of these. Nkrumah spent a number of years during the fifties and, right up to when he was overthrown – that would cover at least ten years – in which he was searching for an ideology. He started out with this mixture of Marxism and Protestantism, he talked about pan-Africanism; he went to Consciencism and then Nkrumahism, and there was everything other than a straight understanding of socialism.[1]

What were the actual consequences of this perception? That is what matters to us. Let us assume that he was searching for something African and that he was trying to avoid the trap of adopting something alien. What were the practical consequences of this attempt to dissociate himself from an international socialist tradition? We saw in Ghana that Nkrumah steadfastly refused to accept that there were classes, that there were class contradictions in Ghana, that these class contradictions were fundamental.

47

For years Nkrumah went along with this mish-mash of philosophy which took some socialist premises but which he refused to pursue to their logical conclusion – that one either had a capitalist system based upon the private ownership of the means of production and the alienation of the product of people's labour, or one had an alternative system which was completely different; and that there was no way of juxtaposing and mixing these two to create anything that was new and viable.

A most-significant test of this position was when Nkrumah himself was overthrown! After he was overthrown, he lived in Guinea-Konakry and before he died, he wrote a small text titled *Class Struggle in Africa*. It is not the greatest philosophical treatise but it is historically important, because it is there that Nkrumah himself in effect admits the consequences, the misleading consequences, of an ideology which espoused an African cause, but which felt, for reasons which he did not understand, an historical necessity to separate itself from Scientific Socialism. It indicated quite clearly the disastrous consequences of that position.

Because Nkrumah denied the existence of classes in Ghana until the petty bourgeoisie as a class overthrew him. And then, in Guinea, he said it was a terrible mistake. Yes, there are classes in Africa. Yes, the petty bourgeoisie is a class with interests fundamentally opposed to workers and peasants in Africa. Yes, the class interest of the petty bourgeoisie is the same or at least is tied in with the class interest of international monopoly capital; and therefore we have in Africa a class struggle within the African continent and a struggle against imperialism.

And if we are to aim at transcending these contradictions, at bringing victory and emancipation to the working peoples, the producers of Africa, we will have to grapple with that ideology, which first of all recognizes and challenges the existence of exploiting and oppressing classes.

It is a very important historical document. It is the closest that Nkrumah comes to a self-critique. It is the record of a genuine nationalist, an African nationalist who wandered for years with this assumption and feeling that somehow he must dissociate himself in one way or another from Scientific Socialism because it originated outside of the boundaries of his own society, and he was afraid of its cultural implications.

This is putting it in the most charitable way. But the fear is due, in fact, to aspects of bourgeois ideology. Due to the fact that he made a distinction between social theory and scientific theory, which is not a necessary distinction. That is the distinction which comes out of the history of bourgeois thought.

People seem to have no difficulty in deciding that they are going to use facets of the material culture that originated in the West, whether it originated in capitalist or socialist society. People have no difficulty relating to electricity, but they say, 'Marx and Engels, that's European!' Was Edison a racist? But they ask the question, 'Was Marx a racist?' They genuinely believe that they are making a fundamental distinction, whereas, in fact, they are obscuring the totality of social development. And the natural sciences are not to be separated from the social sciences. Our interpretation of the social reality can similarly derive a certain, historical law and hence scientific law of society that can be applied irrespective of its origin or its originators.

Of course, it is true, and this is the most appropriate note on which to end – that any ideology, when applied, must be applied with sensitivity. It must be applied with a thorough grasp of the internal realities of a given society.

Marxism comes to the world as an historical fact, and it comes in a cultural nexus. If, for instance, Africans, or let us go back to Asians – when the Chinese first picked up the Marxist texts, they were European texts. They came loaded with conceptions of the historical development of Europe itself. So that method and factual data were obviously interwoven, and the

49

conclusions were in fact in a specific historical and cultural setting.

It was the task of the Chinese to deal with that and to adapt it and to scrutinize it and see how it was applicable to their society. First and foremost, to be scientific, it meant having due regard for the specifics of Chinese historical and social development.

I have already cited Cabral in another context, and he reappears in this context. The way in which he is at all times looking at the particularities of class development in contemporary Guinea-Bissau; looking at the potential of classes in Guinea-Bissau at this point in time. And therefore he is, of course, making sure that Marxism does not simply appear as the summation of other people's history, but appears as a living force within one's history.

And this is a difficult transformation. This is the task of anybody who considers himself or herself a Marxist. However, because it is fraught with so many difficulties and obstacles, many people take the easy route, which is to take it as a finished product rather than an ongoing social product which has to be adapted to their own society.

One finds that in looking at Marxist theory, at its relevance to race, looking at the relevance of Marxist theory to national emancipation, we come up with a very important paradox: that the nationalist, in the strict sense of the word, that is the petty bourgeois nationalist, who aims merely at the recovery of national independence in our epoch, is incapable of giving the people of Africa or the peoples of the Caribbean any participation in liberal democracy.

The petty bourgeois cannot fulfil these historical tasks for national liberation requires a socialist ideology. We cannot separate the two.

Even for national liberation in Africa, Guinea-Bissau and Mozambique very clearly demonstrated the necessity for an ideological development, for conscientization, as they say in

Latin America; and the nationalist struggle was won because it came under the rubric of Scientific Socialist perspective.

As Cabral said: 'There may be revolutions which have had a revolutionary theory and which have failed. But there has certainly been no revolution which has succeeded without a revolutionary theory.'

4

Marxism as a Third World Ideology

This is an appropriate time at which to participate in a further discussion on the question of Marxism, because the amount of interest and the amount of practical attention which has been given to that ideology has increased enormously.

In the process of this increase there has also been, inevitably, a tendency towards factionalism – a tendency towards wanting to adopt, logically enough, a position which the adherents of Marxism or Scientific Socialism consider to be the most theoretical and ultimately practical interpretation of what Marxism is. For my own part, I will at the outset, for the sake of convenience, avoid entering into any discussion which will adjudicate between rival claimants to the title of Marxism. It is not for me at this moment – I do not think it will advance our analysis in the time allocated if we were to launch into trying to determine who is actually Marxist–Leninist between so-called Stalinists and so-called Trotskyites, between one side or the other in the Sino-Soviet dispute, between the old Left and the new Left. That is to say, as a matter of convenience, I will avoid the complications inherent in those very often polemical distinctions. However, more than that, I believe that on principle one can argue that there is a common understanding – or a body of common theoretical understanding – among all of those who are avowedly Marxist, and that there is an area which is smaller, but nevertheless significant, of common practice – common anti-capitalist and anti-imperialist practice – among these rival groups. And this is part of my justification for avoiding that contention. Besides, at a later point in the analysis,

I will go on to suggest that, on principle, the introduction of Marxist factionalism into Third World political discussions in an a priori fashion is usually destructive, and at best is pointless.

So let us attempt – however difficult that may appear to some people who are engaged in Marxist discussion – to take Marxism as though it were homogeneous or as though we do not have a multitude of contenders for the title of Marxism as it were, and focus our attention on the Third World. The Third World, that part of the globe which has been engaged in capitalist relations for centuries, but which has been engaged in capitalist relations in its own peculiar way, qualitatively different from the way in which the metropolitan countries of North America and Europe have been engaged in the capitalist system of relationships. And because of the qualitatively different manner in which the Third World has participated in the international capitalist economy, there are peculiar factors that are described as backwardness or underdevelopment, or what have you. This is a portion of the world without capitalists – without significant indigenous capitalists, without a significant indigenous proletariat, very often having pre-capitalist social formations still existing in various stages of disintegration.

Our enquiry really amounts to trying to determine the relevance of Marxism to that part of the world; and more particularly, understanding the relevance of a Marxist interpretation to strategies designed to transform or speed up the transformation of these parts of the world which are lightly, very often lightly, termed the Third World. So, in trying to answer the question 'How is Marxism relevant to the Third World?' my insistence is that we understand that Africa, Asia and Latin America, when referred to as the Third World, do not constitute a socio-economic system which is distinct from the capitalist centres of the world. If we make that distinction, I believe we will fall into all kinds of traps when we attempt to apply the analysis of Marxism or any other kind of ideology to the Third World. We must see the countries of Africa, most of Asia outside of China, Korea and Vietnam, and virtually all of Latin America outside of Cuba, as still functioning as integral parts of the capitalist world. It is merely that they complement the capitalist centres. And this, after all, is not the thesis that need necessarily be exemplified at great length today in 1975; because, a large number of non-Marxian scholars have also come to accept this complementarity – this dialectical relationship between what is often called the centre and the periphery or the metropolitan heartlands and the colonial or semi-colonial or neo-colonial areas of the world. Looking at this question over several decades, we find that different answers have predominated at different times.

The earliest answers – answers suggested by the colonial powers themselves – were quite simple. They said to Third World peoples: Marxism–Leninism or Scientific Socialism or Communism has absolutely no relevance to your needs and interests. Indeed, this ideology would be completely inimical to your needs and interests. The colonial powers, their spokesmen and ideologies simply said, in effect, that Marxism was not good for the natives; that this was not a vision of the world which should be incorporated into the way in which colonial peoples saw themselves, saw their societies, and saw the world outside. And this was consistent with their position of power. Colonialism sought to ensure that colonized peoples should not wage effective nationalist struggles. They were opposed in the early years, even to the expression of nationalism. So, it follows that they were all the more bitter, all the more concerned to oppose that brand of nationalism which was enlivened by Marxist thought which went beyond saying that we are determined to have independence, but that we are also determined to build a new society which is completely different from the capitalist society we have inherited.

And it is generally true that while colonialists were hostile towards Marxists inside of their own countries, they were doubly hostile to Marxism and to Marxists who might appear in India, in parts of Asia, Africa, Latin America and the Caribbean. Quite obviously, it has not been an easy history for Marxist thought inside of the Western countries – in Britain, France, in North America. Up until today, Western Marxists are discriminated against in institutions such as these. But the bourgeois metropolitan system has certain capacity to accommodate. It sometimes, in fact, goes out of its way to incorporate some individuals who are outside of the so-called mainstream, and it will therefore give and take within the limits of its own maintenance and it will allow some Marxist thought to exist. But the Third World practice for many years, and I think it still remains true, is to resolutely oppose, on the part of the same powers, the development of Marxist thought. It seems to me, then, that the bourgeoisie themselves recognize their vulnerability in the Third World; they recognize that Marxist thought has a double potency, if you like, in the Third World countries.

This attempt on the part of imperialism and the colonial powers to keep Marxism out of the Third World understanding, was not entirely successful. There have always been instances of African, Asian, Latin American and Caribbean Marxists operating in their own societies, operating at an international level – sometimes quite successfully. But, by and large, we must accept that throughout the colonial period – extending right through the 1920s, '30s and '40s – Marxism was an insignificant ideology, lacking both the individuals to articulate Marxist ideas in journals, and the political parties to represent the Marxist–Leninist position.

The colonialists were relatively successful in maintaining the exclusion of Marxist thought. More importantly, they created a generation of Third World scholars who were immersed in bourgeois theory and who peddled all of the understandings which they gained from bourgeois theory.

And this usually meant, for instance, that they were automatically anti-Marxist; without even thinking about it, they were anti-Marxist. They had an idealist vision of the world and they assumed that what they had was a universalistic vision. They saw the capitalist system and they thought that the capitalist system always was, is and always will be. They saw the human being functioning within the constraints of capitalist society, and they said 'there is man'; and they began to talk about human nature and the like, and they did not and cannot perceive that they are speaking about human nature only in a particular social system.

All of these understandings were encrusted in the Third World vision of itself. And that applies irrespective of whether we were trained in these institutions abroad, or whether we were trained in the surrogate institutions such as the University of the West Indies or the University of Ghana or Makerere. Because, one can be brought into line with the bourgeois worldview either by being brought to the metropole itself, or alternatively the bourgeois institutions can be transferred to the metropole to do the job locally, as a sort of forerunner of the international branch plant economy of the multinational corporations.

However, that was an era that I think is disappearing; it is not past. One has to see the trends; one has to see that, today, it is not a simple argument between bourgeois ideology and Marxist ideology. That simple dichotomy between good and bad – the forces of evil and the forces of Christianity, and so on; that kind of argument is no longer very acceptable. A number of factors have intervened. For one thing, when it used to be told to a Ghanian or to a Jamaican that Communism is evil and Marxism–Leninism has no value, it was part of a package in which the bourgeoisie asserted that Marxism–Leninism cannot work. You see, quite apart from the moral, philosophical or ideological arguments, there was this appeal to the so-called practical. It said: Even if we grant the theoretical validity of this system we can prove to you that it is not efficient, that it does not work; that capitalism is efficient and that socialism does not give people food; that there is starvation in Russia and no clothes; and that the Chinese are eating grass. You see, those were years ago in the early period of the development of the revolutionary systems in the world.

But as the Russian Revolution passed those initial years of extreme economic difficulty – the difficulties which they had inherited from Czarist regime, and as the Chinese Revolution grew from strength to strength – again transcending the period of absolute impoverishment of the masses that was characteristic of feudalism and imperialism in China, it was and is no longer possible to seriously propose to any Third World country that socialism does not work – that it is not a practical system, as it were. So the argument must shift; it must in some way come to terms with the ideological dimensions. I believe the argument has shifted and I would like to focus on that shift because it is the contemporary dimension of the discussion of Marxism in the Third World.

This new discussion – the new shift – means that in the first place, Marxism is not posed directly against bourgeois ideology. There is an attempt to avoid this direct confrontation. Marxism in the Third World – I've seen this in Africa, it's happening in the Caribbean, it happens in Asia – is counterposed against some other version or vision of the world. Africans or West Indians will be told: 'We understand that Marxism has some validity, but we do not think that Marxism is relevant for us. We have to look for our own solutions' – which is one of the more important ways of countering the Marxist worldview. And as you can see, it obviously has a greater initial plausibility than the old distinction between Marxism and bourgeois ideology – between socialism and capitalism.

A second variant on the same theme that is often interconnected, is that one can be told that there is some strength in

Marxism and in socialism on the one hand, and there is some strength in capitalism and capitalist theory on the other hand; and that one of our tasks is to borrow intelligently from the two systems. So, here again, you find that Marxism is not posited as something that one runs away from absolutely as an ogre that is painted in certain colours that are very frightening. It is approached rather obliquely, and one is told to choose some elements from either of the two systems.

I believe that these are both sleights of hand and are ideological devices intended to weaken the development of a scientific understanding of the world; and I shall try to indicate where I feel the logical weakness lies in both approaches.

A Peculiar View of the Third World

Let us first examine the approach which suggests that what we need in the Third World is something peculiar. If one is in Ghana, one will think about Ghanaian culture. In Africa, as a whole, there is a need for African socialism, it would be said. In India, in Sri Lanka: let us look for something that relates to our own culture. These are powerful arguments because they address real emotions; they address the colonial in his conception of himself. The colonial, after all, had been challenged as a being; his very identity had been challenged. He had been exposed to cultural imperialism, in addition to the political and economic exploitation. And, therefore, it rings a certain bell and elicits sympathy when one says we must avoid all foreign domination of thought, and we must ensure that that which we create is ours, that we cannot reject capitalism or bourgeois theory and take in its place socialism or Marxist theory, because that is a new form of imposition. And I think that there are a few Africans, a few Asians, who would put forward this kind of argument very ably, and I myself have tried to put it forward without any caricature whatsoever. I

58

think that this is the argument as it would be put forward at its best; and I still feel that, at its best, it is false. For several reasons.

First of all, when these individuals are speaking, they are automatically making the assumption that Scientific Socialist ideology or Marxism–Leninism is limited in time and space – culturally limited. That is the assumption to the argument; because on that assumption one can say Marxism was generated within Western Europe in the nineteenth century. Therefore, if it has any relevance – putting aside that question – its relevance is circumscribed by those factors. It may be relevant to the Europeans, it may have been relevant in the nineteenth century, or perhaps it is still relevant to Europeans in this century; but it is not relevant to us. That is to say an African, a Third World person, is speaking: it is not relevant to us because it is theirs; it is an alien, cultural thing. Later on, we might have to discuss the extent to which Marxism, like any ideology, must of necessity incorporate elements of the culture which produces and fosters and propagates it. But, in this position, the fundamental ideological assumption is a bourgeois assumption.

It's a metaphysical assumption which makes a separation between the application of scientific principles to the society as distinct from the application of scientific principles to the real world – to the natural world. Because the very individuals who would so cogently, and convincingly perhaps, make this kind of argument are individuals who have no qualms about standing before you and using this microphone. They have no qualms of standing before you and using the electricity, the harnessing of the electric energy; and, of course, they may be speaking in an African or Asian or Caribbean country. But they do not make a fanciful argument which suggests that things which originate in the natural world – the harnessing of principles of understanding the motion of the natural world – should be rejected a priori in the Third World because they were initially discovered in the First World or Second or whatever kind of ranking you are applying. And, without recognizing it, they are subscribing to a certain dichotomy which is their bourgeois philosophical worldview – that dichotomy which is perfectly prepared to discover (to seek out at any rate and then discover) the principles of motion in the natural world. The capitalists do that because it aids in production; it is an integral part of the capitalist system that they should maximize production; that they should maximize the efficiency of technology. So they will not mystify (certainly they will not consciously and deliberately mystify) the pursuit of scientific knowledge with regard to the real world.

But then by the same token, the bourgeois class – the capitalist class – has an interest in specifically mystifying the application of scientific principles to society; because the same application of scientific principles to society would suggest that we must understand the changes – the transitions by which capitalism itself came into being, and by which the particular class in power will be removed from power. It would be a study in their own liquidation, if you like, and one perhaps could not reasonably expect the bourgeoisie to promote the study of their own liquidation.

And so, we find that there is always that contradiction in bourgeois thought between the application of scientific principles to society and to the natural world – which is a very artificial distinction. And those who, as I said earlier, are making the argument about cultural validity and cultural uniqueness and peculiarity, are clearly falling victim to this distinction. The moment that we can break beyond that understanding, we can see even further the limitations of a position that tries to see Marxism as culturally distinct and as having no relevance to the Third World.

One of these limitations is that it is necessary first to misunderstand deliberately, to misread Marx in order to conduct their own polemics. They will say, for instance: Marx does not deal with the kinds of society which we have, Marx and Engels were writing about European society which had classes and we don't have the same classes; we don't have any proletarian workers. And they may be right. In some countries of Africa there is hardly any proletariat to speak of. Countries of Latin America and Asia perhaps have larger numbers; but, in any event, they are right in saying that the particular class configuration or even the absence of classes in a Third World country does not conform to the model of analysis that Marx might have organized for Western Europe, and which, of course, is relevant to North America.

In so doing, however, they overlook that which Marx himself had said, because Marx hadn't claimed that he was organizing a philosophical worldview and that he had created categories for Western Europe which were applicable in and of themselves to the Third World – applicable without any new intellectual or analytical effort. Indeed, Marx had to chastise those individuals (some of them calling themselves Marxists) who would like to have applied his understanding of Western Europe in a very uncritical way to the development of Eastern Europe; and he had to warn them that Marxism was not a general historical philosophical understanding of the whole world at all times, in every place. He made it very clear that that which he and Engels had been dealing with was a systematic and detailed formulation of the development of capitalism within Western Europe; and that they had attempted to describe and understand the specific features of capitalism specific to Western Europe. So that the universality which both he and Engels claimed, was not the universality that applied to Western Europe. The 'universality' is the universality of contradiction; the universality which can be determined by utilizing the historical materialist method with relationship to any given society. So that when those individuals say that Marxism claims that all societies must pass through the same processes, and that the important thing is the presence of the given working class in a particular way, and that therefore we must of necessity bypass this because our society is unlike that which Marx describes – I think those individuals have fundamentally failed to come to grips with what he was saying. And I don't think it is merely accidental; I think that there is an element of distortion which is deliberate. And that in itself is a serious reflection on their arguments, because, if you have to engage in deliberate distortion of the opposition's arguments before you can come to terms with the argument, it suggests that you yourself are coming from a very weak position.

Besides, yet another limitation of the attempt to force Marxism into these narrow boundaries of time and place arises out of the fact that these individuals fail to recognize and accept Marxism as a growing ideology. That is to say, just like with any body of science, it is not static; it takes in new ideas, it has new discoveries, it responds to the variations as scientific enquiry continues. That is why one can speak about Marxism–Leninism. The very fact that we couple Lenin's name to Marx's name in a very fundamental way, is a reflection of Lenin's contribution at a different time – his ability to say: Yes, we are looking at capitalism, but we are not looking at the same capitalism which Marx had looked at in the earlier part of the nineteenth century; instead, we are looking at capitalism in its imperialist epoch, and this is a qualitatively different thing. So, in that process, Lenin contributed to the growth of Marxist ideology.

Moreover, the same applies to the contributions by Mao; and the same would apply to the contributions by Che Guevara, or to the contributions by Amilcar Cabral. Contributions which recognize that Marxism is itself a growing body of scientific knowledge, that one has an ontology, one has an epistemology, and that from there one must move towards dealing with the particularities that occur in any given place at any given time. And this would certainly move

Marxism far beyond these mundane, restricted limits which have been forced upon it by some theoreticians.

In the practical day-to-day struggles of the Third World, irrespective of whether people accept some of these arguments – and you may think that they are esoteric and that the day-to-day struggle does necessarily take account of these arguments – Marxism continues to grow as a Third World ideology in spite of the attempts to present it as something alien to the Third World. And it continues to grow as an independent ideology seeking clear alternatives to capitalism, in spite of the attempts to divert this process by focusing on a compromise between capitalism and socialism.

That compromise is something I shan't discuss at any length because, again, the moment that one takes the care to understand Marxist ideology, it becomes immediately obvious that one cannot have a foot in both camps; it is not possible to talk about the coexistence indefinitely of a socialist and capitalist system. There may be, at a certain point of transition, the incorporation of elements which are capitalist in a socialist system or vice versa. But if that is so, then we will have to examine the tendency; we will have to examine which of the contradictory features is manifesting itself ultimately to become the dominant system. But it isn't possible for someone such as Leopold Senghor[1] to say: In Senegal we will have a little bit of capitalism, and a little bit of socialism, and then a little bit of Senegalism; but this is in effect what he says. He says: We're going to have three sectors of our economy. We will have the foreigners owning something, then we will have a section that is publicly owned, and then we will have some joint ownership; and this is put forward as a socialist alternative or an alternative to Marxism; and very consciously Senegal puts this forward as an alternative to Marxism.

Yet one of the many fallacies in this position is that Senegal began as a capitalist country. It is located within the international imperialist order. The Senegalese people were not making any choice about whether they wanted to be either capitalist or socialist; they were in fact capitalist. The only choice they can make is whether they want to continue to be located within the capitalist system or whether they want to escape from it. So it is a false duality to imagine that they are outside of either system, and that they are choosing from both to create a third alternative. And any steps which fail to remove it from the capitalist system are steps which, in effect, support the capitalist system.

The Rise of Marxism in the Third World

Quite apart from examining it at the level of the theoretical implications, one is struck by the sizeable increase in Marxism – or, to put it more effectively, the increase in the adherence to Marxism, the increase in the discussion of Marxism, the increase in the awareness of Marxism, in the Third World. All of these strategies pursued by Africans and Latin Americans and Asians – to stem the tide of Marxism – haven't really been effective. Because, while it may be difficult for anyone to say, for instance, that in Asia, in 1965, there were ten thousand Marxists and now there are twenty thousand (that sort of exact quantitative description we know may not be possible), I am certain that there would be no observers or analysts of the scene who would deny the increase in Marxism, and in adherence to Marxism. And this increase can be measured in a number of indirect ways.

It can be measured, for instance, by seeing the number of scholars who are using the formal tools of Marxist analysis – anthropologists and economists, political scientists, historians from Africa, Asia and Latin America – who, five or ten years ago would never have been found on the scene are today not in a majority, but they are conspicuous in each field. Very often conspicuous by their excellence, because they are engaging in hard original work which challenges bourgeois assumptions and manages to assert itself on the basis of its own internal logic and consistency. So that a glance at the journals – from the point of view of those of us in the academic community – will indicate to you the growing number of Marxists who are practising in every discipline in Third World countries. And this is not because they were encouraged; one can be very sure of that. This is itself a dialectical development, a development over and against the trend of their formulation, because they were formed mentally in bourgeois philosophy, as I said earlier.

A second measure is to look outside of the universities or beyond the level of university academics, at the number of student groups, the number of worker groups or independent intellectual groups that are avowedly Marxist. Not just that – one may say that they are using some Marxist terminology or that they are disguising their Marxist content. Nowadays, in the Third World, there are a large number of groups which come forward and say: We are Marxists. Now again I'm trying to avoid, for the moment, the discussion as to whether they come forward and say they are Maoists or they come forward and say they are something else, but they come forward and say that they are Marxist; that much is certain. And that is a very important change that is part of our contemporary scene; because, in most parts of the Third World, it is still hazardous to identify oneself as a Marxist. And therefore, the fact that it is happening more and more is an indication of a tremendous growth, and a willingness and a capacity to challenge the domination of bourgeois thought.

Alongside these groups – very often as part of the activity of the groups – we have the proliferation of journals which carry Marxist slogans, which carry Marxist analysis. These are things that can be discovered through a random sample, just looking through the Third World, especially if one has the opportunity to see the literature that comes out at what we call the grassroots level. Literature that is not necessarily put in the same glossy format as *Time* or *Fortune* magazines, but literature that comes through the hard sweat and labour of people turning a Gestetner, very often by hand, not even electrically, and producing things that may not be the most attractive to look at, but which carry out the task of Marxist reconsideration of society.

Marxism is growing in the Third World, and I don't think that this is merely because of some theoretical subtlety on the part of the Marxists themselves – if indeed this has any part to play. Rather, it appears to me to derive from the practical experience of the Third World over the last decade and a half – the practical experience gained since countries in Africa and Asia in particular achieved their so-called independence, their nominal constitutional independence. Ever since independence, these countries have had certain experiences; they have set out for instance to develop themselves, whatever that means to anybody else. But they very often had a conscious vision of developing, of advancing, and in so doing, or in attempting to do so, they utilize the well-known bourgeois theoretical assumptions about how one develops, they utilize bourgeois advisors to set up their four- and five-year development plans; they utilize bourgeois international experts to tell them how to take off. And the result is there for everyone to see. It is a failure of bourgeois thought to deliver the goods, if you like.

That is one of the most important considerations in explaining why the alternative philosophical view is gaining ground; because when the bourgeois theorists had before them the new field of independent African countries, then it could be said that they must be given a chance to prove whether they are right or wrong about capitalism being a road of development for everyone. But after ten or fifteen years, in some cases – in Asian countries much longer than that – it is no longer possible to say that bourgeois theory has any possibilities of growth for the Third World countries. Even the liberals, even neo-classical economists themselves, are turning towards Marxist-inspired visions and understandings of what is dependency and what is underdevelopment, and what are the ways out of these states of dependency and underdevelopment, so it is the practice which accounts, in no small measure, for the advance of Marxism in the Third World.

Class Struggle in the Third World

There is also the recognition that the Third World cannot stand outside of the rest of international society. It certainly cannot be considered in isolation from the rest of the capitalist world, nor for that matter, can it isolate itself from those parts of the world which have made socialist revolutions. This recognition came very clearly, or most clearly, and it came at the earlier period in South East Asia – a tremendous development of the Vietnamese struggle.

It came also in Latin America, because the Latin Americans had been independent for a long time and, after this political independence, they have had a long experience of neo-colonialism. An experience which forced them to recognize that there was no way in which they could understand the movement of Latin American society without understanding the interpenetration of foreign – mainly American – capital, monopoly capital into the Latin American environment. So that they began to build into their understanding of their society an understanding of the larger society. And if they had to understand the larger society, they automatically had to go back to understanding capitalism and to seeing why it was or why it is that capitalism enslaves not only its working class but indeed more so, the working class and the dispossessed peoples of the Third World.

One of the interesting choices which has been made by most Third World political spokesmen – choices at the ideological level – is a choice based on their unwillingness to recognize that class can be relevant in their own context. There was some factual basis for that unwillingness. Many Third World countries began their period of political independence with the internal class struggle at a very low level, because the internal classes had been subordinated to external capital, and the operation of internal class struggle had been subordinated to the operation of the nationalist struggle of all classes against the external monopoly capitalists. But, as the years advanced since independence, in each Third World country, the evidence began to grow of the decisive role of internal class struggles – of the growth of indigenous classes playing decisive roles in the motion of the internal societies. And this has also been a potent factor in forcing Third World peoples to come to grips with an analysis which has room for understanding the world in terms of class struggle.

An example which is always very clear and very illustrative, is the example of Ghana and the development of the thought of Kwame Nkrumah. Nkhruma had always had some Marxist overtones before he got into power and when he got into power. There was a time when he used to describe himself as a Marxist and a Christian; there was a time when he used to describe himself as a Consciencist; he spoke of himself as a pan-Africanist. He attempted to incorporate some Marxist insights, but not as a total methodology, not as something that underlay his whole political philosophy and his political practice, largely because he insisted that there were no classes in Ghana. And then he was overthrown and he went to Guinea and he was given aid by his friend Sekou Toure; and in his last days he produced a considerable body of writing. And in this writing he proclaimed: I used to say that there were no classes; but when I was overthrown by the Ghanaian petty bourgeois class, I discovered that there were classes. If you read Nkrumah's *Class Struggles in Africa*, that is basically what he is saying. He very clearly, in his own way, delimits the classes in Africa and accepts that the petty bourgeoisie functions as a class in its own right, with interests hostile to the African working class and peasantry; and he is therefore able to reformulate his vision of Ghana and of Africa, or he did so before he died.

Nkhruma, of course, was one of the foremost nationalists; he stood on the vanguard of nationalist struggle. But that block to his full understanding came because he could not or would not – I think it is a combination of the two – perceive the development of classes inside of Ghana.

Today, the obvious growth of indigenous classes throughout Asia, the Caribbean, Latin America and the rest of the Third World is a clear pointer to the need to grasp a strategy which recognizes, or which is based upon a recognition of the existence of class struggle as a motive force in history; and here again Marxism comes in for additional attention on the part of Third World scholars. Of course, to say that Marxism is relevant does not necessarily say that the body of Marxist thought which exists is adequate to an understanding of the Third World predicament.

These are two different questions, in different order of logic; and I think they have been confused by a number of people. Marxism as an operative methodology in political philosophy, as the ideology which sprang from the working class in Europe, has developed its own. We can measure physically the body of literature which has been produced by Marxists; and that literature has been preoccupied with Western Europe, with North America and with the developed countries, because most of the Marxists came from those countries. And even Third World Marxists in the early days, were concerned with metropolitan society.

So, there is a body of Marxist literature which is inadequate to the needs of the Third World because it just does not deal, for the most part, with the problems of the Third World. So that when one says that Marxism is relevant to the Third

World, it means that the Marxist scholar – whether he be Third World, of Third World origin or not – who attempts to deal with Marxism in the Third World must be operating at the most advanced and creative level. He is not merely transferring known truths from another part of the world to the African or Asian situations; he has to engage in the very difficult task of building from the bottom, an actual body of Marxist enquiry and Marxist analysis of the societies in question. And this is where one has to emphasize – and to emphasize and to emphasize once again – that Marxism can only be of value if whatever it takes to be the universal is applied to the particular; and it is in the very particularity of the exercise that one will demonstrate that the universal is actually universal and that it is applicable.

In the United States for instance, there has been – and no doubt there has been a spillover of the same discussion in Canada – very lengthy, sometimes very violent discussion among black brothers and sisters about the relevance of Marxism. It basically comes from the understanding of whether this Marxism has any validity to black people in their special predicament as an ethnic group. And the arguments against its applicability are rather similar to the arguments which an African or a West Indian might use – the sort of arguments I have outlined above. In other words, those who are opposed would say that: Marxism is about class, and our problem is a racial or ethnic problem. Marxism originated with the same Western society which dominates us and we must reject all forms of white cultural domination, Marxism included.

However, there continues to be the growth of a serious interest in Marxism on the part of Afro-Americans – the black population in the United States. And their task, quite clearly, consists in bringing the tools of Marxism to bear upon the specific history of the United States. In that specific history, a number of contradictions arose; and if the contradiction between races happens to be a fundamental contradiction, then that is the contradiction which will attract their attention. They will have to come up with the formulations which deal with the specifics of their own social situation. Failure to do so does in fact strengthen the arguments of those who try to suggest that Marxism is irrelevant. Because, if you proceed into a situation, whether it be an analysis of Afro-America or an analysis of Pakistan, and you do not attempt to develop with respect to those specific situations, but rather merely to transfer a body of knowledge in a fixed static form from another part of the world, then you will be accused of being irrelevant. You will be accused of cultural hegemony; you will be accused of trying to force the indigenous interpretation into your own external imperialist-oriented model.

The Burden of Third World Marxists

That is why I think that the responsibility which Third World Marxists carry is an extremely heavy responsibility. In Western Europe, in North America, it is possible to plug into an existing body of thought. Any discussion about Marxism in these parts can immediately find some source of established Marxist orthodoxy, they can find the unorthodoxies; they can in fact adjudicate between all kinds of rival versions to Marxism, in its application to their own society. It doesn't mean that the Western Marxist does not function to revitalize and to review the Marxist vision of his own society, but he has something to review. The Third World scholar is more often than not starting from the very beginning, having nothing to review, having nothing else but sometimes inadequate empirical data – empirical data which has to be collated and picked up from bourgeois sources. And because they have to be lifted out of a bourgeois context, you often find yourself in a very difficult position; because it is not entirely impossible to separate the data from the conceptualizations which might have lain behind the enquiries, and which therefore influenced the particular type of data which was collected. So, the Third World Marxists will find themselves starting from scratch. But it is a task that has to be carried out because, to do otherwise, is precisely to fall into the hands of those who want a sort of cultural exceptionalism, who will say that Marxism is not for us because it is inimical or antithetical to our own culture and our own history.

The record so far is very clear that capitalism has been on the retreat; that Marxism–Leninism started out undoubtedly as something within Europe and is today of course embraced by 800 million Chinese – which itself always makes me wonder why it is that people still say that Marxism is a white ideology. One would have thought if the ideology is to be coloured by the colour of the majority of its adherents, then Marxism is to be called a yellow ideology. And if it is a yellow ideology or is capable of being yellow, and if it is capable of being brown in the case of some Asian countries, of being black in the case of Cabral's Guinea or of Mozambique under Frelimo, then immediately one sees that there are very many breaches that are made in this wall which was being built, or which certain people attempt to build around Marxism to keep it from the world's least developed peoples.

My own contribution is merely to bring this to the attention of Third World scholars – for the most part, Third World students; because in an institution such as this, one will of course come into contact with Marxist ideology. But inevitably, Marxist ideology will be the submerged ideology; the dominant ideology is going to be the ideology of the ruling class. As I had cause to tell my students many years ago at the University of Dar es Salaam, when someone asked how they should know which is a bourgeois ideology, which textbook they should take up, which one will have a bourgeois view and which will have the capitalist view, I told them that they could go into the library and close their eyes and stick out their hand and the chances are they would have got a bourgeois book. So that they could proceed on that assumption; they don't have to select, just close your eyes, feel around, grab any number of books, and you're dealing with a bourgeois worldview.

Now, at the same time, there are possibilities; there are possibilities which perhaps, when we live in the metropoles, we do not appreciate them until we go back to the Third World countries from which we came. The possibilities lie in the contradictions of this society and the fact that Marxist thought, irrespective of all these things, is in fact present; and that literature is available, and that facilities for enquiry are available. And one could urge therefore that, even within the realms of institutions that are designed to carry out a particular ideological function, it is possible to conduct a sort of guerrilla intellectual war by which one will have access not to that which was designed specifically for one, but access which hinges upon the dialectical transition beyond that which was intended for one.

There are many things which I believe the Third World scholar can grasp, in spite of the quite conscious attempt on the part of all of our institutions – including those in the Third World – to reformulate us and to continue to programme us as bourgeois thinkers.

5

Labour as a Conceptual Framework for Pan-African Studies

At the most fundamental level, the pan-African historian has to be engaged in the study of either the African continent or the African peoples abroad. It is not at all necessary that he has to be concerned with the links between the two. Nevertheless, there are a number of ways in which the connection can be and has been approached. The two most outstanding would seem to be (a) the choice of a subject that in itself spans Africa and Africans in the New World, such as the slave trade and the pan-African movement; and (b) the search for the African roots of particular New World cultural phenomena, notably religion and music. The proposed use of 'Labour' as a conceptual framework for pan-African studies is in addition to and not a replacement of the already established modes of approach.

The ways in which people organize their labour and the tools with which they work provide an entree to the study of all history from the time that early man was capable of fashioning a crude pebble tool in Eastern Africa. Furthermore, labour is the basis for other global approaches to human history which present their analysis in terms of class and other social formations. This universality has certain advantages, since African history must be evaluated not as a discrete and isolated entity, but as a part of human development. Useful conceptual approaches should therefore facilitate comparisons with other areas of the world. The contention here is that there have been certain peculiarities in the way that Africans have worked or have been forced to work, and those labour patterns over the past few centuries have largely determined the relations between Africans and non-Africans. It is within the present stage of world development that one finds the initial justification for supposing that the labour concept can be of major utility in pan-African history, because no overview of the world today can fail to deal with the contrasts between the rich and the poor nations – between what are essentially the white and non-white peoples of our planet – and underpinning those contrasts are differences in the type of labour performed and the technology of work. What appears in popular jargon as 'the difference between the "haves" and the "have-nots"' is virtually identical with what economists term 'the international division of labour'.

Just as bourgeois intellectuals take the relationship between capital and labour as a 'given' and almost as a 'natural' factor, so they tend to treat the international division of labour in a static fashion, depriving it of its broad historical dimensions. As a result, it is argued that the international trade network (which is so disadvantageous to the underdeveloped countries) is based on different comparative cost advantages in production. It is said that the differences are attributable to different resource endowments, and that world trade enhances the specialization of production in all participating countries. This argument incorporates certain obvious absurdities. Which continent is richer than Africa in natural resources? And yet Africa is the least specialized, except in lines of production that require the least skill, are least remunerative and most vulnerable within the international capitalist system. African peoples everywhere, both within the continent and abroad fall within the category of the poor, the underdeveloped and the under-specialized. The explanation for this must be seen in historical perspective, and it involves a close look at the way Africans have worked prior and subsequent to involvement within Europe and the Americas.

There have indeed been a great deal of scattered studies on African labour, which are illuminating even though they are not necessarily informed by an awareness that similar tendencies were operating wherever Africans worked, and that they were slowly building into an international pattern. What follows below is a mere sketch of the possibilities that might be opened up by looking at the vista of the pan-African past with the labour concept consciously and consistently being utilized as the framework for enquiry. Five broad divisions suggest themselves by way of periodization:

1) Africa before the white man
2) Africans under white slave owners abroad
3) Africa in the epoch of the internationalization of trade (fifteenth to mid-nineteenth century)
4) Africans in post-slavery America
5) The foreign exploitation of African labour within the continent (late nineteenth century to the present).

1. Africa before the White Man

The number of issues to be considered in this category are numerous. Many are brought together within the debate about 'feudalism' in Africa which was once keenly conducted among historians of Africa, and has now virtually petered out as far as English-speaking scholars are concerned. However, within Francophone circles, there is still a stimulating discussion about whether there was a distinctive African mode of production. These issues involve comparisons not only with Europe but also with Asia. Since it was Europe which subsequently came into contact with Africa, it is well to understand the features in African and European society that determined their respective roles of subordination and domination. Naturally, the nature of African work reflected the environment and social interests, and African skills were developed in directions different from those of Europe. For example, West

Africa in the fifteenth century boasted skills in brass casting and plastic arts, advanced techniques in canoe-building and river travel, and notions of agriculture relevant to tropical forests, savannahs and swamps. Europe, on the other hand, had superiority to some extent in arms technology and to an overwhelming extent in shipbuilding, navigation, administration and accounting.

Crudely speaking, it could be said that by the fifteenth century, European labour and technology was more advanced than its African counterpart and hence the European capacity to exploit Africa through trade. But there is scope for a more comprehensive analysis which would pinpoint the precise areas of social dissimilarities vis-à-vis Africa and Europe. It was over a period of time that the dissimilarities transformed themselves into advantages and disadvantages. For instance, Africa lacked a technological dynamic leading towards mass production. When mass production became the norm in Europe and a decisive factor in world trade, then African handicraft skill turned out to be a disadvantage. This did not come into effect until the nineteenth century, when Europe came to define what was developed and what was not, with their own technology and way of life held up as the standard of excellence, for 'those who can define are the masters' and vice versa. In order to start the reconstruction of pan-Africanism with a clean slate, it would be helpful to understand in what direction African labour had been developing at the time that we were our own masters.

2. Africans under White Slave-owners Abroad

An interesting sidelight of the slave trade which has never been brought into view is the extent to which many agricultural, mining and craft skills were transported to the New World. The early slave trade to the Spanish in the New World sought labour to engage in mining and cattle raising in the Greater Antilles and on the Spanish Main. Several of the peoples of the Senegambia who were victims of this phase of the slave trade were experienced as pastoralists and familiar with open-pit mining of gold and iron ore. Crops such as cotton, indigo and rice were produced in the American colonies and the Caribbean by Africans who were already growing those same crops in their own societies. It could hardly be a mere coincidence that rice production was successfully launched in the Brazilian state of Maranhão in the mid-eighteenth century just at the moment when African labour was being brought in from the traditional rice-farming sector of Upper Guinea.

Nevertheless, as has been argued by several scholars, the slave regime was hostile to the formation of new or sophisticated skills within the Western tradition. Slave labour was meant to be the cheapest possible, and it consequently had to be unskilled – carrying out the simplest tasks with the crudest of tools. Otherwise, there would have been specialization and division of labour far beyond the managerial capacity of the overseers and whips. Slavery never evolved beyond backward agriculture, so industrialization was out of the question. Meanwhile, in Europe the bourgeoisie were forced constantly to renovate their means of production, which meant enhancing the skills of their own white workers. The slave sojourn in the Americas, in the Indian Ocean and in Europe by Africans gave the first clear indication of the development of a broad gap in labour performance and technology between the white and the black races.

3. Africa in the Epoch of the Internationalization of Trade

Beginning with the Congo, Europeans showed themselves unwilling to accede to African requests for the importation of new techniques from Europe, although the Congolese requested masons, doctors, apothecaries and teachers. This refusal was repeated when Dahomey and Asante made similar requests in the eighteenth century. Europe was consciously blocking the spread of technology which is a central feature in the emergence of a more scientific mode of production, both in Europe and later in Japan. Africans received cheap consumer goods, while Europe secured gold for expanding its monetary economy and labour to create value and open up a whole brave new world in the Americas.

The impact of the slave trade on the African labouring population is obviously a topic that would of necessity be examined if one is interested in how African labour has fared historically. The only comment offered here is by way of rejection of a recent trend in studies assessing the slave trade. The approach begins by suggestion (with justification) that figures of slaves exported have been greatly exaggerated in the past. There follows the conclusion that the slave trade was therefore far less significant within African history than it was previously made out to have been. The conclusion is a non sequitur, since the impact must be measured for specific places at particular times. At the end of the seventeenth century, the ports of what is now Dahomey[1] were loading 30,000 victims per year, and this was sustained for decades. The hinterland of the Bight of Biafra had its turn at the end of the eighteenth century; while a heavy flow came from Lake Nyasa in the decades before 1850. These are three of many instances, and to find a point of comparison in European history it would be necessary to look at what transpired during the Thirty Years War in Germany, and during the two World Wars in Europe. Besides, in Europe such wars contributed to the development of a particular type of society; so that after all the casualties and all the disruption, opportunities were provided for building bigger things by combining capital, science and skilled labour in ever more daring ways. What did the slave trade build in Africa? Nothing but a bridge leading to the next phase of exploitation where the present international division of labour came into its own.

4. Africans in Post-slavery America

Africans in the New World fared little better after slavery in terms of making their labour more scientific and appropriating more benefits to themselves. In the West Indies and the United States, many ex-slaves were frustrated in their attempts to set up an independent peasantry, and instead they became rural proletariat or quasi-serfs under the name of sharecroppers. There was diversification of black labour into trades and petty commerce, but nothing which could upset the basic pattern of American society where capital came either from whites at home or abroad and where the dominant technology was in the hands of the whites. For the vast majority of New World blacks, phrases such as 'the reserve army of labour', 'labour reservoir' and 'last hired first fired' adequately sum up the position. The reference to the black community in the US as an internal colony has many justifications, not least of which is the remarkable fact that black labour within industrial America has virtually the same relation to whites in terms of skills as does continental African labour with regards to Europe and white America.

Since emancipation, the necessity of obtaining modern scientific labour skills was always appreciated, at different levels of perception, by sectors of the black population in the Americas. There was an awareness that real equality with whites would follow only after the acquisition of a technique that was equal to that of the oppressors, and this explains the tremendous drive towards education within the first generation of legally free black people. Of course, since whites retained political power, there were a thousand ways in which they could thwart the achievement of that objective, and those who broke through the education cordon simply made a contribution to established white technology. The few exceptions to this rule were individuals who sought to aid black political liberation and to build up a tradition of independent black activity on both sides of the Atlantic.

5. The Foreign Exploitation of African Labour within the Continent

Having tired of exploiting African labour abroad in the chattel form, the international capitalist system with Western Europe at its epicentre transferred its interest to African labour on the continent, setting up the political apparatus of colonialism at the same time that European scholars (including non-Marxists) attest to the tremendous role played by capital in imperialist expansion. In industrial society, the concept of capital automatically calls to mind that of labour; but it is worth noting that on the African continent in the colonialist era, labour was held back by the colonialists using several means in addition to the provision of fixed capital and wages. The colonial period is the best documented in African history both from the viewpoint of written records and the accessibility of orally preserved records. Studies to date on forced labour, labour migrations, peasant cash-crop production, the proletarianization of labour in South Africa, and so forth, have tremendous scope to be expanded to cover the whole continent. Those areas of history are so close to the present that their significance in influencing conditions in Africa as they are today is virtually self-evident. Within the field of contemporary history, it becomes even more vital to forge a mature social science approach which attempts to grapple with political economy in its historical perspective. Analytically, the labour factory has the advantage of being valid for several academic disciplines, and it can therefore be pivotal in arriving at an overview of the 'state of the nation' in Africa and in particular parts of the continent.

Conclusion

By re-emphasizing that the above is a mere outline of possibilities, certain criticisms concerning omissions can be avoided. However, there is one particular limitation that is perhaps inherent in the approach: namely that it tends to treat African history using external and largely European frames of reference. For instance, 'Africa before the white man' might suggest that the coming of the whites at a particular point in time marked an entirely new phase in the continent's history. Needless to say, areas of Africa have continued with their own dynamic virtually up to the present and one has to be careful in distinguishing where the European presence was merely one factor among many and where it was the sole or dominant factor. Besides that, there is the danger attendant upon any interpretation based on isolating one variable – the conclusions could be lopsided if a great deal of attention is not paid to the interrelations between that variable and the numerous others which are always involved in any historical reconstruction.

Occasionally, some historians deny that the writing of history is an exercise in contemporary politics. Yet many among those would subscribe to the now-hackneyed adage that 'every generation rewrites its own history according to its own lights', which is another way of saying that the base of operation is always the contemporary socio-political scene. In any event, pan-African historians have largely taken it upon themselves to make it explicitly clear that history and the writing of history must be used as a means of liberation of our people. This does not necessarily mean that the historian qua historian is in the front line of the struggle, or that he has ready solutions, but at least he should be called upon to investigate areas relevant to an understanding of the present predicament of black peoples around the world. Looking at our labour history should provide some further insights into the differentiation in labour skills and technology which is now so characteristic of black/white relations, and it has the added advantage of underscoring the sameness of historical experience of a people scattered in different parts of the world.

6

The Angolan Question

I would like to come to the situation in the United States and to look at the types of responses, and to look at what I consider to be some fairly horrendous mistakes which were made by certain forces in this country, the United States, in their approach to the Angolan question.

Again, I will dismiss at least one element. We can dismiss those who are attempting to hire black mercenaries for the FNLA (National Liberation Front of Angola) and UNITA (the National Union for the Total Independence of Angola). When this individual (Roy Innis, who took over the Congress of Racial Equality in 1968) purports to be organizing black mercenaries to go and fight in Africa, and then we know that mercenaries cost, whether they are black or white – and we know that this particular black functionary cannot afford to pay anybody – we know that these black mercenaries would have been paid by imperialism, to go and fight in Angola.

However, I think we can dismiss that as an aberrant phenomenon – as the expression of a particularly reactionary and unresponsive force within the black American political environment. So, we should really concentrate attention on those elements that are serious. With serious people, one engages in serious debate. And I think there were a large number of serious people throughout the Afro-American community who supported UNITA when they should have been lending uncompromising support to the MPLA (People's Movement for the Liberation of Angola) at that particular historical juncture.

It was immediately obvious that there was a startling coincidence – a startling convergence – between the positions of certain individuals who call themselves progressive, revolutionaries, and who in fact regarded themselves as the essence of revolution – yet their positions converged with that of US imperialism. And this amazing historical convergence needs to be understood.

I assume that there are elements within the audience who took that position, and I'm not going to engage in any abuse of those elements. I am simply going to say I believe the position was historically completely incorrect. I will indicate how I believe that error took place.

The first thing is UNITA gained a certain popularity in this country in the very late sixties and the early seventies, particularly in the period of the rise of the African liberation movement, and the like. I was following the process, so I know that they were becoming more exposed and more popular in this country. And that they used certain, very opportunist political tactics and techniques. They simply appealed to the growing black consciousness by saying, 'Inside of Angola we stand for the elevation of the black man to a position of dignity and rule, and the MPLA stands for the elevation of whites and mulattoes over the indigenous African people.' That was the standard line in the late sixties and early seventies.

And they would then say, 'Look at the MPLA. It has so-and-so, who is in its executive, who is a white, who is a Portuguese. It has so many mulattoes who are on the Central Committee, it has so-and-so who is married to a white woman, President Neto, and so on and so forth.'

And in the context of the US, I think that those are very telling points. In the context of the black struggle in this country, when brothers and sisters were going through that terrible period of self-identification, trying to extract themselves out of the dominant white culture, I think that those points made a great deal of impact. Particularly because the MPLA was not really seeking to influence the Afro-American population. Or much of the American population.

So that is one reason why the UNITA gained in popularity. And when we examine that very carefully, we must of course admit that to declare blackness is a very easy thing to do. I mean the same character who was mobilizing black mercenaries was also in the forefront of declaring his blackness – and he would call himself Garveyite, and so on and so forth.

To declare for blackness is one of the easier things to do. Once one recognizes the opportunities inherent in that situation.

But surely we need to go further than that. We need to examine, first, whether the reality in Angola was the reality as portrayed by UNITA. We need to go further and ask whether the historical experience of Angola could be so easily assimilated into the historical experience of black people in the US that Afro-Americans should run to make a judgement on Angola on the basis of some knowledge they had that so-and-so was married to a white. Or that so-and-so was a mulatto.

Because the central understanding that we must reach is that any situation must be examined on its own historical merits. What is called 'race' in the US is not the same thing as what might be called race in Angola. In fact, in this country, those who are all called black, or used to be called Negro – if they went to Angola, they would be distinguished, many, as mulattoes. If we want to understand Angola and the complex of the relationships between social strata and race, and so forth, we must then understand Angola. We cannot sit in Washington or in Detroit and imagine that what we are seeing around the block is Angolan society.

And this seems to me to be one of the mistakes which the brothers made when they tried to transform a very simplistic understanding of black–white relationships in the judgement of whether they would support the MPLA or support UNITA.

One is reminded here of some of the things which Fanon wrote in regard to Africa, when he was talking about the pitfalls of national consciousness. He was talking about the pitfalls of African national consciousness. Now we can apply that to the pitfalls of black national consciousness. Which is to say that national consciousness is clearly a liberating force, but at a certain point it can provide blinkers. It can turn into blinkers and constitute a barrier for further understanding of the real world.

The second and more widespread factor, and one that ultimately proved to be most decisive for many black progressives, was the notion that UNITA was a Maoist movement. And these left forces who opposed the MPLA were moving from the starting point of supporting Marxism–Leninism, Mao Zedong thought.

In their own words, they have a vision and an analysis of contemporary society wherein they identify as the principal contradiction between the two superpowers. They argue further that the more dangerous force is Soviet socialist imperialism, because it's more covert, it's more subtle, and because it ultimately can be more powerful, since capitalist imperialism is on the wane. And therefore, in a situation in which the Soviets are involved, one has to take a stand on the opposite side.

Now, what is my disagreement with that position? I shall not go into all my disagreements, because I do not want any sort of global confrontation. I am not in favour of trying to resolve all the problems of the world at the same time, in a single stroke. So that I'm not going to attempt to deal with that postulation about the principal contradiction and its implication.

What we are going to ask is how does that relate to Angola with its specific characteristics. If someone holds that belief as a sincere revolutionary tenet, when that person approaches Angola, how is it that such a belief ends by placing such forces on the side of those who have for 500 years oppressed the African people?

What explanation does such a person give to the Angolans who have been engaged since 1960 in armed struggle against the Portuguese, against NATO, who at the end of that struggle found they were faced with the South Africans and with an escalation of US support to the so-called liberation movement which had been harassing the genuine freedom fighters for many years?

So that from a dialectical perspective and a scientific perspective we struggle and work to discover the correct line. It is only from a theological perspective that one knows the correct line because of revealed truth. And it seems to me that the limitations of that position were very clearly revealed in the Angolan situation. I have not seen a single analysis from forces claiming that they had the 'correct' line, which meant opposing the Soviets – not a single analysis of what was going on inside of Angola. It was purely external. And I do not believe we can proceed on that basis.

II

Development and Underdevelopment

7

The Historical Roots of African Underdevelopment

Tomas Szentes, in his survey of *Interpretations of Economic Development*, observed that, in contrast to bourgeois theories, Marxist writing 'explains the phenomenon of economic underdevelopment, the perspectives of eliminating it and the concrete questions on further development, always in relation to *history*, within the framework of historical interrelations, by concentrating on *the main driving forces* of social and economic development, and by analyzing phenomena and their causes as *dialectical* interdependencies'. He then goes on to draw attention to the fact that 'it is particularly and *naturally* the national theoreticians of the underdeveloped countries themselves, who stress the international aspects of economic underdevelopment, and the latter's relations with colonialism, even if without any sign of Marxist mentality.' It is no accident that the Tanzanian, Justinian Rweyemamu, puts forward the view that the poverty of 'developing' countries is to be largely traced to the historical relationships of the metropolitan countries and the former colonial countries. The West Indian, Norman Givan, in a study of 'Multinational Corporations and Dependent Underdevelopment in Mineral Export Economies', also urges that the origins of institutional dependence must be sought in the historical evolution of the economies for centuries before. Both are products of and spokesmen for colonized portions of the globe, reacting against the metropolitan bias of standard bourgeois approaches to the problem of development.

Unfortunately, historical dimensions to the analysis of the African economy are lacking, because enquiry into the African past, as conducted by historians, has seldom concerned itself with seeking explanations for the present international division of labour and all that goes with it. My examination here does not pretend to be exhaustive, but hopefully it will shed some light on the coming into being of the structural features associated with development and underdevelopment, as instanced in the economies of Western Europe and Africa. Because the economic history of Europe is better known, more emphasis will be placed on African underdevelopment; and for similar reasons, the colonial period will be neglected relative to the centuries commonly referred to as 'pre-colonial'.

The first significant thing about the internationalization of trade in the late fifteenth century was that Europeans took the initiative and went to other parts of the world. No Chinese junks reached Europe, and if any African canoes reached the Americas (as is sometimes maintained) they did not establish two-way links. This meant that what was called international trade was nothing but the extension overseas of European interests. Insofar as there was a strategy to international trade and the production that supported it, that strategy was firmly in European hands, and specifically in the hands of the maritime nations from the North Sea to the Mediterranean. They owned and directed the great majority of the world's ocean-going vessels, and they controlled the financing of trade between four continents. Africans had little clue as to the tri-continental linkages between Africa, Europe and the Americas; nor did the inhabitants of the Moluccas have any notion of the European markets into which their species were directed by European ships. Europe had a monopoly of economic intelligence of the international exchange system seen as a whole, for Western Europe was the only sector capable of viewing the system as a whole.

Europeans used the superiority of their ships and cannon to gain control of all the world's waterways. For instance, force was necessary in the case of the Sino-Japanese trade and with regards to the Arabs in East Africa. Once European hegemony was achieved, it gave them the power to allocate roles to every other part of the world, so that the various inputs intermingled with the benefits of Western Europe. Even the whites in the Americas were for three centuries on the periphery of a system whose centre of power was in Western Europe. Initially, the Portuguese, Spanish and Dutch had the most far-flung interests. When the Iberians were still in command of a major sector of world trade in the first half of the seventeenth century, they engaged in buying cotton clothes in India to exchange for slaves in Africa to mine gold in America. Part of the gold in the Americas would then be used to purchase spices and silks from the Far East. The concept of metropole and colony did not require European settlement. In Africa (and Asia) it was sufficient that local economies were in some way drawn into the web of international commerce.

It is interesting to note that what is called 'international law' also reflected the early division of the trading world into metropoles and dependencies. The law recognized by different states as governing the high seas was understandably European and not Indonesian or African. On the Atlantic and in the Indian Ocean, the African more likely than not was an object rather than subject or master of the law. Slavers in a Dutch slave ship were legally protected against piracy, because they were Dutch property. The law of the metropoles became the law of international relations. This is yet another reflection of the commercial hegemony established by Europe at the onset of the epoch of international trade.

Africa had little say in the determination of the import and export content of its commerce with Europeans. Europe's exports were an extension of domestic production of and demand for a wide range of articles, such as Dutch linen,

Spanish iron, English pewter, Portuguese wines, French brandy, Venetian glass beads, German muskets, and so forth. Europeans were also able to unload on the African continent goods which had become unsalable in Europe. Thus, items like old sheets, cast-off uniforms, technologically outdated firearms, and a whole range of *pacotille* found guaranteed markets in Africa. Africans slowly became aware of the possibility of demanding and obtaining better imported goods, and pressure was exerted on the captains of ships, but the interplay between African buyer and European supplier was extremely circumscribed. Europeans were most concerned about regional variants like the demand for copper in Eastern Nigeria and iron on the Upper Guinea Coast. They also took into account shifting tastes within any given region; but the overall range of trade goods which left Hamburg, Copenhagen and Liverpool was determined almost exclusively by the pattern of production and consumption within Europe itself.

The effectiveness of Europe's power to make decisions within the international trading system was best seen in the way that it selected what Africa would export. A complete list of African export commodities since the fifteenth century would include things such as civet perfume, ambergris, indigo, monkeys and feathers: but, of course, those were mere curiosities. The economically significant commodities were very few and were chosen by Europeans in accordance with European needs.

The ships of the Portuguese discoverers gave the search for gold the highest priority; partly on the basis of well-known information that West African gold reached Europe across the Sahara, and partly on the basis of speculation. The Portuguese were successful in abstaining gold in parts of West Africa and in eastern Central Africa; and it was the 'Gold Coast' which attracted the greatest attention from Europeans in the sixteenth and seventeenth centuries. The number of forts built there was testimony to this, and the nations involved included

the Scandinavians and the German principality of Branden-
burg, as well as other colonial stalwarts such as the British,
Dutch and Portuguese. However, since gold was limited to
very small areas of Africa as far as Europeans were aware, the
principal export was human beings.

Only in a very few places at given times was there the export
of another commodity of equal or greater importance. For
instance, in Senegal there was gum, in Sierra Leone camwood,
and in Mozambique ivory.

Why Europeans were anxious to acquire gold would appear
to require no explanation, but, apart from the universal fas-
cination with the yellow metal, one must take into account
that it was a direct response to a pressing need in Europe:
namely, the need for gold coins within the growing capitalist
money economy. Camwood was also called into existence as
a West African export because of the expanding capitalism in
Europe. It was mainly utilized for its yield of red dye, and it
ceased to be of value in the nineteenth century when European
technological advance created substitutes. Ivory from Africa
passed into European industry (as distinct from artwork)
during and after the sixteenth century, once the lathe had
made precision-cutting possible. Its export to Europe continued well into the colonial period, until plastic substitutes
undermined important sectors such as billiard and bowling
ball manufacture. It is in the light of its own needs and technology that Europe has always made the decisions concerning
what Africa should export and concerning the beginning and
decline of each export commodity. The most crucial of these
decisions for 'pre-colonial' African trade was Europe's allocation to Africa of the role of supplier of human captives to be
used as slaves in various parts of the world.

It is a valid question to ask why Africans accepted the terms of
what they should export, and particularly with regard to the
sale of human beings. One suggestion which was at one time

widely accepted and unchallenged was that African society already had slaves which were simply handed over to European buyers. The institution of slavery has co-existed with and formed part of communal, feudal and capitalist societies; but its widest incidence occurred when communalism was extensively broken down, which was not the case in Africa in the fifteenth and sixteenth centuries. The most likely explanation is that captives were made in war, and it is reasonable to assume that such *fresh* captives (as distinct from those who had earned a place in their captors' society and family structure) would have been considered readily expendable to European buyers.

One has also to take into account the offer of European commodities as a pole of attraction. Paradoxically enough, the influence of European goods can scarcely be attributed to their quality. On the contrary, things such as cheap European fabrics were inferior to African products and this was recognized by buyers. However, they were brought to Africa in large quantities, so availability was the crucial factor. No doubt, the novelty of European commodities also led to their being accepted in exchange for gold or human beings. Estaban Montejo, an African who ran away from a Cuban slave plantation in the nineteenth century, recalled that his people were wooed into slavery by the colour red. Diverting as his recollection may appear, it should not be dismissed lightly. He wrote as follows:

It was the scarlet which did for the Africans; both the kings and the rest surrendered without a struggle. When the kings saw that whites – I think the Portuguese were the first – were taking out these scarlet handkerchiefs, and the blacks were so excited by the scarlet they ran down to the ships like sheep and there they were captured. The Negro has always liked scarlet. It was the fault of this colour that they put them in chains and sent them to America.

In the Congo, the slave trade did not get under way without grave doubts and opposition from Africans who had established contact with the Europeans. The king of the state of Kongo clearly defied the nature of his expectations from Europe. He asked for masons, priests, clerks, physicians, and the like; but instead he was overwhelmed by slave ships sent by his Catholic brothers in Portugal, and a vicious trade was opened up by exploiting contradictions within the loosely structured Kongo kingdom. It might be objected that the Kongo king who took this stand against slavery had been converted to Christianity and was speaking as a Catholic. But there was little in Catholicism either in Portugal or among the missionaries in Kongo which would have raised any sanguine hopes that the Christian religion was in any way a barrier to the enslavement of Africans. With the date of the Kongo episode being at the beginning of the sixteenth century it can legitimately be interpreted as rare surviving evidence of an important aspect of the initial confrontation between Europeans and Africans at the onset of the internationalization of trade and the onset of the Atlantic slave trade in particular. An African ruler had conceived of possibilities of mutually beneficial interchange between his people and a European state, but the latter imposed an export specialization in human cargo.

Once Africa and Europe became interlocked on the latter's terms, it was beyond the capacity of any given African state or society to change the status quo, because Europeans reacted by force and other means to maintain their position. This was exemplified in Angola, where the Portuguese employed an unusual number of their own troops and tried to wrest political power from Africans – with a resolution that was not customary in the epoch before colonial rule. The Angolan state of Matamba on the river Kwango was founded around 1630 as a direct reaction against the Portuguese. With Queen Nzinga at its head, Matamba tried to coordinate resistance against the Portuguese in Angola, especially in the 1640s when the Dutch offensive against the Portuguese provided a European ally. Portugal gained the upper hand in 1648, but Matamba remained hostile, and participation in the slave trade was largely in abeyance as far as that state was concerned for a quarter of a century. But, slaving having become a major activity of the region, Matamba could not forever stand aside. So long as it opposed trade with the Portuguese, it was an object of hostility from neighbouring African states which had a modus vivendi with Europeans and slave trading. When Queen Nzinga resumed business with the Portuguese in 1656, it was undoubtedly a major victory for the latter. Her change of name to Dona Ana de Sousa was a very nominal concession to Christianity, but it symbolized a major decision-making role of the Portuguese within the Angolan economy.

A smaller but more specific example of African resistance to continued European imposition of trade in slaves comes from the Baga people in what is now the Republic of Guinea. The Baga lived in mini-states, and in circa 1720 one of their leaders attempted to secure an alliance to stop the slave traffic. He was apparently defeated by local European resident traders, mulattoes and other slave-trading Africans. It is not difficult to understand why Europeans would have taken immediate steps to see that Tomba and his Baga followers did not opt out of the role allocated to them by Europe. A parallel which presents itself is the manner in which Europeans got together to wage the 'Opium War' against China in order to ensure that the Chinese would continue to import the addictive drug that was so profitable for Western capital.

Of course, it is only as a last resort that the capitalist metropoles need to use armed force to ensure the pursuit of favourable policies in the periphery. Normally, economic weapons are sufficient. Within the same context of opposition to the slave trade, Dahomey[1] found itself being brought to terms by being deprived of European imports – some of which had become necessities by the time that Dahomey had its altercation with European slave traders in the 1970s. The episode is worth careful scrutiny because the conventional interpretations portray Dahomey as nothing but a bloody slave-trading state, and make absolutely no mention of the determined opposition to the trade that was carried out by Dahomey's greatest king, Agadja Trudo.

The fundamental pillar of the Dahomean conception of the state was that all Dahomeans were inalienable. The king required of his subjects complete obedience, and they asked in turn for unqualified protection. Adadja Trudo appreciated that European demand for slaves and the pursuit of slaving in and around Dahomey was incompatible with Dahomey's development. Between 1724 and 1726, he looted and burnt European forts and slave barracoons; and he reduced the trade from the 'Slave Coast' to a mere trickle, by blocking the paths leading to sources of supply in the interior. European slave dealers were very bitter, and they tried to sponsor some African collaborators against Agadja Trudo. They failed to unseat him or crush the Dahomean state, but in turn Agadja failed to persuade them to develop new lines of economic activity, such as local plantation agriculture; and, being anxious to acquire firearms and cowries through the Europeans, he had to acquiesce in the resumption of slave trading in 1730.

In 1730, Dahomean slaving was placed under royal control and was far more restricted than previously. Yet, the failure of this determined effort illustrated that a single African state at the time could not emancipate itself from European hegemony. The small size of the polities and the numerous political divisions made it so much easier for Europe to make the decisions about Africa's role in world production and trade.

Because the nature of African exports was determined from outside the continent, questions such as the level of output and prices were also decided outside Africa. Time and time again, trade in slaves responded to various external stimuli.

At first, the labour was needed in Iberia and in the Atlantic islands such as São Tomé, Cape Verde and the Canaries; then came this period when the Greater Antilles and the Spanish American mainland needed replacements for the Indians who were victims of genocide; and then the demands of Caribbean and mainland plantation societies had to be met. The records show direct correlations between levels of exports from Africa and European demand for slave labour in this or that part of the American plantation economy. When the Dutch took Pernambuco in 1634, the directors of the Dutch West India Company immediately informed their agents on the 'Gold Coast' that they were to take the necessary steps to pursue the trade in slaves on the adjacent coast east of the Volta – thereby creating the infamous 'Slave Coast'. When the British islands of the Caribbean took to growing sugarcane, the Gambia was one of the first places to respond. Examples of this kind of external control can be instanced right up to the end of the trade, and this embraces Eastern Africa also, since European markets in the Indian Ocean islands became important in the eighteenth and nineteenth centuries, and since American demand caused Mozambicans to be shipped around the Cape of Good Hope.

Even medium and short-run fluctuations in the volume of African trade were usually reflections of European conditions. The incessant European wars of the mercantilist epoch were particularly decisive in this respect. There was a drastic fall in French shipping to Africa during the Seven Years War (1748–55); while both British and French shipping was absent from regular trade during the American War of Independence and the years of Anglo-French struggle that followed. The African 'producer' of a commodity such as captives was quite helpless in the face of these European practices. During the American War of Independence, Futa Djallon and the neighbouring countries in Sierra Leone became full of captives, who had of necessity to be incorporated into a local system of production because they were kept hanging around for a long time with no ships in sight.

It might seem to be labouring the obvious to emphasize that a fundamental characteristic of centuries of Afro-European trade was that its dimensions were determined outside of Africa. But, it is equally obvious that local conditions were bound in some ways to affect output, price and the European choice of particular parts of the continent at particular times. Thus, the local conditions around (say) the Bight of Biafra or Lake Nyasar would certainly have influenced the rate of extraction of captives at any given time. The emphasis on the overall global determinants is necessary in order to situate the mechanics of trade within Africa and their proper international perspective, and in so doing one can immediately perceive the striking similarity between the early commerce and the subsequent colonial and neo-colonial trades.

The kind of benefits which Europe derived from its control of world commerce are well known, although it is curious that the recognition of Africa's major contribution to European development is usually made in works devoted specifically to that subject; while European scholars of Europe often treat the European economy as if it were entirely autonomous. European economists of the nineteenth century certainly had no illusions about the interconnections between their national economies and the world at large. J.S. Mill went so far as to assert that as far as England was concerned, 'the trade of the West Indies is hardly to be considered as external trade, but more resembles the traffic between town and country.'

Marx can be cited in the same context, not as heretic or as the ultimate authority, but merely because of the frankness of his comments. It was Marx who wrote that 'the discovery of gold and silver in America, the extirpation, enslavement and entombment in mines of the aboriginal populations ... the turning of Africa into a commercial warren for the hunting of black skins signalised the rosy dawn of the era of capitalist production.'

Central and South American gold and silver played a crucial role in meeting the need for coin in the expanding capitalist money economy, while African gold was also significant in this respect. African gold helped the Portuguese to finance further navigations around the Cape of Good Hope and into Asia; it was the main source for the Dutch mint in the seventeenth century (which helped to secure Amsterdam as the financial capital of Europe in that period); and it is no coincidence that when the English struck a new gold coin in 1663 they called it the 'guinea'.

Throughout the seventeenth and eighteenth centuries, and for the most part of the nineteenth, the exploitation of Africa and African labour continued to be a source for the accumulation of capital to be reinvested in Western Europe. The African contribution to European capitalist growth extended over such vital sectors as shopping, insurance, the association of capital, capitalist agriculture and the capital goods industry. Sometimes, the efforts were modest and localized. Thus, the St Malo fishing industry was stimulated by the opening up of markets in the French slave plantations; while the Portuguese fishing industry also gained new buoyancy. Then there were more spectacular developments like the growth of seaport towns connected with Atlantic trade – notably Bristol, Liverpool, Nantes, Bordeaux and Seville. Behind those ports there often emerged the manufacturing centres that gave rise to the notion of the 'industrial revolution'. As Mantoux put it, 'the growth of Lancashire, of all English countries the one most deserving to be called the cradle of the factory system, depended first of all on the development of Liverpool and her trade.'

The connections between capitalism and slavery as far as England is concerned are adequately documented by Eric Williams. A similar picture would emerge from any detailed study of French capitalism and slavery, given the fact that during the eighteenth century the West Indies accounted for 20 per cent of France's external trade – much more than the whole of Africa in the present century. Of course, benefits were not always directly proportional to the amount of involvement of a given European state in the Atlantic trade – for instance, the enormous profits of the Portuguese economy went into the hands of the more developed Western European capitalist nations who supplied Portugal with capital, ships and trade goods. Germany was included in this category, along with England, the Dutch Provinces and France.

Commerce deriving from Africa helped a great deal to strengthen transnational links within the Western European economy, bearing in mind that American produce was the consequence of African labour. Brazilian dyewoods, for example, were re-exported from Portugal into the Mediterranean, the North Sea and the Baltic, and passed into the continental cloth industry of the seventeenth century. Sugar from the Caribbean was re-exported from England and France to other parts of Europe to such an extent that Hamburg was the biggest sugar-refining centre in Europe in the first half of the eighteenth century. Germany supplied manufacturers to Scandinavia, Holland, England, France and Portugal, for resale in Africa. England, France and Holland (in spite of competing mercantilist systems) found it necessary to exchange various classes of goods to better deal with Africans for gold, slaves and ivory. The financiers and merchants of Genoa were the powers behind the markets of Lisbon and Seville; while Dutch bankers played a similar role with respect to Scandinavia and England.

Western Europe, after all, was more than just an arbitrary geographical connotation. It was that part of Europe in which by the fifteenth century embryo capitalist relations already posed a challenge to feudalism, marking a further departure from the natural, self-sufficient autarchic economies of previous modes of production. When the Western European nations moved overseas, it was the product of an internal dynamic, which was not navigated or even deflected by new trades with Africa, Asia and the Americas. Enclosures continued in the English countryside, and agriculture in Western Europe generally continued its slow rate of evolution, serving to support a larger population and to provide a more effective basis for the wool and linen industries in particular. The rate of transformation in technology and in the socio-economic organization of industry was more rapid. African trade hindered none of these things. On the contrary, it speeded up several aspects, including the integration of Western Europe – as noted above. That is why the African connection contributed not merely to economic growth (which relates only to quantitative dimensions) but also to real development in a structural sense. Conversely, it can be demonstrated that the contacts with Europe had no organic relationship to what Africa was doing previously nor did they permit the reemergence of any rational continental or regional ties within Africa itself. Trade within Europe meant historical disruption and disintegration, and those things proved crucial to Africa's underdevelopment.

Africa's external trade was very limited up to the fifteenth century. Apart from northern Africa (the Horn included), it was only East Africa that had foreign trade relations. The Portuguese sought with some success to replace the Arabs as the merchants who tied East Africa to India and to the rest of Asia. It was the Portuguese who came to carry most of the ivory which was marketed in India; while Indian clothes and beads were sold in East and West Africa by the Portuguese and the Dutch. The same applied to cowry shells from the East Indies. A new trade route between Africa and the Americas was an extension neither of the indigenous American economy nor of the African economy. Its total rationale lay in Europe. In effect, therefore, Europe took the first steps towards transforming Africa, Asia and America into economic satellites. It was at the very outset of international trade that there was established that radical pattern with Europe at the centre and very few independent connections between the non-European territories.

Inside Africa itself, the period of trade which preceded the establishment of colonial rule was also determined by the state of affairs where there were ties between colony and metropole but none between colony and colony. It will shortly be illustrated that trade with Europe arrested the development of numerous small African economies. Lack of economic integration in Africa is mainly a result of that fact, because social formations in given geographical areas were not permitted to extend their production and economic boundaries so as to generate trade with each other comparable in importance to that between each area and Europe. There is no doubt that the potential for independent economic development was present in a large number of localities, based on local resources and skills. As those local economies multiplied and grew closer together, they were bound to create regional and continental markets as in Europe and parts of Asia that had gone further along the same evolutionary path. In addition to blocking the possibilities of continued evolution, European trade also set in motion a process of active disintegration. Certain interterritorial links established on the continent were broken down because of European trade. Several examples arose on the West African coast down to Angola, because in those parts European trade was most voluminous, and the surviving written record is also more extensive.

When the Portuguese arrived in the region of modern Ghana in the 1470s, they had few commodities to offer local inhabitants in exchange for the coveted gold. However, they were able to trans-ship from Dahomey supplies of cotton cloths, beads and female slaves which were saleable on the 'Gold Coast'. The indications are that the Portuguese were responding to a given demand in the 'Gold Coast', so that a previous trade must have been in existence between the two regions. The Akan were gold producers, and the people of

Benin were specialist craftsmen who had a surplus of cloth and beads which they manufactured themselves. As an expansionist state, Dahomey also had access to prisoners of war; while the Akan seemed concerned with building their own population and labour force, so they acquired female captives from Dahomey and rapidly integrated them as wives. When the Portuguese intervened in this exchange, it was subordinated to the overall interests of European trade. As soon as Portugal and other European nations had sufficient goods so as not to be dependent on the re-export of certain commodities from Dahomey, then all that remained were the links between the 'Gold Coast' and Europe on the one hand, and between Dahomey and Europe on the other. That represented the destruction of whatever potential existed for creating a regional market with its own internal logic.

Probably, Dahomey products reached the 'Gold Coast' by percolating through what is now Benin and Togo, using as far as possible the creeks behind the coast. Therefore, it would have been more convenient when Europeans established a direct link across the open sea. The superiority of Europeans at sea was of the greatest strategic value, along with their organizational ability. This was illustrated in several places, beginning with the Upper Guinea Coast and the Cape Verde islands, where Portuguese settlers broke into the pattern of local trade ever since the 1460s. They intervened in the transfers of raw cotton and indigo dye from one African community to another, and the Cape Verdean settlers went a step further in establishing a flourishing cotton-growing and cotton-manufacturing industry. They used labour and techniques from the mainland and exported the finished product along the length of the coast down to El Mina.

The Portuguese also took over the trade in local cowries in Kongo, the trade in salt along the Angolan coast, and the trade in high-quality palm cloth between Loango and southern Angola. In some instances, they achieved dominance not just because of their ships and commercial skills but also by the use of force – providing they were operating on the littoral and could bring their cannon into play. The disruption of transactions between the 'Gold Coast' and the 'Ivory Coast' followed that pattern. A strong coastal canoe trade existed between these two regions, with people of Cape Lahou sailing past Cape Three Points to sell their cloth as far east as Accra. The Portuguese set up a fort at Axim near Cape Three Points, to service gold trade with the hinterland; and one of its incidental functions was to restrict the east–west coastal African trade. They prohibited Axim residents from going to Cape Lahou, and they stopped canoes from the 'Ivory Coast' from travelling east beyond Axim. The purpose was obviously to make both areas discrete economic entities exclusively tied to Europe.

The Portuguese were not successful in destroying this African commerce, and the Dutch inherited the problem when they took over Axim in 1673. The servants of the Dutch West India company which was operating on the Gold Coast hovered between two alternatives. If possible, they wanted a complete cessation of the African trade; and when that was not achieved, they tried to force the people of the 'Ivory Coast' to buy a certain amount of Dutch goods in addition to the local products they received on the 'Gold Coast'. The Dutch stipulated that each Axim canoeman going to Cape Lahou should carry Dutch goods worth at least four ounces of gold. In effect, that converted a purely inter-African exchange into a European/African trade.

What was doubly detrimental to African attempts to integrate their own economies was the fact that when Europeans became middlemen in local trade networks, they did so mainly to facilitate the extraction of captives, and thereby subordinated the whole economy to the slave trade. In Upper Guinea, the Portuguese and their mulatto descendants in the Cape Verde islands and on the coast engaged in a large variety of trade permutations – involving cotton, dyes, kola nuts and European products. The purpose of it all was to fill the holds of slave-ships calling at Gambia, Cacheu, Bissau, the Bay of Sierra Leone, and so on. In Congo/Angola, the same picture emerges. The salt, *nzimbu* shells and palm cloth that came into Portuguese hands made up for their shortage of trade goods and served to purchase captives on different parts of the coast and deep in the interior. This element of subordination and dependence is crucial to an understanding of African under-development today, and its roots lie far back in the era of international trade. It is also worth noting that there is a type of pseudo-integration which is compatible with dependence. In contemporary times, it takes the form of Free Trade areas in the 'Third World', which are made to order for the penetration of multinational corporations; while from the fifteenth century onwards this pseudo-integration took the form of the interlocking of African economics over long distances from the coast, so as to allow the passage of human captives and ivory from a given point inland to a given port on the Atlantic or Indian ocean.

The West African gold trade was not destroyed but it became directly dependent on European buyers, by being diverted from the northward routes across the Sahara. Within the savannah belt of the 'Western Sudan', the trans-Saharan gold trade had nourished one of the most highly developed political zones in all Africa from the fifth century onwards. But it was more convenient for Europe to obtain its gold on the West Coast than through North African intermediaries, and one is left to speculate on what might have occurred in the 'Western Sudan' if there had been a steady increase in the gold trade over the seventeenth and eighteenth centuries. Nevertheless, there is something to be said in favour of African trade with Europe in this particular commodity: gold production involves mining and an ordered system of distribution within

Africa. Akan country and parts of Zimbabwe and Mozambique sustained flourishing socio-political systems up to the nineteenth century, largely because of gold production. It was the trade in slaves that completely undermined the situation in West, East and Central Africa, for the procurement of captives was based on warfare, banditry and social distortions.

A considerable body of writing is now coming into existence on the topic of the consequence of the Atlantic slave trade on Africa; and much of it purports to show that earlier views of the completely negative impact of the trade are ill-founded. Indeed, some individuals are preoccupying themselves with highlighting the many beneficial effects of the slave trade on Africa. The white-washing trend is another facet of the distortions produced when capitalism tries to provide itself with moral justification. Apologists rely on such flimsy arguments as 'Africans benefited by getting European goods' and 'new food crops were introduced' – as though Europe had to be enslaved before it got to enjoy the potato from the Native American Indian. This genre of scholarship stresses the fact that certain African kingdoms grew stronger during the centuries of slaving, and it assumes that the connection was a positive one. The truth is that some areas *continued* to develop and they did so *in spite of* slave trading; although all who participated were warped to a greater or lesser extent, and all were reduced to a state of dependence.

Many things remain uncertain about the slave trade and its consequences for Africa, but the overall picture of destructiveness is clear, and that destructiveness can be shown to be the logical consequence of the recruitment of captives in Africa (as distinct from their sale at coastal ports).

One of the uncertainties concerns the basic question of how many Africans were exported. This has long been an object of speculation, with estimates ranging from a few millions to 100 million. A study by Philip Curtin, *The Atlantic Slave Trade: A Census*, has suggested the figure of about ten million Africans landed alive in the Americas, the Atlantic islands and Europe. That figure may well be low, in spite of the author's assertions to the contrary, because so many of the import figures in the Americas were given out by individuals who were deliberately minimizing numbers in order to defraud revenue collection, and the volume of 'contraband' arrivals is difficult to measure. However, if this low figure was accepted as a basis for evaluating the impact of slaving on Africa as a whole, the conclusions that could legitimately be drawn would confound those attempting to make light of the experience. As Curtin was aware, 'the cost of the slave trade in human life was many times the number of slaves landed in the Americas. For every slave landed alive, other people died in warfare, along the bush pats leading to the coast, awaiting shipment, or in the crowded and insanitary conditions of the middle passage.'

On any base figure of Africans who landed alive in the Americas, one would have to make an increment to cover mortality in trans-shipment, which averaged in the vicinity of 15 to 20 per cent. There were also other deaths between time of capture and time of embarkation. Most important of all, given that warfare was the principal means of obtaining captives, it is necessary to estimate the number of people killed or maimed in order to appreciate the extent of the millions who were taken alive. The resultant figure (a considerable multiple of 10 million) would represent the number from the population and labour force of Africa because of the establishment of slave production by Europeans in the Americas. It is a loss that would have to be evaluated in the light of age and sex selection and other features. Slave traders preferred their victims between fifteen and thirty-five years of age, with a ratio of two men to one woman. They often accepted younger children but rarely any older person. They shipped the most healthy wherever possible, and even took pains to choose those who had had smallpox and were thereby immunized.

Absence of data about the size of Africa's population in the fifteenth century makes it impossible to carry out any scientific assessment of the results of the population outflow. But, nothing suggests that there was any increase in the continent's population over the centuries of slaving, although that was the trend in other parts of the world. Lack of increase or even slight increases would have represented a 'deficit' in terms of a population projection, since fewer babies were born that would otherwise have been the case if millions of childbearing age had not been eliminated. Finally, on this particular topic, it is essential to recognize that the Atlantic slave trade on the Indian Ocean has been called 'The East African slave trade' and 'the Arab slave trade' for so long that it obscures the extent to which it was the European slave trade. When the slave trade from East Africa was at its height in the late eighteenth century and in the early nineteenth century, the destination of captives was the plantation societies of Mauritius, Reunion and Seychelles as well as the New World, via the Cape of Good Hope. Besides, Africans labouring as slaves from Zanzibar to Persia in the sixteenth and nineteenth centuries were all ultimately serving the European capitalist system which had become all pervasive. The Sultan of Zanzibar did not eat from cloves himself.

An emphasis on population loss as such is highly relevant to the question of socio-economic development. In recent times, since imperial agencies have decided on a Malthusian line for the 'Third World', it is being forgotten that population growth played a major role in European development in providing labour, markets and the pressures which led to further advance. The Japanese population growth had similar positive effects; while in other parts of Asia which remained pre-capitalist, the size of the population led to a much more intensive exploration of the land than has ever been the case in what is still a sparsely peopled African continent. Even in the absence of statistics, it seems that West Africa was always a more densely populated section of the continent than either Central or East Africa; and it was there that the brunt of the slaving fell, warping the development of some of the most advanced areas in all Africa, such as Yorubaland, Igboland and Akan country.

African economic activities were affected both directly by population loss and indirectly by other features of slave trading – notably the violence and insecurity that it engendered. Before the eighteenth century, the Portuguese and Dutch actually discouraged slaving on the 'Gold Coast', for they recognized that it would be incompatible with the gold trade. However, by the end of the seventeenth century, gold had been discovered in Brazil, and the importance of gold supplies from Africa was lessened. Within the total Atlantic pattern, African slaves became more important than gold, and Brazilian gold was offered for African captives at Whydah and Accra. At that point, slaving began undermining the 'Gold Coast' economy, and made large inroads into the gold trade. Slave-raiding and kidnapping made it unsafe to mine and to travel; and in any event the resort to warfare for captives proved more profitable than gold mining. One contemporary European observer noted that 'as one fortunate marauding makes a native rich in a day, they therefore exert themselves rather in war, robbery and plunder than in their old business of digging and collecting gold.'

What was so clearly evidenced in the above example must have been true for all other branches of economic activity, and especially for agriculture. Occasionally in certain localities, food production was stimulated to provide supplies for slave ships, but the overall consequence of slaving on agricultural activities in Western and Central Africa were negative. Europeans on the scene did not commit to that effort, and where such comments are not available the inference is nonetheless inescapable. Labour was drawn off from agriculture and for those remaining, conditions were unsettled. Dahomey, which in the sixteenth century was renowned for exporting food to parts of what is now Togo, was suffering through famines in the nineteenth century. An enlightening parallel is the way migrant labour and cash crops affected the food economy of colonial Africa and made famine endemic in some districts. Just as the slave trade and overseas trade in general had multiplier effects on European development, so it had multiplier effects on African underdevelopment. Where there was integration across national boundaries in Europe, there was disintegration in Africa. The creation of growing points in the European economy and the establishment of backward and forward linkages were all out of the question in Africa, because foreign trade was not a logical extension of internal production and exchange. On the contrary, a great deal of time and energy went into activities like slaving and elephant hunting, which were not designed to permit an expansion of Africa's ability to produce foodstuffs and other essentials of human consumption.

Special attention needs to be paid to ivory exports, because they are more important than the sport of captives as far as most East African societies were concerned and because it is necessary to determine the extent to which the ivory trade had consequences comparable to the slave trade. There was definitely a qualitative difference between the two. The ivory trade led to professionalization just like the slave trade, but bands of elephant hunters (found for example among the Cokwo, Baganda, Nyamwezi and Bambara) were positive additions to the social structure while bands of professional raiders and man-stealers were threats to established society. Andrew Roberts's study of the evidence relating to Nyamwezi ivory trade has shown that this long-distance trade sparked off other beneficial developments, such as increased trading goods, food and salt. There were other African exports such as gum, rubber, camwood and wax which also had certain beneficial effects on socio-economic patterns when they were traded, showing clearly that slaving was in a category by itself. Many of the other commodities were accommodated within the colonial trade of the late nineteenth century, indicating that their export was comparable with the exploitation of African labour within Africa – an objective with which slave trading obviously came into sharp conflict.

On the other hand, ivory was an asset that was rapidly exhausted in any given region, and the struggle to secure new supplies sometimes brought violence almost indistinguishable from that produced by slaving. Besides, the most decisive limitation of the ivory trade was the fact that it was not an outgrowth of local product, and it caused restructuring dependent upon an overseas market. The Nyamwezi were trading articles of African manufacture among Africans long before the export of trade opened up. In a sense, regional trade provided the 'capital' for the long-distance ivory trade, but from then on any expansion of local manufacturing was incidental to, rather than the goal of, local economies caught up in the international trading network, and the expansion was very limited. This kind of conceptualization is completely lacking in reconstructions of African history. In a sizable volume of essays devoted to 'trade in Central and Eastern Africa before 1900', there is nowhere expressed any awareness that the professionalization of trade per se is no great thing, and that it meant not development but the subordination of local economies in the case of Africa's relations with Europe. Andrew Roberts ends his study of Nyamwezi trade as follows:

> It would seem, then, that we are obliged yet again to conclude that only rule by representatives of superior technology could provide the conditions for sustained advance from the subsistence economy. This was, indeed, partly due to the very manner in which the region had become already linked to, and in a sense dependent on, the economies of the industrialized world.

The writer of those lines should be given credit for at least a hesitant acknowledgement of the notion of 'dependence', which is so central to an understanding of underdevelopment. For the rest, the statement is timid and confusing. Why is it that representatives of superior technology were required to carry Africans out of the subsistence economy, and they were not necessary to perform similar functions for Europeans and most Asians? It was precisely the external links which precluded the possibility of independent self-sustaining advice, and that was true of the Nyamwezi ivory trade as it was of the Kazembe trade in captives. Besides, at all times one must keep in mind the dialectical opposite of the trade in Africa: namely, production in Europe or in the Americas under European control. The few socially desirable by-products of elephant hunting within Africa were chickenfeed in comparison with the profits, technology and skills associated with the product in Europe. The ivory marts of Minping Lane were the centres where real profits on ivory trade were made. The tusks then augmented in value when they were turned into billiard balls and piano keys in London, and when they went to Sheffield to be transformed into knife handles and to Dieppe and Geislingen to be made into hundreds of different artifacts by marine processes. Europe was strengthened by these and numerous other foreign-fed industries to carry Africa out of their own developing capitalist economy in the most disadvantaged situation possible.

European technology was not as superior to that in other parts of the world in the fifteenth century as is often assumed. Their supremacy in that aspect at the present time is itself more a consequence than the cause of their hegemony over the rest of the world. In the fifteenth century, Europe merely had the edge over humanity elsewhere in the scientific understanding of the universe, the making of tools and the rational organization of work. One of the major shortcomings of Europeans in the fifteenth and sixteenth centuries was a shortage of commodities for exchange, as has already been illustrated. They were forced to make use of Asian and (to a lesser extent) African consumer goods, which were often of superior quality. Yet, as is also implicit in earlier sections of this analysis, European superiority in certain sectors proved decisive. African and Polynesian canoes were of high standard, but the relevant sphere of operations was the ocean, where European ships could take command. West Africans had developed metal-casting to a fine artistic perfection in many parts of Nigeria, but when it came to the meeting with Europe, beautiful bronzes were far less relevant than the crudest of cannon. African wooden utensils were sometimes works of great sensitivity, but Europe produced pots and pans that had many functional advantages. Literacy, numeracy, organizational experience and the capacity to produce on an ever-expanding scale (even under the domestic system) were also very meaningful advantages on the European side of the scale.

Once Africa was drawn into the orbit of Western Europe, the latter's technological development was speeded up, as already noted in the case of several other aspects of their economy. For example, the evolution of European shipbuilding from the sixteenth to the nineteenth centuries was a logical consequence of their monopoly of sea commerce after the fifteenth century. During the same period, the North Africans were bottled up in the Mediterranean, and although it was from there that Europe borrowed a great deal of nautical instrumentation, the North Africans made no further worthwhile advances. Where the initial European advantage was not sufficient to assume supremacy, they deliberately undermined other people's efforts. The Indian navy, for instance, suffered from the rigid enforcement of the English Navigation Laws. Yet, the expenses involved in building new and better European ships were met by the profits of overseas trade such as with India and Africa. The Dutch were pioneers in improving upon the caravels which took the Spanish and Portuguese out across the Atlantic, and the succession of Dutch trading companies operating in Asia, Africa and America were the ones responsible for experimentation. By the eighteenth century, the British were using Dutch know-how as a basis for surpassing the Dutch themselves, and the Atlantic was their laboratory. It used to be said that the slave trade was a training ground for British seamen. It is probably more significant to note that the Atlantic trade was the stimulator of consistent advances in naval technology.

We know a fair amount about the evolution of science in Europe prior to overseas expansion, and it is possible to evaluate the catalytic contribution of the non-European world in the epoch of mercantilism. The technological revolution of the eighteenth and nineteenth centuries in Europe sprung from the interplay of numerous variables rooted entirely in the European experience, but they all have to be placed in the context of capitalist development; and it is no mere coincidence that the crucial engineering inventions of the late eighteenth century followed after the profits from external trade had been internalized by Western European capitalism. We know far less about the evolution of African technology, but commerce with Europe could have had no positive effect in this sphere.

In the first place, craft skills would have suffered from the plague of slaving in the areas directly affected. Much has been made of the destructive aspect of the Ngoni incursion northwards into East Africa. In the Lake Nyasa/Lake Tanganyika corridor, warfare and raiding virtually obliterated cloth and hoe-making. Slave recruitment was warfare and pillage on a grand scale, and must have had analogous effects for the vast areas concerned. Of greater importance, however, were the indirect consequences of trade as such, including the impact of imports and the European subversion of local trade.

The relationship of African technology to cloth manufacture is worthy of note, given the strategic role that textiles have played in economic development in Western Europe, Japan and the US. From the fifteenth to the nineteenth century, the demand for cloth in Africa was constantly expanding. All areas experienced a shift from car nudity through animal skins and bark cloth to cotton. Indian and European textiles helped meet this expanding demand, while areas like Senegambia, Ivory Coast, Benin, Yorubaland and Loango were exporters to other parts of Africa (through European intermediaries for the most part). But the volume of European production was so constantly increasing, along with the skill, so that Dutch and English manufacturers in the eighteenth century copied fashionable Indian and African patterns. Since they had established a stranglehold on local distribution, the products they brought had to be accepted even though they were inferior to the originals. By the late nineteenth century, European textiles were being imported in sufficient quantities to swamp local production and to make regions such as Senegambia into exporters of raw cotton and importers of finished cotton cloths. Wherever remnants of the industry survived, production was in the same technological mould of earlier centuries, because the narrow looms were never permitted to respond to the kind of demand which would have forced a breakthrough.

With regard to textiles as well as iron, European imports were presumably viewed by Africans as supplementary to their own production of those items so long as there was a sufficient market. One would expect that if the foreign commodity became a threat to local manufacture, the affected African would make a stand. An example to this effect was the salt industry of Sierra Leone, which was protected by local African edict excluding salt as an import in the eighteenth century. The reasoning was sound, because in the early nineteenth century, British ships sailing to Nigeria carried cheap salt – to the detriment of local production.

Yet the industry and skills which actually existed and were destroyed were probably of less consequence than the loss of the development *opportunity*. This cannot be calculated, but it must not be ignored.

The editors of the aforementioned volume on East and Central African trade illustrate the disruption of industry and skills in Congo/Angola through the intervention of the Portuguese and their mulatto and black servants (*pombeiros*) in African commerce. They recognize that the demands of the Atlantic trade 'ended by subverting the whole commercial structure with its attendant local industries' but in the same breath they contend that 'the opening of the overseas market does not seem to have altered in any radical way the role which commerce played in the economy of the area'. Here again, the basic weakness is a failure to distinguish between an independent economy in evolution and one that is being transformed into a satellite. In the former, commercial activity is entirely the consequence of the level of the development of the productive forces, whereas in the latter it is mainly a reflection of external needs. For slaving regions like Congo/Angola in the sixteenth and seventeenth centuries, it means that the role of commercial activity was no longer simply the distribution of local products, nor was it the export of those products, nor was it the export compatible with the old. That is what *cut off the possibility of evolution along previous lines,* even though the worst effects were deferred for a considerable period until Europe itself was powerful enough to take complete control through such means as the sending of commodities to replace those that had formerly been locally made.

Any trade in Africa which was an extension of European production was largely irrelevant to the technological advance within Africa. When Britain was the world's leading economic power, it used to be referred to as a nation of shopkeepers. Most of the goods in their ships were produced by themselves. Africans from Senegal to the Cunene and from the Limpopo to the Tana busied themselves selling godos that they had not produced. They were agents for distributing European imports and for organizing the export of a few staples which were not in demand within the continent. The Afro-Portuguese middlemen of Upper Guinea, the Akan market women, the Aro traders of the Bight of Biafra, the *pombeiros* of Angola, the Yao traders of Mozambique, the Swahili and Nyamwezi of East Africa were not performing a function which is essentially the same as that being carried out today by members of the disproportionality large service sector. Their contribution to technological development was nil because they were on the fringes of production.

Commerce with Europe was not propitious to independent technological invention on the African side, nor did it create any consistent demand for the import of European technology, except for firearms. Europeans responded to that with the cheapest of muskets. What they deliberately ignored were the exceptional African requests that Europe should place certain skills and techniques at the disposal of Africa. This was an element in the Kongo situation, already alluded to. When Agadja Trudo sought to stop the slave trade, he also made an appeal to European craftsmen, and he sent an ambassador to London for that purpose. One European who stayed at the court of Dahomey in the late 1720s told his countrymen that 'if any tailor, carpenter, smith or any other sort of white man that is free be willing to come here, he will find very good encouragement.'

At about the same time that Agadja Trudo was seeking new skills from Europe, the Asantehene, Opuku Ware (1720–50), was also thinking along those lines. He asked Europeans to set up factories and distilleries in Ashtai country and got no response. Those requests were coming from the areas of Africa that were sufficiently developed to have been able to incorporate new production techniques without any great dysfunctions. This was also true of Ethiopia. A Portuguese embassy reached the Ethiopian court in 1520. Having examined Portuguese swords, muskets, clothes, books and other objects, the Emperor Lebna Dengel felt the need to introduce European technical knowledge into Ethiopia. Correspondence exists between Emperor and European dignitaries such as Diego de Albuquerque (Portuguese Viceroy in India), Kings Manuel I and John III of Portugal, and Pope Leo X, in which requests were made for European assistance to Ethiopian industry. Until late in the nineteenth century, Ethiopian petitions to that effect were being repeated with scant success.

One of the most profound facets of the cultural arrogance of European colonialists in Africa was their boastfulness about technological accomplishments and their contemptuous attitude towards what they considered as African non-achievements in that sphere. 'They (Africans) had no plough, no wheel, and no means of transportation except human head porterage and dugout canoes on rivers and lakes. These people had built nothing, nothing of any kind in material more durable than mud, poles, and hatch!' The above words of a British colonial governor are relatively mild specimens of the technological superiority syndrome. Such statements sprung from and strengthened the racist assumption that African people were incapable of the discovery and application of scientific laws. Yet, the evidence suggests that it was the connection between Europe and Africa which aided the technological maturation of the former, while inducing a period of technological marking time and even regression in Africa. Furthermore, the issue of inventiveness is subordinate to the diffusion of techniques. Europeans did not invent the wheel – it spread from China. Both because of the structure of international trade and because of the conscious decisions of European states, Africa was robbed of the opportunity to benefit from the scientific heritage of man.

In the centuries before colonial rule, Europe's scientific and technical capacity increased by progressions, while Africa appeared to have been almost static. What was a slight edge when the Portuguese rounded Cape Bojador in 1444 was a huge gap by the time that European robber statesmen sat down at Berlin 440 years later.

The growing technological gap between Western Europe and Africa was consistent with the trend of capitalism to polarize wealth and power on the one hand, and poverty and dependence on the other. In a present imperialist epoch, super-profits from the dependencies have to some extent improved the standards of living of the metropolitan workers but in the earlier period internal exploitation strengthened external exploitation, and vice versa. At the national level within Western Europe, the unevenness of development had already been noted. This was sharply in evidence by the nineteenth century, with areas such as Portugal, Spain and Ireland playing colonial roles with respect to Britain, France and Germany. Inside of national economies, the polarization also expressed itself in the elimination of small producers and the rise of monopolies. The monopolies, therefore, were at the pinnacle of a system that knew nothing but profit-making and domination as its guiding principles. The monopolies set the tone for international political economy in the late nineteenth century. They intervened directly in Central and Eastern Europe through massive investments; and on a slightly smaller scale Western European monopolies sought financial and economic opportunities in Asia and Latin America. They were joined in this imperialist partition of the world by North American capital – the US having been transformed from an outpost of Europe into one of the command centres of capitalism.

Africa by then was somewhat in the doldrums as far as Europe was concerned. Its great period accumulating primary capital for European development was over. Nevertheless, Europe still had a place for Africa within the new imperialist scheme of things. A few areas of the continent became crucial for European investment: namely, Algeria, Egypt, South Africa and Congo. Elsewhere, smaller European entrepreneurs were permitted to operate, although ultimately they too were tied to the big banking and industrial concerns which controlled the Western European economy, and they were under the umbrella of nation states that bargained consciously and unconsciously as agents of monopoly capital. Thus, the clash of Anglo-French financial interests in Egypt and the potential for investment in Congo were keys which opened the doors to the 'Scramble for Africa' – that is, to the transformation of the continent into political colonies to protect economic spheres.

Apart from the Suez Canal and the South African and Congolese mines, the investment in the African continent in the late nineteenth century and subsequently was primarily to facilitate the production of agricultural staples to be utilized by the new industries of Europe. The expansion of soap-making, the rise of a wider market for cooking fats, and the need for lubricants in railway and engineering works led to the exploitation of the palm oil resources of West Africa; while the German machine industry could produce plants for crushing palm-kernels to provide stock-feed for capitalist agriculture. The extension of demand for cooking oils and fats also affected groundnuts – the opportunity being exploited by the financiers and industrialists of Marseilles. The Lancashire cotton industry, after its long partnership with the American slave South, was in the late nineteenth century anxious to promote the growing of cotton in Egypt and the Sudan and in East and West Africa. The invention of the pneumatic tube, the arrival of the motorcar, and the increase in the rubber-wheeled transport of all sorts taxed the rubber-producing capacities of the Dutch East Indies, Malaya, Brazil and Africa. Such examples could be multiplied. They all demonstrate that Europe's needs by the late nineteenth century were themselves a product of the immense quickening of economic life over the previous four centuries, and one of the factors in that quickening was the unequal association with Africa.

Equally significant is the fact that Europe derived the power to exploit Africa in new ways. Trade in slaves, ivory and gold was conducted from the coasts. There, European ships could dominate the scene, and, when necessary, forts could be built. Before the nineteenth century, Europe was incapable of penetrating the African continent, because the balance of force at their disposal was inadequate. But the same technological changes which created the *need* to penetrate Africa, also created the *power* to conquer Africa. The firearms of the imperialist epoch marked a qualitative leap forward. Breech-loading rifles and machine guns were a far cry from the smooth-bore muzzle loaders and flintlocks of the previous era. It is no wonder that Europeans had no hesitation in selling Africans antediluvian models of firearms. Hillaire Belloc spoke on behalf of his fellow Europeans when he said that 'what matters is that we have the Maxim [machine gun] and they have not.'

Curiously, Europeans often derived the *moral justification* for imperialism and colonialism from features of the international trade as conducted up to the eve of colonial rule in Africa. The British were the major exponents of the view that the desire to colonize was largely based on their good intentions in wanting to put up a stop to the slave trade. True enough, they were by then as opposed to the slave trade as they were once in favour of it. Technological changes had dialectically transformed the seventeenth century necessity for slaves into the nineteenth century necessity to clear the remnants of slaving from Africa so as to organize the local exploitation of land and labour. Leopold in the Congo also used the anti-slavery pretext to introduce into Congo itself forced labour and 'slavery-like practices'; while at a deeper level all Europeans had derived notions of racial and cultural superiority between the fifteenth and nineteenth centuries so that even the Portuguese presumed that they were historically destined to 'civilize the natives'.

Africans fought alien political rule and had to be subdued by superior force. But a sizable minority did not insist that their trade connections with Europe should remain unbroken, for that was a measure of the extent to which they were already dependent on Europe. The most dramatic illustration of that dependence was the tenacity with which some Africans fought the termination of slave trading. For most European capitalist states, the enslavement of Africans had served its purpose by the middle of the nineteenth century, but for those Africans who dealt in captives the abrupt termination of the trade at any given point was a crisis of the greatest magnitude. In many areas, major social changes had taken place to gear the region to the service of the slave-trade – one of the most significant being the rise of 'domestic slavery' and various forms of class and caste subjugation. African rulers and traders who found their social existence threatened by the earliest legal edicts such as Britain's Abolition of the Slave Trade Act in 1807 found ways of making contact with Europeans who still wanted salves. Where other commodities were suggested, tremendous effort went into organizing those alternatives: ivory, rubber, palm oil, groundnuts, cotton, and so on.

The transition to forms of production that used African labour inside Africa resulted in the rise of economic and social institutions that ensured the partition of a large number of Africans in the money economy, and also ensured that the value created would be siphoned off to capitalist Europe. That gave rise to the particular forms of structural dependence which we know today – visibly seen in the bank branches, the import/export agencies, the manufacturing subsidiaries, the mining companies, the pattern of road and railway networks, and so on. Needless to say, it is the intensive study of the colonial period which will answer most of the questions about underdevelopment as we know it today, but the extent to which the situation was being set up for centuries before is often underestimated. Anthropologists were the worst offenders in this regard, with their ahistorical prediction for describing everything that they found in colonial Africa as 'traditional'. But historians are also guilty of making a distinction between colonial and 'pre-colonial' Africa, in such a way as to cloud the fact that there was continuity from one phase to the other.

The notion that the first four centuries of Afro-European trade represent the *roots* of African underdevelopment is doubly attractive because there was an actual carry-over of some of the mechanisms that connect the two spheres of metropole and dependency. At the metropolitan end, there were the insurance companies and the shipping companies; while in Africa itself there had arisen certain social formations that were immediately available to operate within the colonial enclave economies from the 1880s onwards. Those are the African traders already mentioned as the forerunners of the modern service sector. Some were highly placed within African society; many were new men of previously low status; while many others were literally products of foreign trades, being the children of Europeans and Arabs. The mulatto element was very pronounced in Western Africa, and it continued to be prominent in the early colonial period and for much later. In what was called the French Sudan, to take one specific example, all economic activity spread inland from the four communes on the Senegalese coast, inhabited by blacks and mulattoes having long connections with Atlantic trade. So long as it is not based on settlement, a colonial system requires compradors. Throughout most of Africa, those compradors at the start of the colonial period were already performing that function in the dependent trade economy.

Besides, the Africans conducting trade on behalf of Europeans were inevitably influenced by European thought and values. The quest for European education did not begin in colonial Africa. It started when coastal rulers and traders recognized the need to penetrate more deeply into the way of life of the white men who came from across the sea. The mulatto sons of white traders and the sons of African rulers were the ones who went furthest along this line. At one level, it was strictly functional. The Sierra Leone chief in the eighteenth century explained that he wished 'to learn book to be rogue as good as white man'. At another level, it meant imbibing those values which led to further African subjugation. The Rev. Thomas Thompson was the first European educator on the 'Gold Coast', and he wrote in 1772 a pamphlet entitled *The African Trade for Negro Slaves Shown to be Consistent with the Principles of Humanity and the Laws of Revealed Religion*. The returned Africans who played such a crucial role in Sierra Leone and throughout West Africa in the period of the establishment of colonial rule were also in varying degrees products of Western culture and education – strikingly embodying potentialities of both enlightenment and mental confusion springing from deculturalization. Unfortunately, the latter trend was no more operative, and with the coming of colonial rule they became conscious and naive agents of foreign domination. The cultural nexus, therefore, provides further reason for seeking the roots of African underdevelopment and dependence in the early centuries of Afro-European trade.

8

Problems of Third World Development

On reflecting on the problem of Third World development, I recall an incident many months ago when the Republic of Guinea was invaded by the Portuguese. As soon as the Chinese heard about the invasion, the Xinhua News Agency put out a report denouncing American imperialism. America's name had not as yet been called by Guineans, but the Chinese from objective analysis decided that if the Portuguese were invading Guinea, it had something to do with American imperialism. And in like vein, I would suggest that if we are talking about the problems of development in the Third World, the major problem is the United States of America, because it crowns the whole structure of world imperialism. I will leave this as an assertion, because to go into a justification would consume time. However, I would like to illustrate in some ways the connections between imperialism and underdevelopment.

In the United Nations, a certain euphemism is in use. They speak about the 'developed' and the 'developing' market economies. These two collectively constitute the imperialist world: the developed market economy being the United States, the Western European countries and Japan; and the curious category of the developing market economy includes the rest of what we commonly refer to as the Third World, the economies of which are hooked into the metropolitan structures of North America, Western Europe and Japan. Some of the mechanisms for exploiting the so-called developing countries have been known for a long time. For instance, unequal trade has been a common subject of discussion, and in recent times it has received more careful analysis, so that we know rather more than we used to about exactly how the captains of trade contributed to the exploitation of the underdeveloped world. This is not a position that is merely adopted by Marxists or radical nationalists; it is a position which is commonly asserted even by the United Nations Conference on Trade and Development (UNCTAD).

A second well-known mechanism of exploitation within the structure of imperialism is the transfer of profits from underdeveloped areas towards the metropoles. My only comment on this is to note that what is called 'profits' is in fact 'capital'. For too long most of us, including people who would call themselves leftists, have created an idiom of 'capital export' from the colonies and semi-colonies; and the very idiom obscures part of the reality, indeed, perhaps the whole reality. I am of the opinion that we cannot refer to the export of capital from the metropoles to the underdeveloped sector of the world except in a limited sense. Historically, the movement of capital has always been on balance from the external or peripheral sectors of the imperialist economy to its epicentres. This began with the trade in slaves, while later it took the form of grossly unequal trade between Europe and the rest of the world. The most that can be said about European capital export is that Europe has been the centre for the redistribution and reallocation of capital that is produced throughout the world. Capital produced in, say, the Caribbean or in North America in the epoch of slavery, was shifted to Europe, and – at a later date – was redistributed from Western Europe to Eastern Europe; or capital that was obtained by forcing the Chinese to smoke opium was redistributed into the Indian sector of the British imperialist economy; and so on and so forth. But, strictly speaking, there never has been any export of capital from the developed areas in the sense of capital being engendered and originating in the metropolitan sectors for export overseas. So, my point about profit is that when we look at its mechanism closely, we find that it is always a means of transferring to the metropolitan economy capital produced out of the material and human resources of the Third World.

Unequal trade and capital flows away from the underdeveloped countries are two of the principal mechanisms of imperialism. There are others that are proving to be significant in their own ways, which tend to be left out of the literature, and which are very operative when we come to think in terms of changing the status quo. One of these, for instance, is the blockage of technology. This takes a number of forms: it could mean actual technological retardation or arrest in the underdeveloped countries; or it could mean simply the blockage of the movement of technology from the metropolitan to the colonial economy. The best examples of the actual destruction and retardation of technology would come from Asia – notably China and India – and to a lesser extent from Africa. Examples of the failure to allow the transfer of whatever technology has developed in Europe itself to the Third World can be taken at random. Particularly in the more recent epoch, we have had in Africa striking instances of the refusal of the metropolitan capitalist/imperialist countries to allow the transfer of technology in certain critical areas which would pose a threat to their own exploitation and domination. In Africa today, one of the biggest and best-known projects is that of the Tanzania–Zambian railway. The whole history of this railway is one in which metropolitan countries set out to interfere with the movement of this particular aspect of technology to a part of the Third World, and they failed because in this instance the People's Republic of China was available as an alternative source. The corollary to the blockage of skills and technology is that of the international division of labor under imperialism has always ensured the development of world technology within certain specific sectors, namely the metropolis, and more recently in particular parts of the metropoles, allowing the United States to assume hegemony in most fields. This is an important phenomenon when we come to examine the contemporary evolution of imperialism, because the changes in technology which were possible in the last decade have made it possible for the imperialist countries to begin to adopt radically new strategies in terms of international division of labour and in terms of the kinds of political controls which they exercise over the Third World.

Yet another general feature to which attention should be drawn is the way in which imperialism has restructured the world economy so that within the Third World there is no cohesion with respect to production and exchange. As one moves from colony or semi-colony to another colony or semi-colony, one finds the breaking of the ties which formerly integrated one with the other – that is to say, the breaking of the trade ties which integrated the productive resources. One finds within each colony also the same disjunction, the same disaggregation of the consistent parts of a colonized economy. Instead, the linkages are with the metropolitan economy, and are determined exclusively by the latter in its own interest – an interest which proves incompatible with the independence and any real development of the Third World.

Moving on from the essentially economic concerns, I wish to highlight the political facet of imperialism. A number of writers on Latin America and to a lesser extent on Africa have paid considerable attention to the creation in the Third World of certain strata, or certain classes, which reflect the interest of the metropoles and which allow the requisite kinds of penetration and exploitation. This political control takes a number of forms: there is the classical colonial form, there is the utilization of white settlers, and most important in the recent period, there has emerged in Africa and Asia an indigenous strata who conduct locally the activity required to support the international economy. These are people who – in Fanon's words – perform the function of transmission lines for international monopoly capital.

The foregoing represents a very brief portrayal of the mechanisms of imperialism. I am not attempting to go into any serious theoretical justification of why imperialism is the big problem of Third World development, because – hopefully – we understand that. So perhaps we could proceed to look rather more closely at the movement of contemporary Third World history, in order to better appreciate the problems and possible antidote to underdevelopment. In the last decade, we have been in a sense in a counter-revolutionary epoch, in spite of many of the festivities that have taken place celebrating the so-called independence in various parts of Africa and Asia, and in spite of certain foci of liberation. We can say that a general movement of history in the Third World has been counter to any direction that one may term independence. This I will illustrate using a number of criteria. First of all, one can apply the Western bourgeois measurements of growth rates, although these are very limited and skewed. One finds that the growth of the Third World economy has failed to keep up with those norms which have been established by groups such as the Pearson Commission. Most Third World countries do not get that ratio of growth in bourgeois economic terms which is supposed to represent their march forward. Very, very few have achieved the percentages – 6 or 8 per cent growth rate – which are set by the bourgeois economists as prerequisites for development. Second, and more important, is the fact that those criteria, where they are satisfied, do not lead to anything that the people of the country would call development. Hence the rise of the term 'growth without development', which has already become current in the writings on West Africa.

It has been seen that by using the criteria of GNP (gross national product) and per capita income, one finds a certain amount of growth undoubtedly taking place, but when this is examined in any serious detail, it is proved to be entirely misleading. As long as the local economy is part of the imperialist world economy, there is still the export of surplus – that

PROBLEMS OF THIRD WORLD DEVELOPMENT

is, the actual export of capital – and the redistribution of wealth within these so-called developing Third World countries is such that the vast majority of the people can and do experience an actual lowering of their living standards while the GNP and per capita income are supposedly rising. A few economists looking at the problems of economic development are beginning to apply the simplest of yardsticks by returning to factors such as housing, food and clothing – the principal elements of man's existence and the things that human beings have been striving for from the very onset of their attempts to deal with the material environment. In Jamaica, for example, it has been found that the units of housing for the vast majority of the people have been decreasing; more people are suffering from protein deficiency than was true of an earlier period; and more people are going about without shoes or without proper clothing than has been true earlier. All this in spite of significant increases in GDP (gross domestic product). In Africa one can readily cite Ivory Coast and Kenya in this respect, for such growth as shown by the statistical indices in these parts of Africa is not matched by any increases in the wellbeing of the mass of the population.

The most animus factor undermining attempts to achieve independence and development in the Third World has been the rise of new forms of exploitation and domination within the global capitalist economy. One of them is tourism. It has a nasty history in the Caribbean, particularly in Cuba, but in more recent times it is becoming very extensive. By 1969, tourism was one of the biggest economic factors in Tanzania of all places. Someone observed that, just as in Latin America there used to be 'Banana Republics', so international imperialism was threatening to transform Kenya, Uganda and Tanzania into the 'Wildlife Republics'. Every effort was made to attract tourists to look at the animals, and the animals assumed priorities higher than human beings. Incidentally, it is not at all true that it is the indigenous people who are responsible for such diminution in the wildlife population as has occurred in recent years, because groups like the Maasai have always coexisted with the lions and wild game. And in recent times, the problem of game conservation is of far lesser magnitude than that of human development and that of the survival and creativity of peoples of the region. Certainly, tourism in all its aspects is proving to be one of the new areas of expansion of the imperialism economy. It is a new way of confirming the dependence and subjugation of Third World economies, being seen in its most arrant and vicious forms in the Caribbean territories. Several islands in the Caribbean have been transformed into backwaters of the world economy; they are no longer central to the development of the world economy, because they have lost the priority that they had a long time ago when Sugar was king. It is a relatively simple task to transform them into cesspools, which is what the tourism economy is all about.

A more significant aspect of the new trend of domination is that which economists are calling the 'branch-plant economy'. It made its impact felt first in Latin America and then in Asia, and it is slowly beginning to touch on the African continent. This is a very subtle development, the negative effects of which remain unperceived for some time, because many people have been preoccupied with looking at the *old forms* of the international division of labor, whereby the underdeveloped countries were allocated roles connected either with agriculture or with the production of raw materials in the extractive mineral industry. It was felt by leaders like Nkrumah when he came to power in Ghana that the answer was to create industry in Africa. The dichotomy was simply industry versus agriculture or processing versus the export of unprocessed goods. Now imperialism has been able to circumvent the criticism that it reduces the Third World merely to primary production. The international bourgeoisie and their agents have been able to start 'industrialization' of a sort within Third World countries.

Looking at the development plans of every African nation, one finds that a beer factory will usually figure number one or number two on the list.

Building a beer factory is considered as the first step towards industrialization. Quite apart from the fact that I don't know of beer as having developed any nation, one has to realize the fallacy on which the claims are based. The underlying notion is that industrialization per se is the answer to underdevelopment. Therefore, the logic of that argument is that if the country ceases to import beer and instead develops an import substitute by making the beer locally, then a step has been made in the direction of development. This resort to import substitution has characterized a lot of the development plans of the Third World outside of the really progressive areas, and what in fact it means is that the capitalist structures in the metropoles have reached the stage where the export of consumer goods is no longer really critical, but the export of certain capital in goods is much more crucial. The capital goods sector has experienced tremendous growth in the period of colonial exploitation and the period of semicolonial exploitation, and there is now an objective necessity for the metropoles to export these capital goods; namely the plants that manufacture the beer, cigarettes or even textiles. Of course, the metropole seeks to incorporate their productive enterprises within the total structure of monopoly capital, which takes the form of the multinational corporation. The multinational corporation perceives the advantage of extending its operations into various other parts of the globe. Today it is not considered opportune merely to produce in the United States and Germany and to sell abroad. More markets can be explored by actually setting up the 'branch plants' in Brazil, in Singapore, in Ivory Coast, and so forth.

The movement of contemporary Third World political development throughout Africa and throughout Asia also shows tremendous deterioration. Latin America is exceptional only because it had its formal independence ever since the early nineteenth century, and Latin America has gone through the kinds of trauma which Africa and parts of Asia are only now beginning to experience. The dictators and the coups in Latin America were the butt of jokes even in the colonial world. In the West Indies, we used to say that if there was no coup in Latin America on a particular day, it would be announced on the radio as an item of significance – 'no coup anywhere in Latin America today'. In Latin America, countries have perhaps settled down to a pattern of more stable dictatorships, but they certainly have not in most places begun to tackle the problem of political stability in terms of the development of their own people. In any event, what I have to say relates more to Asia and Africa, and I will pick my examples mainly from Africa and from the Caribbean. In these instances, constitutional independence took place during the last decade. Subsequently, we have witnessed the realization of political dependency and economic dependency in much sharper forms, and of course the two cannot be separated. It is an allusion to put forward the notion of political independence without economic independence because politics is about making choices, and it seems to be incredible that someone should say, 'We have no control over our economy but we can make political choices.'

What happened after *constitutional* independence was of course the rise of new forms of political manipulation on the part of imperialism. Deterioration of this independence has been taking place because of a number of factors. First, under the control of imperialism, Third World countries have a sort of political vacuum nationally that arises from the fact that power does not reside locally. The national government of the petty bourgeoisie has little control over production and is endowed with a very feeble political base. They of course have police and military forces which are intended to serve as means of coercion of the population, but nothing else. An appreciation of these facts is fundamental to an understanding of the trends towards militarism, because if a political regime is so bankrupt that it is entirely dependent upon the military, if it has to resort to authoritarianism, then who is more authoritarian than the army? So, the army frequently decides to take over the role of governing, rather than merely being the police force of the civilians in power. We also find that the petty bourgeoisie in the Third World countries are not as capable as the bourgeoisie in the metropoles when it comes to playing a certain kind of political game. They are not capable of granting to their own population participation in bourgeois democracy, because the colonial situation is antithetical to any form of democracy – even to bourgeois democracy. The American bourgeoisie – to use this example – is powerful enough to realize that it can afford certain forms of bourgeois democracy, unless the stage is reached where the system is so eroded that they must take to fascist alternatives. But, normally, the bourgeoisie will of necessity engage the large middle-class sector and a large segment of the working population in parliamentarianism, free speech, and the like. In the Third World, this is seldom possible. The petty bourgeoisie who reside in Accra and in Kingston and in Singapore cannot afford to have any formal exercise of democracy. They do not have the power. They do not have the economic base. They are entirely dependent on two things: first, their external support; and second, whatever local police forces they can muster. Increasingly, the political situation in these Third World countries becomes more openly authoritarian. A striking example has been the regime of Forbes Burham in Guyana. He began some years ago by trying to convince some folk that he was about nationalism and even about socialism. To a large extent, he succeeded in the mystification, but after just a few years, the mask has been removed, and it is now apparent that Guyana has the makings of a kind of Haitian situation, given the trend towards the creation of a *Ton-Ton*

Macoute, aiming at political intimidation and assassinations. This and other indications in most of Africa and Asia suggest that neo-colonialism is not merely a state but – like all historical forms – it has its own motion, and both politically and economically the motion is in a negative direction.

I would like to try and explore some of the difficulties facing politically progressive groups within Third World territories – groups who analyse the situation and problems of development and who ask themselves the classic question, 'What is to be done?' How do they function, or how have they been functioning, and what kinds of projections can be made for the near and distant future? Using the crude distinction between the political and economic facets of the problem, I will suggest that the real issue at the moment – and for the foreseeable future – is not an economic issue but a political one.

It has already been affirmed that the fundamental nature of the development problem in the Third World is the relationship with the metropolitan economies and the nature of dependency, lack of internal integration, absence of technology, and so on, which are all essentially or primarily economic phenomena. Nevertheless, we should distinguish between what may be fundamental – which I think is economic – and what has a priority. The latter refers to the question of timing and that is where politics takes precedence. It will be necessary to look briefly at some of the economic problems, but the emphasis here will be on the political ones.

Progressives residing within Third World countries virtually without exception now pose the problem of economic development in terms of 'disengagement'. How do you break with the dominant imperialist system? This question marks a change from a lot of the preoccupations of a decade or five years ago, because it has become clear to a minority at any rate that some kinds of proposed solutions are not solutions at all, but rather an intensification of the problem. That is to say, solutions by way of aid, by way of further foreign entanglements, by way of so-called local capitalist development are not really solutions. An awareness of their insidious nature springs from a correct historical appraisal of the form of involvement between, on the one hand, Africa, Asia and Latin America, and, on the other hand, the European and North American economies plus Japan. Historically, this involvement has been the determinant of the Third World countries; and therefore, it becomes odd to suggest that further involvement, that an intensification of the involvement, would provide a solution. The solution lies in disengaging and disentangling from the historical bonds. In other words, if the answer is not in further engagement, if it is not in aid, if it is not in increasing one's traditional exports, if it is not merely in import substitution, then it must lie in terms of rebuilding one's economy so that it becomes a logical integrated whole. It must lie in terms of creating linkages between Third World economies, starting from a continental base within Latin America and within Africa. It must lie in rebuilding or regenerating, or starting afresh if necessary, the technological development of the Third World which has been arrested or which has been side-stepped in one way or another. These are undoubtedly tremendous tasks. Certain kinds of solutions are already being indicated but the main thing is to identify the direction in which one has to investigate. As long as so many poor economists have been looking at aid theories and at forms of playing around with devaluing or revaluing currencies or other techniques which all have as their basis a preoccupation with sustaining links with the imperialist economy, then for so long we have not been looking at the real problems and we have not been turning up any valid solutions.

However, before any progressive within the Third World can get down to working out the economic minutiae, they have to deal with the political problems. Indeed, the tendency on the part of progressive groups within these Third

World countries to evade the issue of getting at the political preconditions to economic development is itself a problem of underdevelopment. In my own days as an undergraduate at the University of the West Indies, several of us did sit down and try to work out a schema concerning what the new political economy would look like. There was no dearth of talk about what society should look like. Many socialists in Africa, Asia and Latin America have been dealing with that issue for a long time, but it is only a very tiny minority who have been concerned with trying to analyse the movement of history as it is subsequently to determine what action was needed to obtain political leverage. In other words, the question of power was being avoided, and without that one is only talking about blueprints which is essentially an occupation for idle bourgeois philosophers.

With respect to tackling the problem of power, there is required more detailed social analysis than merely saying that we have, on the one hand, the enemy who are the metropolitan capitalist, and, on the other hand, the exploited Third World. We have to make a closer analysis of the types of society which have been created within the Third World, to enquire as to what are the potential openings for a struggle to change the situation. Nationalist movements almost by definition tended to obscure and paper over the kinds of internal contradictions that existed in their societies, and when they achieved constitutional independence it very often came as a shock to realize that the internal contradictions were playing a much more crucial and determining role than had previously been allocated to them. Only a small number of progressives in the Third World are exempted from this stricture. The majority failed to make a clear analysis of the society which would allow them to locate within their own society the forces of change and the forces of reaction. The probable reason is that the social strata existing in Third World countries manifest a variety of forms that were not necessarily encountered in the metropoles. So the Third World intellectuals who may have taken a progressive orientation forming from a Marxist framework still found themselves unable to understand their own society, to the extent that they failed to distinguish between the tools that they acquired from abroad and the conclusions that they were introducing from abroad. This is a very common misconception. Having adopted Marxism or Scientific Socialism as a framework of analysis, one may or may not apply it creatively to one's own environment. Besides, Third World intellectuals are very fascinated by models, models that were historically applicable to societies outside of their own. The principal model was Russia at one time, while later it became China. There are very few who have had the courage – because it does take a lot of courage and a lot of energy – to deal with their own situations and to come up with the relevant answers.

One of the Third World social groups readily identified as having its own peculiarities is the petty bourgeoisie. There is a national bourgeoisie in India and Brazil, and in parts of Latin America; but it is not a general phenomenon within the Third World. By and large, the personnel who control the reins of power undoubtedly adhere to the norms and values of the bourgeoisie in the metropoles. But they do not control any capital formations. At best, they own two or three houses, and they own one Mercedes-Benz plus a Volkswagen, and so forth. But these are not capitalists. We must formulate a position that allows us to see the dependency of this class, its roots in the international bourgeoisie and the peculiarities which develop from that. I myself prefer to portray them as a stratum within the international capitalist class, a stratum serving that international capitalist class; and in each situation one has to examine their particular characteristics, including their behaviour patterns. In Africa and the West Indies, the petty bourgeoisie display characteristics such as self-hate, because they are usually black men who have a certain white

orientation. They have what is correctly identified as imita-
tiveness and lack of creativity, which were not characteristic of
the European bourgeoisie in its heyday. The European bourgeoisie was an entrepreneurial bourgeoisie. In the Caribbean
or in Africa the only entrepreneurship that the petty bourgeoisie are capable of is buying a truck or investing in real estate.
They have neither the capital nor the kind of aggressiveness
which is required to engage in capital enterprise. The point at
issue is that progressives within Third World countries have
to confront the problems of development almost exclusively
in relationship to local particularisms. What are the forces
existing in the society and how does one begin to organize
to confront the recognized enemy? How does one begin to
reach the masses, who are essentially peasant masses, with a
very small minority of workers in the traditional (industrial)
sense of the word? I would like to reflect briefly on these questions with regard to one part of East Africa, one where I am
fortunate to possess first-hand or very reliable second-hand
information: Uganda.

Uganda is an intriguing case. In Uganda, under Milton
Obote, progressive groups were in existence and had to make
a decision on how to participate in actualizing Uganda's
development. Looking at their national society, they saw a
phenomenon that is becoming increasingly evident in the
Third World: namely, a government that could not easily be
classified as being either fish or fowl – a government that was
making certain rhetorical statements about socialism, about
'moving to the left' – a government that within the context
of African liberation was anti-apartheid, anti-Smith regime,
anti-imperialist *in its rhetoric* – and therefore a government
that one could not place in the same anti-communist and pro-
Western bracket as that of Malawi's Hastings Banda or that
led by Felix Houphouët-Boigny in the Ivory Coast. And yet
at the same time when these Ugandan progressives looked at
Ugandan society they knew that it was no different from the

society in Ivory Coast or very little different from the society of Malawi. There was the same continuation of the exploitation of the peasantry in the Ugandan countryside and the same rapid increase in wealth – in terms of consumer goods and land – of a small elite. It was an elite that to some extent had a base in the 'traditional', quasi-feudal structures, along with a new elite of intellectuals, the government officials, the new party officials, and so on. In effect, Ugandan militants recognized that neo-colonialism was running rampant within Ugandan society. Any ambivalence on their part derided from the ambiguity caused by Obote's preempting of certain socialist terminology, thus making it difficult for socialists to come out and completely denounce him. So, the socialists in Uganda began to work out a strategy for their particular situation.

It was a strategy for immediate political action and it was tantamount to a strategy of development. They recognized that first they needed to establish an organization of their own. This is a real problem in Third World countries, especially where the government is playing games. How does one establish an organization of one's own? It appears that there were groups in Uganda who were concentrating on resolving that problem. At the same time, they had to decide that they must participate to a certain extent within the politics of Uganda and within the politics of the ruling party, Obote's Uganda People's Congress (UPC). Some of these individuals were in fact prepared to run in the elections scheduled by Obote – he had scheduled a very fancy election where a single candidate was to appear in about four constituencies simultaneously. The election never materialized because of the coup. But some of these individuals were prepared to participate in those elections. Eventually of course, the coup interrupted this, and Ugandan progressives were then faced with the situation where a government that was more clearly rightist, a government that was more clearly neo-colonialist, had come to power.

Some Ugandan militants had predicted the military coup – a testimony to their insights into their own society – and yet their response to the new clique was far from uncompromising. Several among them produced rationalizations which permitted them to associate with a regime that was more blatantly opposed to the interests of the 'common man' in Uganda than was the case under Obote. Kobode, who was appointed foreign minister, was previously one of the shining lights of the Uganda Left, and apparently still retains pretensions to socialism. Only a tiny fragment denounced the coup and began to take steps which qualify to be called revolutionary, and which kept in sight the objective of people's power. Why did this ineptness, disintegration and collaboration arise on the part of groups who claimed to perceive the essential lines of solution to their own development problems? It does suggest a lack of serious analytical framework, although many of those involved claim to be Marxist. Besides that, however, lack of self-confidence and a degree of opportunism also enter the picture. The new situation posed by the Idi Amin takeover[1] would have required the boldness to break completely with the state machinery and to operate entirely outside of the boundaries of petty bourgeois politics. Instead, several of the progressives came up with the lame alternative of 'working within the system', and fobbed off many revolutionary Ugandan youth by saying that Amin was amenable to the advice from the 'Leftists'.

The paradox of progressives seeking to give advice to reactionary governments is not new. There is a long history of this in Latin America, because Latin America has had many progressive economists and other social scientists who spent a lot of time advising the curious governments that arise in that part of the world. The paradox reveals that from the viewpoint of groups grappling with the problem of development in the Third World, the roots of the problem are political, being inextricably linked with the question of political power.

The Ugandans would seem to have accepted this under Obote and then to have reneged on their responsibility in this regard subsequent to the coup. Nevertheless, one does not have to be pessimistic about the outcome. What is happening in Uganda and other arenas is that contradictions keep multiplying day by day. The creation of a militaristic or police state itself polarizes the forces and causes people to react against the regime, if only for the sake of survival. If, on the other hand, the regime is flirting with anti-imperialist and socialist ideas without any commitment, then it requires only a few years before the rhetoric is exhausted and the period of reckoning begins. Inevitably, behind the facade of pseudo-progressive assertions, corruption increases and police brutality also. I am not at all pessimistic about the long-term prospects for liberation and development in the Third World. The propping up of regimes by imperialism is a short-term solution. Objective conditions in the Third World are worsening, as I suggested earlier. The living conditions of the vast majority of people are deteriorating. That is what will maintain the initiative towards change and propel the Third World out of the counter-revolutionary phase which arose after formal independence. Besides there is the factor of racism which is all pervasive throughout the Third World, which is particularly strong where black people live in Africa and the Caribbean. It is a unifying factor. Imperialism has used racism in its own interest, but it turns out to be a double-edged blade, and the very unity that is engendered among black people – the unity of common conditions and common exploitation and oppression – is being turned around as a weapon to be used against imperialism.

To conclude, perhaps the most important reason for confidence and for revolutionary optimism – with respect to both the political problem which is immediate and the long-term economic problem – is that the peoples of the Third World have not been dehumanized, in spite of everything: in spite of slavery, in spite of colonialism. The historical record will show that it is the peoples of the metropoles who have gone through the most dehumanization. That's the way it is. Slavery has dehumanized slave masters more than it has dehumanized slaves. Colonialism has dehumanized the colonialist more than it has dehumanized the colonial people. The working class in the metropoles is more confused, more alienated and less in control of their own destiny than the peasants in the African countryside and the workers on plantations in the Third World countries. The latter do not have any crumbs or fruits that have been thrown at them to increase their confusion. Nor have they been living within a society which assails them on all sides with a variety of myths that cloud exploitation under the banner of God and country, and so on. Ultimately, it seems to me that freedom will come from those who are the most oppressed. Slaves rather than slave masters are the repositories of freedom; liberation will come from those who are not yet liberated, and human dignity will be reasserted by those who are not yet dehumanized.

Q&A

Question: Would you consider the more important problems of imperialism to be the ones created by neo-colonialism or those belonging to the old capitalist experience of imperialism?

Answer: The old imperialism is falling apart, one has to be more sensitive about the new changes. There are very powerful existing areas of old imperialism as in South Africa, but there the issues are clearly defined. Whatever the strength of the white minority regimes and of Portuguese colonialism backed by NATO and by foreign monopoly capital, the stage is set and armed struggles are already unleashed in those areas. I think it is easier to mobilize politically where colonialism is open and blatant in the old-fashioned form.

The new colonialism is sometimes so difficult to decipher that one might think that one is doing something progressive when in fact one is really being co-opted by the system. Take nationalization as an example. There was a time, back in the early fifties, when people who nationalized were automatically regarded as progressive nationalists and socialists, and imperialism moved against them to squash them immediately. But now nationalization has become a technique that can just as well be used by the enemy, as by progressive Africans, Asians or Latin Americans. Nationalizing a plant within the context of the international division of labour and the international allocation of resources could well mean that production is no more independent than if it had remained in the hands of foreign enterprises. A joint venture in which the government takes over 51 per cent of the shares may superficially suggest control, while in practice the 51 per cent comprises the problems of labour management and their 49 per cent comprises the profits. There are all kinds of new techniques that are being devised by international capital. After all, mosquitos today are able to cope with the DDT insecticide. Similarly, imperialism has a certain flexibility, and I think the new forms and adjustments are maybe more difficult to combat because they are subtle, and there is a time lag before it can be appreciated that imperialism can also turn retreat into success.

Question: Could you analyse the Tanzanian situation?

Answer: Tanzania is one of the few instances where I think that a nationalist government, which inherited power at independence, does provide a framework within which a struggle can be conducted. Both things have to be recognized: first, that this nationalist government does provide a legitimate framework for onward development; and second, that a struggle is nevertheless necessary. One then has to determine what exactly is the struggle? Who is struggling against whom? What is the alignment of forces? There is a very useful analysis by a young Tanzanian which is entitled *Tanzania: The Silent Class Struggle*. It is a silent class struggle because it does not take the form of armed struggle. Instead, it takes the form of a great deal of manoeuvring within the structure between on the one hand the bureaucracy and the reactionary elements of the petty bourgeoisie, and on the other hand a much smaller group committed to socialism, who are attempting very slowly and with a great deal of difficulty to try and establish some links with the vast majority of the people. Meanwhile, the workers themselves have to find ways and means of confronting the petty bourgeoisie. Within this structure, within the idiom of socialism, a struggle is going on all the time. Many individuals who are justifiably happy about what is going on in Tanzania sometimes romanticize the situation, because they do not know how difficult the struggle is and they do not realize that it is a struggle that has produced not only gains for the working people but also many setbacks from day to day.

Question: What role is being played by the nationalized sector and by the trade unions in Tanzania?

Answer: Nationalization is a step in a forward direction. The next issue becomes the method of running these enterprises. Nationalized industry is a fairly small sector, because Tanzania is not an industrialized country, but what goes on within it is significant in ideological and political terms, apart from the economic implications. A bureaucracy has been developing. This is not unique; it happened in the Soviet Union, it happened in China, it happened in Cuba. The bureaucracy has emerged as a social formation crucial to socialist development – or lack thereof – even where the property base of an exploiting class has been liquidated. So that is a very real problem in the nationalized sector. How does one deal with it? In Tanzania, there has been talk about workers' control in the factories. It has never reached the point of workers' control in practice, but there has been over the past year a very healthy self-assertion by the workers. This has not taken place through the trade union, which is virtually defunct. Workers in their own factories have been reasserting themselves in Tanzania, particularly since the Tami Guidelines, which Tanzanians refer to as the *Mwongozo*. There has been a spate of worker manifestations which have taken these guidelines as their credo, because the guidelines say that the country has to create new styles of work, new kinds of relationships between the party, the government, the officials and the bureaucrats, and the workers and peasants; and this is getting at the root of the problem of the rise of a new bureaucracy and its relationship politically and socially to the rest of the population. Workers in their factories, using *Mwongozo* as a sort of article of faith, have been attacking the bureaucracy, have been attacking the managers and the officials who have been placed over them. Strikes and work stoppages therefore often mirror, in a small way, the ongoing struggle between the people who are directly at the production line and those who are supposedly making policy in the society. That is one facet of this silent class struggle.

9

Slavery and Underdevelopment

In evaluating the two connected concepts of slavery and underdevelopment, the principal emphasis must necessarily be on underdevelopment. Slavery – as institution, as epoch, as mode of production – acquires its significance in this formulation from an awareness of the implications of inequality and dependence in the modern world. Failure to grasp the multiple manifestations of underdevelopment as a contemporary phenomenon inevitably leads to an obscuring of the historical issues. Multinational corporations, management contracts, blockages of technology transfers and the rise of new dependent class structures in the so-called Third World provide the logical starting point for historical enquiry. No doubt it is for this reason that within the field of African studies the most effective analyses of the development process have been authored by economists, cultural anthropologists and political scientists, while historians remained locked within time capsules. It is against the background of the considerable advance in theoretical and scientific work on underdevelopment that one might resume in a new way the already long-established debate on the role of slavery.

The notion of underdevelopment has emerged out of a series of debates. There have been varying empirical observations from territory to territory and varying emphases on the constituents of underdevelopment.[1] Yet, all approaches to underdevelopment as a historical process have discerned the presence of given tendencies towards inequality, backwardness and dependence. These tendencies are operative at most times, although they might ultimately be transcended.

It is, for instance, observable that inequality and dependence are self-reinforcing; but a decisive and obvious exception is provided by the transition from a peripheral role in colonial North America to the hegemonic position of the US within the capitalist/imperialist world. Today, the discussion continues – focusing on potentialities in Brazil, in India, and in other 'semi-industrialized' or 'intermediary' economies. In terms of modern monopoly capital, it is preferable to identify the forms of surplus realization and accumulation without prejudice to the possibility that 'underdevelopment' can give way to 'dependent development' in certain sectors of the periphery. These modifications in the approach to underdevelopment hardly apply to the period of slavery, since it predates monopoly capitalism. As a premise of this chapter, underdevelopment will be held to be an integral part of the development of capitalism on a world scale.[2] This is not necessarily self-evident, but the arguments to this effect have been made at such length elsewhere that they have to be taken as a given in this context.

The expanded reproduction of capital and the creation of a world-system involved the realization of surplus and its extraction from all regions within the ambit of capital. This meant not merely the extension of economic activity from one continent to another but also the juxtaposition of several different social formations and modes of production, articulated in such a way as to secure the dominance of capitalist relations as well as the transfer of value to the capitalist class in the core areas.[3] The search for greater precision in determining when capitalism became the dominant mode in Europe is beyond the present exercise and so too is an estimation of the impact of New World slavery on the emergence of capitalism in Europe. However, these questions do have relevance to the distinction between 'commercial capital' and 'industrial capital' and to that between commodity production by wage labour and commodity production by means other than wage labour. These latter issues are directly pertinent to the role of slavery in the history of underdevelopment in Africa and the Americas.

The slavery which existed in the Americas between the sixteenth and the nineteenth centuries coexisted with other modes of production in Europe, Africa and America. These were articulated to constitute a system with a capacity for further physical expansion and one which achieved inter alia the following:

1) the accumulation of capital;
2) new forms of combining and organizing capital;
3) qualitative leaps in the production of technology;
4) the development of the bourgeoisie and the proletariat; and
5) a strengthening of the state and other basic social institutions.

Any exploration of the links between slavery and underdevelopment should seek to assess the contribution of slavery to the lop-sidedness of the above points. More than that, one needs to be more confident that the contribution by slavery was essential and unique at decisive junctures.

No scholars have expressed doubt as to the enormous significance of European overseas expansion and of Atlantic trade in particular. The stumbling blocks are to be found beyond these innocuous phrases when attempting to assign weight to slavery and the slave trade.

Africa still receives short shrift in conventional texts on the subject of Atlantic trade.[4] Yet, whenever the subject has been explored, it emerges that Africa was historically indispensable to the leading class forces in Europe. The feudal landed classes who participated in overseas expansion would have been unable to renew themselves (in the form of quasi-feudal plantations and land grants) and the nascent capitalist class needed the New World to redress the social balance in the Old. They did so by integrating the Americas into a network of financial and market relations dominated by themselves in the metropolitan centres. Africa also helped to extend the market for cheap European manufactures and to strengthen the techniques of guaranteeing capital and credit; but, of course, Africa's key role was as supplier of labour for which there were no alternatives at the time.

Africa was *structurally* marginal to the emergent world system of the sixteenth and seventeenth centuries. In strict terms, one could not in fact say that African societies had become integrated into the world economy. Wallerstein argues persuasively as follows:

> But why Africans as the new slaves? Because Europe needed a source of labor from a reasonably well-populated region that was accessible and relatively near the region of usage. But it had to be from a region which was outside its world-economy so that Europe could feel unconcerned about the economic consequences for the breeding region of wide-scale removal of manpower as slaves.[5]

Only rarely did Africa supply values and labour directly to Europe; and for the most part its linkages were via the American continent. In the apt terms of Samir Amin, Africa functioned as a periphery of the American periphery.[6] As a periphery of a periphery, Africa was raided rather than cultivated. The politico-commercial nexus was rather fragile. European forts changed hands among the different nation states and sometimes fell under the sway of the local African rulers. The more vulnerable slave barracoons were in effect tolerated by African authorities; while both the European and African trading factors on the coast had to be allocated considerable amounts of commercial credit on mere trust. But the paradox of structural marginality and immense historical significance also applied with regard to the impact of the slave trade on Africa itself. Large parts of the continent supplied labour at a cost to itself which must be measured in terms of production and physical and social reproduction.

Unfortunately, there has been no appreciable accumulation

of new data to clarify the question of the slave trade within African societies. Available statistical information was compiled and tabulated as a 'Slave Trade Census' by Philip Curtin. This was hailed in some quarters as indicating that prior estimates were grossly exaggerated and that consequently one must scale down considerably conceptions of the destructive effect of slaving on African society. The Curtin figures were of course oriented towards the Americas; and he indicated that they could not be held to be definitive for Africa.[7] Give or take their own imperfections, figures for Africans landed alive in the Americas or even embarked on slave ships offered no more than a framework in which further extrapolations are required to approximate numbers lost to African societies and to relate quantity to quality. This would have called for further regional and general studies to examine the mechanisms of slave procurement and the indirect consequences in the demographic, social, economic and political spheres. One is still left with the necessity to speculate, partly because of the insufficiency of studies and partly because certain data may well be irrecoverable.

Surmising or theorizing about the relationship of slaving to African development may be done plausibly by inferring from general principles or perversely by hiding behind the supposed lack of proof. Thus, Inikori contends that a much higher population loss must be inferred from projections having to do with the removal of Africans in their reproductive prime. He contends further that the diseconomies in the utilization of a basic factor of production (labour) meant that even a neo-classical theoretical approach should logically deduce that the slave trade applied a brake on African growth and development.[8] John Fage, on the other hand, emphasizes that there is no evidence to suggest that the operations of slaving caused marked devastation and loss of life; while with respect to the labour factor, he hypothesizes that it is even conceivable that it may have been more profitable for some parts of this area [of West Africa] to have exported the equivalent of its natural growth of population rather than to have kept it at home.[9]

No indication is provided by Fage as to the relationship between labour and development or that between population densities and the social and natural environment.

I have argued elsewhere at some length with respect to the underdeveloping tendencies of the slave trade in Upper Guinea and in Africa as a whole.[10] Slavery in the Americas was of course ultimately responsible for whatever consequences flowed from the Atlantic slave trade in Africa; but what needs to be recognized is that slave exportation from Africa was not a system of production comparable to slavery in the New World or anywhere else in prior epochs. For Africa, the critical activity centred around the mechanisms for the reduction of human beings into captives and chattel. These mechanisms reduced or destroyed production, as has graphically been illustrated by the effects of slave procurement on the gold mining industry of the Gold Coast in the eighteenth century.[11] One frequently encounters African sayings that people, subjects or hands make for strength. With relatively low population densities and little labour-saving technology, it followed that labour rather than land was the scarce factor of reduction – to use the neo-classical formulation. In Marxist terms, the removal of human beings constituted the removal of the most important of the productive forces.

Sections of the current scholarly literature continue to affirm that what took place in Africa was 'trade' and that this trade *ipso facto* contained developmental potential.[12] John Fage argues that 'in the first place, the European slave traders were traders, who bought their slaves from coastal African merchants'.[13] More recently, A.G. Hopkins has elaborated on this theme.[14] By insisting that the exchange of human beings for commodities on the coast comprised trade, the analysis directs attention away from the mode of acquiring captives.[15] It also saves the way for the assumption that trade always benefits both parties – that is to say, the concept of comparative advantage is accepted without question. Yet, all recent work on development on a world scale (of varying ideological perspectives) confirms that 'unequal trade' is entrenched as between developed and underdeveloped countries; and hence the near-universal appeal for a New International Economic Order. With regard to slavery, trade and market theories which have no power to explain the present are invoked to explain the past.

The search for comparative advantage deriving to Africa from the trade in slaves gives rise to arguments which are both trivial and contrived. For instance, Hopkins places great store on the African production of food for provisioning slave ships, as though the quantum would have been greater or the process more dynamic than in the case of food production to feed the same Africans for the duration of their lives in Africa. Under colonial rule, the underdeveloping tendencies persisted for as long as African production was designed primarily for an external market, while the withdrawal of manpower as migrant labour has been abundantly illustrated as serving to enhance backwardness and dependence in which labour is recruited.[16] One of the principal differences between slave trading and colonialism is that the latter introduced the hegemony of capital within African societies. Slavery began the destruction of the coherence of African social formations without offering any alternatives. Colonialism actively pursued the destruction while counterposing a new coherence of capitalist structures in which eleven social formations and modes were reconstituted to confirm capitalist market relations and ultimately wage relations. Slavery began the incorporation of Africa into the periphery of the world-system without any notable intrusion of capitalist forms inside Africa itself.

The terms 'periphery' and 'core' are only rough approximations as descriptions of parts of the world economy at any given time. It is acknowledged that there were always gradations of centrality and importance, so that the American periphery of the slavery era falls into a category different from that of the African periphery. In the Americas, slavery undoubtedly constituted one of the modes of appropriation integral to the capitalist system; and for this reason, the discussion of slavery and underdevelopment should concentrate on the American sector. The exercise can usefully be prefaced by an indication of the essential and recurring features of (capitalist) underdevelopment expressed as laws of motion of the societies concerned. Clive Thomas offers invaluable insights when he identifies underdevelopment and dependence as basically involving:

1. the lack of an organic link between domestic resources and domestic demand; and
2. the divergence between domestic demand and the needs of the broad majority of the population.[17]

At this point I will focus on the example of Guyana with the intention of providing some specificity within the context of the broader study of trans-Atlantic slavery. The available literature on West Indian slave plantations has usually found little difficulty in fitting Guyana into the main generalizations covering the region. In Guyana, as elsewhere, sugar seemed inevitably to go hand in hand with slavery. For all practical purposes, the strip of coastland which circumscribed the slave plantations of Guyana in the eighteenth century was another small island where the master–slave relationship was almost exclusive. Production in Guyana was subject to the same colonial and market constraints as were characteristic of the West Indian islands.

Yet, Guyana did have its peculiarities. It was not a small island in which continuous sugar growing had exhausted the cultivable soils before or soon after slavery ended; nor was it debt-ridden and burdened by multiple mortgages by the turn of the nineteenth century. On the contrary, the soils were not easily exhaustible and there was no question about the economic viability of the slave-based sugar industry on the eve of emancipation. The relatively large plantation units were well capitalized and, with the aid of compensation payments, the industry survived the first major market crisis of the equalization of UK sugar duties in 1846. Above all, Guyana had a substantial hinterland which set it off from the West Indian islands. There is every reason to investigate why a large continental area remained a colonial enclave during and after slavery.

Guyana had large areas of living space which were not occupied by slave plantations. In these thinly populated areas, the prior communal modes of the Amerindians persisted – albeit deformed under the pressure of European conquest and colonization. Slave plantations were established on the littoral from which the indigenous Amerindian population had been cleared. But the frontier was static and there was no expansion of capitalist relations or transplanted peoples into the hinterland. Among the characteristics of Guyanese underdevelopment one notes the incomplete inventory and exploitation of hinterland resources and the limited nature of new settlements. These features were marked during the heyday of slavery and are to be attributed to the political economy of slavery.

Slavery required secure conditions for the reproduction of slave labour after that labour had been introduced. The problem of runaways varied in acuteness depending mainly on the environment. The forested areas of Guyana offered conditions no less favourable to runaways than did Suriname and Brazil. In the period of Dutch ascendancy, intermingling between Amerindians and Africans produced the mixed 'Boviander' communities which were highly rebellious and constituted poles of attraction for runaways. This was the

experience of the seventeenth century when small slave plantations were established on the middle and upper reaches of the
Guyanese rivers. After the Dutch resolved upon coastal agriculture in the mid-eighteenth century, the Guyanese economy
turned away from the hinterland. Even the necessary activity
of slaves 'aback', such as cutting palm leaves for thatch, was
considered dangerous since it facilitated escape.[18] The enslavement of distant Amerindian ethnicities and the importation
of Africans on a large scale were compatible with the maintenance of friendly relations between European slave owners
and the neighbouring Amerindian communities. Indeed, the
latter were then prevailed upon to undertake certain police
functions in apprehending and returning escaped slaves. The
choice of the coastlands for the development of slave plantations was premised upon ecological factors; but, having been
made, this choice was reinforced by the demand of the slave
system for security – to the prejudice of interior development.

Slavery arrived full-blown on the Guyanese coast, attracting both Dutch and English capital and settlers already in the
Caribbean. There was no question of replacing independent
small producers by slaves and the rise of such cultivators was
inconceivable once the slave plantation held sway. The plantation system continually sought to exercise monopoly over land
and labour, a feature which was perceptible only after slavery
ended. Although Guyanese history is badly under-researched,
it has recently been served by two scholarly texts which address
themselves to the plantations after slavery. Both confirm the
perverse role of the plantation owners in seeking to hold on
to all cultivable land and in providing disincentives to any
alternative economic ventures which would reduce planter
dominance over the labour market.[19] Even a casual examination of the slavery era shows that these tendencies were most
pronounced and that it was the slave-based plantation which
was the principal stumbling block to hinterland development
and to the balanced development of the economy.

The dependent slave economy failed to utilize resources which were readily at hand within the domestic environment, while relying on the import of goods which could have derived from these same resources. The buildings of the coast were made from wood, but for the most part that wood was not cut from the forests of Guyana. The same could be said for the furniture within the houses. It was not until the 1850s that the export of greenheart was established and several more decades passed before there was a local timber industry seeking to fulfill local demands. As late as 1902, the administration was unable to answer a query from the Colonial Office as to the existence of particular woods. On that occasion, the governor observed: 'It is clearly unsatisfactory that we should be without complete and suitable specimens of all the woods of this Colony.'[20]

The spectacle of importing North American white pine into a forested colony was startling enough; but the policy towards the gold industry is more striking still. In spite of the El Dorado legend and the tremendous stimulus provided by the search for gold in the Americas, the gold industry in Guyana was pursued with a remarkable lack of vigour. African slaves and Bovianders had mined gold under the direction of the Dutch in the mid-eighteenth century. After the move to the coastal plantations, Dutch planters were apparently so fearful of any competition to their plantation labour supplies that they closed gold mining operations completely. Nothing was revived until exploration resumed in 1864; and in the 1880s Guyanese were still rediscovering that the territory had alluvial gold. At that point, the planter class was reluctant to release public funds to advance the gold industry. Their command over public policy and the public treasury was unchallenged during the epoch of slavery, and this ensured that slavery had profound effects in vitiating the links between production and resource base in the Guyanese situation.

Underdevelopment is a form of development – dependent and asymmetrical, but development nonetheless within the socio-historical context of the capitalist world system. The slave plantations of Guyana transformed the coastlands from thinly inhabited marshland to productive plantation zones. This was a development of resources hitherto *underdeveloped* by the sparse settlements of communally organized Amerindians who were farming, fishing and hunting. While contributing to the burgeoning growth of the capitalist cores, slave plantations imposed constraints on extending capitalist relations within Guyana itself. Discussion on the precise relationship of slavery to capitalism has advanced beyond the polarization of slavery as either capitalist or non-capitalist. It is self-evident that slavery stood in the way of the commoditization of labour and yet the internal hierarchical structure of the slave plantation was significantly influenced by capitalist forms in Europe. At all times, slavery remained independent on the markets, financial infrastructure and technology of the world capitalist centres.

Hindess and Hirst seek to abstract the essence of slavery in the Americas as follows:

> It is a mode of production subordinated to the capitalist mode of production within the international division of labour and the world market created by capitalism. The conditions of reproduction of the Slave Mode of Production under these circumstances depend upon the capitalist system; upon world demand for the commodities it produces, competing regions and methods of production, alternative sources of investment, etc.[21]

Paula Beiguelman simply and effectively defines modern (New World) slavery as 'capitalist slavery';[22] while Clive Thomas emphasizes another crucial dimension when he designates it as a 'colonial slave mode of production', given the fact that colonialism became 'the mediatory structure through which the influences of emerging capitalism in Europe were transmitted'.[23] There is a wide area of agreement that slavery was an essential component of peripheral capitalism and that as such it could not develop enough internal momentum to ensure that its surpluses were used for the development of capitalism in a territory such as Guyana.

For sugar, there was only one market, which lay more often than not in a single metropolitan centre. The nature of surplus realization imposed a relentless dependency on the planter class vis-à-vis the metropoles. Dependency is a colonial characteristic; but it must be noted that slavery in the colonies was bound to be heavily dependent because the slave economy stood no chance of creating an internal market. The tied market was also the source of capital and credit. Commercial and financial institutions were never autonomous within Guyana. Technology, too, was externally derived and there was little room for innovation or even adaptation of the type which could be termed developmental. Improvements to factory technology were very slow in coming to Guyana, while field husbandry remained wedded to the utilization of heavy inputs of cheap labour. In his unique study of Cuban sugar technology, Manuel Moreno Fraginals makes it clear that the major force in inducing growth in eighteenth-century Cuba was more manpower and slavery – in contrast to metropolitan capitalism – which lacked the dynamic to constantly revolutionize production methods.[24]

These remarks are also applicable to Guyana. There was a proliferation of artisan skills on the Guyanese slave plantations and there were slaves who mastered the boiling of the sugar; but, of course, they were not exposed to scientific principles or experimentation. Besides, sugar technology was industry-specific and confirmed the mono-cultural dimension of the economy. The slave planters pursued policies which made it impossible for other branches of economic activity to be established and they were able to create barriers to the free entry of capital into agriculture, industry and distribution.

The legal essence of slavery – ownership and legal coercion – and its political expression in a narrow planter-controlled state both contributed to holding back development in Guyana. The local state institutions under planter management were weak in their relation to the external world but they were powerful instruments in the hands of the masters for use against the slaves. The plantocracy was given free rein in its domestic policies. Without a domestic market and forms of petty commodity production, intermediary strata were extremely weak and closely tied to the planter class. Obviously, slavery stood in the way of the emergence of a wage-earning proletariat, but in addition it also inhibited the growth of other classes and strata associated with the maturation of capitalism in the metropoles.

Initially, reference was made to the necessity to premise the evaluation of slavery on contemporary underdevelopment. It is, however, just as important to pursue the historical enquiry into the post-slavery decades of the nineteenth century, where continuity and change gave meaning to previous trends.

For nearly 100 years, sugar planters bitterly resisted the creation of a free labour market as implied by emancipation. They succeeded (with metropolitan backing) in importing indentured labour from various sources and in having that labour force heavily subsidized from state revenues. Briefly in 1848 and then systematically from 1846, the planters organized large-scale state-aided immigration from India. Until the last indentureship terminated in 1921, planters maintained a strategic section of the labour force on fixed wages and contracts outside the labour market. Their efforts were directed against the emergence of a proletariat which could make industrial and social demands on the owners of capital. Inevitably, the free section of the labour force found its initiatives frustrated by the immense control which planters wielded over indentured workers and hence the ease with which those workers were deployed to break the unity of working-class struggle. Interestingly enough, planter resistance against the commoditization of labour was spearheaded in the late nineteenth century by plantation companies which were an integral part of the new monopoly forms of the imperialist era.

The post-slavery plantations also showed a determination to retain a monopoly over land and to keep agricultural land in particular from coming onto the market. The conditions of tenure of the 'frontlands' of the coastal strip were such that each estate had an automatic option on the 'backlands' of potential polder husbandry. Until these options were taken up, the land belonged to the Crown, as did the forests and savannahs of the interior. Planters moved quickly to raise the price at which Crown land could be sold to a prohibitive level and to restrict the terms under which it could be leased. These measures blocked non-plantation capitalist development of the land and they militated severely against the emergence of a peasantry.

Nevertheless, it is equally important to recognize that the planter monopoly over land and labour was breached in the nineteenth century and that growth and development registered in the post-slavery epoch were due precisely to the small ways in which that monopoly had been successfully challenged. Ex-slaves immediately assumed the role of a modern proletariat in presenting their own terms for wages and conditions of work. They did not make a great deal of headway in the face of state-aided indentured immigration, but their wage level was usually slightly higher than that of indentured bondsmen whose rate of one shilling per day remained unchanged from 1838 to 1921. African exslaves moved into a variety of occupations in the villages and towns and to some extent in the hinterland also. Their first objective was not to escape from estate employment, but they at least supplemented estate earnings by functioning part-time as artisans and in petty commodity self-employment of one sort or another. Ex-indentured Indians, Chinese and Madeirans took similar routes. One infers from all this the extraordinary importance of legal coercion in the slavery epoch. Recent research has firmly concluded that it was the plantation structure that was the key element in underdevelopment in Guyana.[25] This should be modified, and the emphasis shifted to the slave mode of production – colonial and capitalist – with which the plantation was first associated. The plantation remained a factor inducing backwardness mainly to the extent that legal extra-economic extraction of surplus did continue after slavery; but the new situation lacked the comprehensiveness of slavery and was slowly undermined by wage labour.

Former slaves and ex-indentured workers were able to express their own demands for goods and services. Their demand created an internal market for land and houses as well as for food, clothing and other consumer items. The immediate post-slavery activities of Africans in Guyana have long been a subject of scholarly attention, but misapprehensions still prevail. In general, the first postemancipation decade is presented as the era in which ex-slaves fled the plantations and set themselves up as peasants in the villages.[26] This simplifies and virtually inverts a reality in which Africans were still primarily sugar workers but had withdrawn their residence from estate housing and were making strident demands to support their conception of a tolerable standard of living – demands which included higher wages, education and access to cultivable land for those who wished to become full-time or part-time agricultural producers for local consumption. Distribution and other service sectors expanded because of these post-slavery trends, and intermediary classes began to make their presence felt.

However slow hinterland development may have been in the nineteenth century, it was only possible because of the energy released by emancipation. As wage earners and as petty entrepreneurs, former plantation workers were responsible for the growth of the timber and mining industries. When the middle strata acquired a small economic base outside the direct control of the plantation, they also started to challenge the political hegemony which restricted their further growth. A new Constitution in 1891 was the consequence of protracted 'populist' agitation on the part of all strata outside the planter class. Legislators were thereafter elected on a slightly widened franchise, and they were persuaded to remove some of the stumbling blocks towards the acquisition of Crown land, towards the establishment of a peasant-based rice industry and towards the development of a gold and diamond mining industry. Once more, the role of the state serves to emphasize the historical significance of the political exclusiveness which necessarily went along with slavery in Guyana and wherever slavery was not merely one institution but the basis of peripheral capitalism in any given territory.

Because New World slavery was a colonial phenomenon, it is sometimes difficult to separate the specific consequences of slavery from those which accrued from colonialism. The evidence on Guyana seems to support the conclusion that underdeveloping tendencies can uniquely be identified with slavery. First, when they relate to the central fact that labour was not a commodity and to the absence of efforts to achieve this – in contrast to primitive accumulation when indigenous pre-capitalist societies were colonized in Africa and Asia. And second, when the tendencies stem from the monopoly over land and labour in the hands of slave owners, who placed restraints on the development of other forms of private property. This again falls short of being a common feature of colonialism per se. The colonial state – in the history of capitalism – guaranteed slavery or migrant labour or peasant production, depending upon the mode of labour appropriation which evolved. But the colonial slave state was more monolithic than others because there were no competing class interests which had to be reconciled at the level of the state and because uncompromising authoritarianism was necessary to reproduce the relationship between master and slave.

III

Their Pedagogy and Ours

10

The British Colonialist School of African Historiography and the Question of African Independence

Views on African independence can be divided into three major categories, as follows:

1. The colonial rulers, out of *goodwill*, granted independence, for which Africans had previously been given the necessary *training*.
2. The African people, through *mass nationalist* parties, wrested political independence from the colonizers through *struggle*.
3. With *malice* and deep strategy, the colonial powers themselves promoted the handover of the trappings of sovereignty, so that African independence meant *false decolonization*.

In terms of intrinsic merit, the second and third categories above are of much greater importance than the first, because they reveal more about the historic processes which they set out to explain and they contribute more to an understanding of 'the present as history'. One embarks on a critique of the colonial-goodwill training school mainly because the view is widespread and still in the ascendant in certain quarters. Besides, chronologically speaking, it was the earliest view; and the others cannot be fully comprehended without contemplating their relationship to the colonialist position.

Two principal protagonists have been selected here to represent British colonial writing on this subject: namely, Sir Alan Burns and Lady Margery Perham. In the opening sentence of his book, *Colonial Civil Servant,* Sir Alan Burns announced, 'I was practically born into the Colonial Civil Service. My grandfather and my father were both members of that Service.' As a former governor of Gold Coast and Nigeria, and as a high-ranking official in the Colonial Office itself, Sir Alan Burns is an unimpeachable spokesman for British colonialism.

Lady Margery Perham is well known as a friend of the Colonial Office. She was for many years the most active 'Africanist' at Oxford, offering courses to Colonial Office civil servants, as well as training the present generation of colonist-minded fellows at Oxford who write on African history.

Independence and nationalism came to Africa as European imports, so they tell us. African peoples previously lacked all common elements of nationalism, except common territory; and the requisite ingredients were provided by the presence of the colonizing powers. According to Margery Perham, African nations now owe to Europe the form of their existence as nation states. In effect, the argument suggests that both formal and informal education given by the British brought to Africa the ideas of freedom and democracy and the conception of the nation state. Margery Perham notes that schools in British colonies taught 'the assertion of liberties from Magna Carta to the Reform Act of 1832 and beyond'.[1]

Nationalism is a sense of common identity that arises as human groups seek to resolve the basic contradiction between man and nature. It is a definition of the in-group, as against all competitors in the struggle for scarce resources. Nation states grew up in Europe, Asia and Africa. What was Ethiopia other than a nation state? And what about Egypt long before colonial rule? Several African states destroyed by colonialism were as large as and often larger than the succeeding territories arbitrarily defined by Europeans. Even if, for the sake of argument, one were to deny that states like those of the Zulu, the Baganda, the Asante and the Mandinga under Samori Touré were not nations, it would be impossible to deny that they were 'nationalities' at an advanced stage of evolution towards nationhood per se. They were at least comparable to Ireland and Ukraine in the nineteenth century; and they had more people sharing a common culture than many microstates in Europe, Africa and Latin America at the present time. What European colonialism provided was a new context for nationalism in Africa, after having destroyed the old. The boundaries drawn at Berlin became in most instances the borders of the new African nations of our time, because reaction against colonial administrations dictated the *form* of African nationalism. There is a vast difference between form and substance.

Another extravagant assertion of the colonial-goodwill-training school is that Africans were taught 'freedom', or (more modestly) 'the democratic freedoms'. Sir Alan Burns states categorically that 'the Sudan, under Anglo-Egyptian condominium, owes everything – including independence – to British tutelage.'[2] Do the concepts of freedom and independence really involve tuition and learning? It has aptly been pointed out that throughout history, there is no evidence of any individuals or groups being against the idea of freedom, though there are countless numbers who have been against the freedom of others. Claiming freedom on behalf of the people of Tanganyika at the United Nations in 1956, Mwalimu Julius Nyerere spoke of freedom in terms of 'a natural call, a call of the spirit, ringing in the hearts of all men, and of all times, educated or uneducated, to rebel against foreign domination'. He was then making a reference to the great Haji Maji wars by the people of southern Tanganyika against the Germans; and the thesis can be amply illustrated by the wide-ranging African resistance to the imposition of colonial rule in the last two decades of the nineteenth century and the first decade of the twentieth.

With respect to 'democratic freedom', one can say that the issue is much narrower than that of relaxing to 'freedom'.

Liberal or bourgeois democratic freedoms are a specific set of civil rights which emerged at a particular period in the history of capitalist Europe. Leaving aside the question of how far those rights were implemented in practice in Europe itself, it is certainly true that African leaders articulated African demands for freedom in the terminology of bourgeois democracy. Here again, what is at issue is the form of the demands. And, even at that superficial level, one must be careful to notice the sleight of hand by which the dialectical opposite of a particular position is presented as conscious policy. The British taught those who emerged as nationalist leaders with the purpose of facilitating exploitation, not so that they would advance the cause of African freedom. British colonialism in Africa produced Nkrumah, Kaunda and even Banda (of anti-federation fame) in spite of and not because of British colonialist intentions.

At one point in her analysis of African and Indian nationalism, Margery Perham comments on the ideas of nationalist leaders as follows: 'Like other weapons turned against the West, they have been purloined from the West. And the ideal of democratic freedom and an almost indefinable sense of moral obligation towards the weak, have been learned very largely from Britain herself.'

That statement is redolent with bourgeois and colonialist assumptions, confusion and deceit. In the first place, the bourgeois notion of private property is extended to political and moral standards and the ideal of democracy. They have been taken out of patents for those aspects of the universal striving of man, and the Africans have come by them only through theft – that is, 'purloined'. But, in the very next breath, the Lady says that the ideas were 'learned', thereby reintroducing the duality of teaching/learning and the implication that it was a conscious handing over on Britain's part.

Indirect rule is a topic much favoured by British colonialist historians.

Sir Alan Burns calls indirect rule 'local government' and claims that 'indirect rule is an excellent school in which the difficult art of self-government can be learned'. Whatever indirect rule was, it was *not* training in self-government, because power and responsibility was always in the hands of the colonizers. Indeed, it marked the termination of the exercise of political power by the African people or by strata of the African population on behalf of others. In its northern Nigerian form and other variations, indirect rule was a tool of convenience for governing Africa cheaply and with the minimum of effort. It is quite incredible that it should be interpreted as one of Britain's gifts of backward Africa, and as offering the training that would lead to independence.

It might appear more plausible to suggest that the legislatures which were set up in the colonies offered training for independence. Legislative councils allowed for a few nominated Africans, and later on for a few elected African representatives. Undoubtedly, the few learned about Westminster procedure and about when bills went into committee, when they had their second reading, and so on. But, that is hardly enough grounds for concluding that the legislative councils were the 'educational prototype of centralized parliamentary government', to use the words of Margery Perham. Up until the time that internal self-government was constitutionally made possible, all other legislative experiments wore variations on the theme of metropolitan domination via the governor of the colony. The basic question is whether Africans were participating in the exercise of power and responsibility, to which the answer is 'no'.

All colonial constitutions stressed the 'reserve', 'paramount' or 'overriding' powers of the governor, thus guaranteeing that African members would be frustrated, in the few instances where honest and courageous African nationalists were permitted to enter.

In its extreme form, the colonial-goodwill-training thesis

amounts to the assertion that colonialism from the outset was consciously liquidating itself. Sir Alan Burns implies this by observing that in the very process of colonizing Africa, Britain was 'bringing under its protection backward peoples and leading them towards civilisation'. With reference to Nigeria, he wrote that 'we are in Nigeria merely as trustees for the people, and it is our business to train them as rapidly as possible for self-government.'

A writer who claims that British education in the colonies was education for freedom and that indirect rule was practice in the art of self-government, should also maintain that Britain was planning decolonization virtually from the word 'go'. In that regard, Burns maintains consistency, at the price of holding the laughable view that the British conquered only so as to plan decolonization. Margery Perham is more cautious and less consistent. When it comes to timing the moment when imperial Britain decided on the policy on self-government as a possibility, she moves much closer to the end of the colonial period.

If admittance of Africans to the legislative councils was part of the preparation for self-government and independence, then the timing of Britain's goodwill-training programme should at least date from the 1920s. However, Perham concedes that colonial administration hardly got under way properly until the 1930s, and it was not until after the Second World War that Britain began to timetable independence. 'The war had subtly changed Britain's attitude, though the authorities hardly knew it until faced with the decision', she writes. So now we know that there was a *change* post-1944, that there could not therefore have been a previous *policy* to contemplate independence, and that even after 1944 this change does not become effective until the colonial authorities were faced by 'the decision': namely, what to do with the great African and Asian humanity which said 'enough' to colonial overlordship.

In parts of her work, Perham unreservedly admits that 'anti-colonialism and anti-imperialism represents the latest phase in the reaction of the rest of the world against the long domination of the West.' She concedes the basic desire for freedom on the part of all peoples, and actually uses the term 'regaining of independence' with reference to the movement for African sovereignty in the late fifties. A reading of several texts from this British colonial historiographical school shows the same ambivalence and inconsistency. On the one hand, there are the vague and far-reaching claims to British uniqueness in preparing Africans for independence or self-government from a very early date. On the other hand, when more specific statements are made, they never mention a date earlier than the post-war epoch as the point when conscious policy came into being; and (on a lower key) they admit that the initiative for change came from the colonized peoples.

Sir Arthur Creech-Jones, as secretary of state for the colonies in 1948, put forward the first public policy statement to the effect that the central purpose of British colonial policy was to guide the colonial territories to responsible self-government within the Commonwealth. That statement is often cited by the British colonialist school of historiography under discussion, and Perham places considerable emphasis on the role of the Labour Party in that respect. With the experience of India, Ceylon and Burma behind them, British policymakers had apparently anticipated the goal of eventual African self-government within the Commonwealth and the rapid and full constitutional independence which actually came to Africa. It is the contention here that the nature and degree of independence and the timing of that eventually as conceived by some British policymakers in 1948 were all significantly different from what did occur in the years to follow.

The most dramatic testimony that Africans rather than the British were the ones who set the main patterns of constitutional change in the 1960s is provided by the remarks of colonial officials right up to the eve of those changes – remarks showing blissful unawareness that the end of colonialism was in sight. Burns addressed a seminar of colonial officials at Oxford in 1947, in the capacity of governor of the Gold Coast. He began as follows:

> I have been asked to speak to you this morning on the future of the Colonial Service as I think it must develop if it is to meet the growing demands that will be made on it during the next twenty or thirty years ... There have even been suggestions that our Empire is coming to an end, that our colonies are now anxious and ready to stand by themselves, and there will shortly be no more need for a Colonial Civil Service. I don't believe it.

Virtually all the statements that Britain was actively contemplating granting African self-government from the latter part of the 1940s are made with hindsight by the writer faced with the reality of independent Ghana and other comparable changes. For instance, Sir Charles Jeffries explained in 1960 that 'the writing was on the wall' in the Gold Coast in 1947, but he confessed that he did not see it, and he justified his own lack of perception as being part of a general phenomenon. He notes that Martin Wight, an 'expert' on colonial constitutions, had written in 1947 that the Gold Coast Constitution of 1946 would last for decades! So, while Wight, Jeffries, Burns and Creech-Jones were contemplating self-government perhaps at the end of this century, the people of the Gold Coast came out on the streets in 1948 and upset those plans. The same picture can be obtained for other colonial territories which later played very dynamic roles in the independence struggle. Sir Hugh Foot said of Nigeria: 'In 1945 many people thought that the most Nigeria could hope for was a continuation of paternal administration, a few decades of marking time, at most a slow and steady development of the policy of indirect rule.'

With hardly any exceptions, the British colonial historians would join Perham in acknowledging that the nationalist movements developed with 'unexpected speed and power'. This is explained away by the colonial-goodwill training school as something that did not contradict the substance of British plans but was 'merely a matter of timing'. However, that is a very frail rationalization, because the rate of change was so drastically affected by the efforts of the colonized that in effect the guide was being led. It would be naive and anti-historical to overlook the role of the colonizers in the last years of colonialism.

Governors like Arden-Clarke, Renison, Turnbull and Hugh Foot presided over the dissolution of the British Empire with unquestioned skill; but it is certainly questionable whether they led or guided towards independence, as distinct from compromising with a reality that had outrun expectations.

A great deal usually hinges on the example of the rise of Ghana out of this Gold Coast colony. It is there that one can pinpoint the earliest plans and reactions of British colonialism faced with African nationalism. Events in Ghana up to 1957 cannot be measured in exactly the same way as events leading to the independence of Lesotho in 1966 or even to that of Uganda in 1962 or Sierra Leone in 1961, because the later stages of the process gave the colonizers much more time to readjust and resume the initiative. The detailed history of the Gold Coast from 1947 to 1957 is one of British back-peddling on the specific issue of constitutional independence. It was rioting by working elements that led to the Coussey Commission; 'Self-Government Now' meant a great deal more than eventual self-government; and the leap from self-government to independence was also, from the British viewpoint, a major concession. The sequence of events is incompatible with the notion that the process reflected the central purpose of British colonial policy.

British colonialist historians consistently propose the most disinterested of motives as lying behind British colonialism in Africa. In their interpretations of British decolonization, they merely assert the factor of goodwill, and never contemplate the possibility of self-interest. Thus, Margery Perham writes:

> Nowhere, except in the regions of white settlement, did Britain even attempt to refuse the demand once her government was convinced of its strength. The problem was essentially one of timing. With her stands of efficiency and her sense of obligation to minority groups, British governments wanted to see the transfer of power carried out by gradual and orderly stages.

A reconsideration of the supposedly philanthropic reasons for colonizing Africa would automatically weaken the credibility of this line of argument, and whatever little remains would disappear in the face of *British manoeuvers* during that period when Africans were pushing for independence. Why were so many African nationalism leaders jailed? What about the attempts to interfere with the character of the regimes that would rule the independent African states? Without going into the details, one can cite Zanzibar as a blatant example of the way in which the British tried to manipulate the granting of independence so as to frustrate the will of the African majority and leave local power in the hands of a trusted Arab elite. British colonialists withdrew only when faced with a challenge, they beat a strategic retreat in the light of their own interests, seeking to preserve as much as was possible. That was entirely natural, and is to be expected in any such political situation. It needs to be argued only because certain high priests have suggested otherwise.

British colonialist writers on the period of decolonization in Africa invariably refer to the notions of 'mandate', 'trusteeship', 'welfare' and 'development' as being integral to the purpose of colonial rule. Some of the actors in the colonizing drama had made such claims from the outset – notably, Livingston, in his emphasis on Christianity and commerce, and

Lord Lugard, in his thesis on *Dual Mandate*. However, it was not until after the last war that policy statements consistently included the welfare of Africans as one of the motivations of colonial rule, coinciding with the establishment of Colonial Development and Welfare (C.D. & W.). Sir Alan Burns adds this concern of the British for African economic independence to the list of other noble motives. In 1957, he asserted that:

> The avowed British Policy is today, as it has been for many decades, to lead all dependent territories up to self-government, and in the meantime to teach the peoples of the countries concerned the difficult art of governing themselves, and to improve the economic condition of each territory so that it may be able to face the future unaided.

The C.D. & W. fund is generally projected by writers of this school as Britain's contribution to the socio-economic welfare of the colonies and to their economic self-sufficiency. But C.D. & W. loans were not intended to make the colonies more independent, nor did they accidentally achieve that end. The loans were meant to develop certain social services and infrastructure in the colonies, so as to maximize their potential within the imperial context. The French were doing the same with their fund, and so both operations were following the line of thought advanced most cogently by the colonial minister, Albert Sarrault, in 1914 – the policy of *mise en valeur* or economic maximization of the potentiality of the colonies in the interests of the metropoles. Britain and France made no bones about the fact that the colonies were required to bail the metropoles out of the desperate post-war economic situation. To a considerable extent, the colonies did serve that purpose. Discerning Africans saw the whole C.D. & W. scheme as a fraud, having nothing to do with African development and a great deal to do with the welfare of Europe; but, in any event, none of its British planners ever asserted more than the aim to develop both the colonies and British in terms of their *continued association.* Economic development for political independence was never raised as an issue.

Undoubtedly, no nationalist movements in Africa so far as advanced to constitution and juridical independence entirely through armed struggle – not even Algeria. Apart from Algeria and perhaps Kenya, it cannot be said that violence was the dominant element within any one colony. Yet, in spite of all that, it is misleading to characterize the independence movements as non-violent. The emphasis on non-violence overlooks the fact that the concept of violence in any operational sense includes also the threat of violence and the example of violence; and, within the colonialist camp, additional confusion is deliberately generated to obscure the fact that colonialism was violence in a form hardly less distilled than slavery.

Colonialism was violently imposed on Africa, and it was violently maintained. Land-grabbing was violence, forced labour was violence, tax collection was violence. Certain juridical fictions emanating from the colonizing power placed only the briefest of lion-clothes to cover the nakedness of violent colonial oppression. If the colonized exposed the legal fictions of 'law and order', then there was the Riot Act and the colonial police. If the local forces were inadequate, then a troop-carrying gunboat was forthcoming. In spite of all that, there was a pattern of violence in the colonies, stemming from worker and peasant actions such as strikes and boycotts. There were enough of those in the inter-war years and in the post-war epoch to make the colonialist extremely apprehensive.

Nationalists and anti-colonialists inside and outside the African continent naturally draw attention to the evidence of that African resistance against European exploitation which took the form of strikes and violent demonstrations. However, colonialist historians, and especially those with administrative backgrounds, were well aware of the same phenomena. Burns dedicated a chapter in his *Colonial Civil Servant* to 'Wars and Riots'. He noted the seriousness of the Egba Rebellion in western Nigeria in 1918 and of the Aba women's riots in eastern Nigeria in 1929. He admitted that the 'Gold Coast has a bad reputation for wars and civil disturbances, some of which were against the alien government'. He was acting-governor of Nigeria in 1942 when the trade unions mobilized against the government; and he went on the air to broadcast a typical governor's appeal for 'reasonableness' and 'loyalty' while promising that he must do his 'duty' if anyone dared to go on strike. The increasing intensity of such strikes and confrontations after the war must have necessarily entered into British calculations as to how long unadulterated colonialism could last.

The winning of constitutional independence in any given African territory has to be correlated with winning of independence everywhere else on the continent and in Asia, so as to determine to what extent the so-called peaceful handover of power was really peaceful and was due to the goodness of the colonizers, and to what extent it was an option forced on them by examples of violence in particular colonies and by the threat of violence implicit in any nationalist movement which had shaped the people into a single resolute force. It is, for example, palpably obvious that the French learned from defeats in Vietnam that they should quit the whole of Indo-china 'peacefully', rather than perish at other Dien Bien-Phus. The French repeated their high-handed actions in Africa and found that the national war of liberation threatened to reduce the French 100-franc note to a piece of worthless paper, and had already bequeathed the National Assembly in Paris with a succession of jack-in-the-box premiers. There was clearly a connection with the unsuccessful French wars of repression in Algeria and the hate with which they tried to establish acceptable African governments in West Africa.

As for the British, Malaya haunted them in Asia and the example of Kenya gave them diarrhoea in Africa. True, they did suppress the Mau Mau land and freedom army, but at what cost! Imperialism is not imperialism if it costs more to suppress the exploited than the imperialists receive in surplus. The British knew that it was wise to proceed with African independence rather than court more Mau Mau. Even in far-off British Guiana, the popular movement of the 1950s could exert some leverage on the British by threatening them with Mau Mau.

India is often given as the classic example of non-violent transfer of power from the imperial power to the indigenous nationalist forces. But it should be remembered that India had a powerful current of mutinous soldiers and other political traditions opposed to the non-violence of Gandhi. The British retreated as much from the threat of millions of Indians lying peacefully on the roads and railways as from the possibility that they might get up and strike back, given the example of those nationalists who were attacking British life and property before and during the Second World War. Some insight into that situation and its relevance to Africa is provided by W.R. Crocker in his book *Self-Government for the Colonies*, written in 1949.

Crocker was a colonial official in Africa, and shared many of the general assumptions of his professional group. Yet, his emphasis is quite different from Burns's, under whom Crocker worked for some time. His book was an attempt to explain to his countrymen the force of nationalism as he saw it in the colonies. The question that he posed was 'suppress or appease?', and he followed that up by asking whether suppression by the British stood any chance of success. His own answer was that:

> The lesson from India is that nationalist agitation can be carried to such a length as to result in a breakdown of government, or what is so near to a breakdown that law and order and essential social measures can no longer be properly executed.

Crocker also made reference to the cost and difficulty of putting down the early armed African movements for independence in Algeria in the 1920s and in Madagascar in 1946, as well as the people's war in Indochina. Besides, the international situation had changed, and he warned that Western Europe lacked the power and will to suppress. Therefore, it was essential to 'appease', and he explained:

> By appease I mean that the existence and the reality of the nationalist movement must be taken very seriously and that efforts must be bent to controlling it, guiding it, and competing with it, up until the moment when power can be transferred with a reasonable prospect of inflicting no undue sufferings upon the docile majority, or up until the moment when the retain of power is no longer practicable.

Apart from the gratuitous solicitude for the welfare of the 'docile' colonized, the above statement really gets down to the nitty-gritty. Crocker goes into a few more details where he warns that to oppose the agitators is to make them more popular, and that to hold back too long in granting African demands for independence would be dangerous. In one sense, Crocker was a liberal among reactionaries; while in another sense, he was no more progressive – save that his line was a frank exposure of what the colonialists were doing, while others were trying to say that the hyena was only a goat. For what Margery Perham tries to hide under the rubric of 'transfer of power' is what he exposes in his definition of 'appease'. He showed an awareness that constitutional independence in India and Burma had not weakened the ties between those territories and Britain. The problem was how and when to step down, so as to secure the best of the situation. As he explains it:

> The conundrum of when to the transfer authority, and how to in any given territory, will require the highest political qualities

... But English history is in many ways a history of political genius ... If the British are true to their genius, the British colonial problem can be solved.

The limitations of this British colonialist school of historians are manifold. Most of them flow logically from the bourgeois worldview. There is no piece of this writing which is free of references to the Soviet Union and Communism. Explicitly and implicitly, there is the recognition that their interpretation of what happened in Africa is part of the struggle to determine whether capitalism or socialism shall triumph. Indeed, an interesting side-alley into which many of these writers divert is a discussion of the 'colonial' and 'nationality' question of the Soviet Union, with a view to demonstrating that Russian exploitation of non-Russians existed inside the Soviet Union, and with a view to warning Africans about the Soviet wolf.

Needless to say, the British colonialist school has a metropolitan and racial bias. It comes out most clearly in their references to pre-colonial Africa, but it is also present in their analysis of decolonization in a patronizing form. This is implicit in many statements already quoted in this discussion and is generally well enough known that the issue need not be flogged in this context.

In highlighting the dominant features of this type of scholarship, attention should be drawn to the fact that it springs from the British political ruling elite, who are bourgeois but more than just bourgeois. Throughout British history, there has been a unique interpretation of classes and class values at the level of the political elite. The English bourgeois partly pushed aside but partly absorbed the feudal nobility, whose deportment and norms were adopted. Writers who fall into the colonial-goodwill-training school were nearly all colonial civil servants at one time or another and were very much part of the political ruling class. One of the distinguishing marks of this scholarship is the use of the royal 'we' – clearly referring not even to the British people as a whole but to the policymakers. They scarcely bother to mention the economic exploitation of the colonies, which metropolitan rule was intended to protect; and one suspects that they were often ignorant of or indifferent to the economic reality of colonialism. Be that as it may, this school of interpretation is concerned above all to justify itself as a good ruling class – both in a practical and moral sense.

In the final analysis, the value of the work under discussion is virtually nil. Because of its narrow focus on constitutional decolonization, it completely fails to mention other forms of integration between the colonies and the metropole in the economic sphere. Because of its concentration on British activity, it tells us nothing about African participation and the African role. There are a few hints that they perceived the class fissures within the nationalist movements; and, whatever their class perspective, it would have been valuable to get the views of the British rulers on this matter. However, such issues are simply defined out of the picture.

On the specific issue of constitutional decolonization projected as British activity, the colonial-goodwill-training school tells us nothing about the pull and shove of the critical years when the question of African Independence was indeed a political game. British colonialist writers cannot say anything meaningful about the process because they have conspired beforehand to affirm that it was nothing but sweet reasonableness on the part of Britain. With that sort of approach the result is a 'scholarship' devoid of even the saving grace of 'facts' unearthed by bourgeois empiricism. It reveals nothing. At every turn, there is a bland expression about trusteeship, mandate, guidance, partnership, transfer – like soothing music for the milch-cows.

As indicated from the outset, the obligation to deal critically with the school of British colonialist historians is imposed by the wide vogue which it enjoys. It is probably still the majority position among European scholars in the metropole, and there is a significant neo-colonialist school whose work involves a revamping and refurbishing of the old interpretations, after jettisoning a few of the more objectionable and unsaleable points. Besides, a historical view is not the property of historians. It is the expression of class, national, racial and other presuppositions, and it returns to strengthen the said presuppositions. The vast majority of Englishmen will never give a thought to African history, but, whenever they react to an issue involving Africa or Africans, their judgement is shot through by the colonialist historical interpretation.

Supposedly in the new spirit of independence, African research historians have taken to compiling texts for schools, sometimes in collaboration with whites who are very much tied to the old colonial structures. Thus, Joseph Anane of Nigeria got together with Godfrey Brown to edit *West Africa in the Nineteenth and Twentieth Centuries*, and they handed over a chapter on 'Colonial Rule in West Africa' to W.E.F. Ward, a former educational officer on the staff of the British Colonial Office. Understandably, Ward spoke on behalf of his own country and class, and restarted the colonial-goodwill-training myth:

> When I joined the British Colonial Service in 1924 the fashionable slogan was 'trusteeship': I was told that West Africa was not yet ready for self-government, but that it would be one day. Meanwhile Britain was in the position of a trustee, and I must look on my work as directed to helping Africa to take the government into its own hands ... We were expected to work ourselves out of a job, though it cannot be claimed that all of us realised it, or that all of those who did not realise it approved of the idea.

The last sentence is a characteristic piece of double talk; while the 'we' simply means that the oppressor continues to write history for the oppressed.

In East Africa, the volume by Gideon Wese and Derek Wilson, *East Africa Through a Thousand Years*, is in some ways a counterpart of the Anane and Brown volume – Wese being a Kenyan and Wilson an English history master at a white settler-oriented Nairobi school. This time, however, it is just not inviting a particular British colonialist, but the advancement of a coherent colonialist view of decolonization, made more dangerous because it will infiltrate under the name of an African historian.

East Africa Through a Thousand Years completely accepts the frame of reference of British colonialist historians, whereby constitutional matters were the focus of the decolonization process. It presents to African school certificate pupils the notion that 'the path to independence' in Tanganyika began in 1945, when two African members were admitted to the legislative council. Wese and Wilson credit Burns and Perham when they assert that:

> The major concern of the British government was that each new state should be *ready* for independence, i.e. that it should be a stable government, acceptable to its people, under wise and capable leadership.

Must another generation of African youth be asked to write and believe in such European fairy tales?

11

Education in Colonial Africa

The separation of knowledge has been entrenched within the structures of bourgeois universities in such a way that scholars in the humanities and social sciences can only pay lip-service to the concept of multidisciplinary approaches. It would appear that education as a subject or department is particularly alienated and cut off from other disciplines. Certainly, on the development issue, the little that is written hardly ever integrates the aspect of education. At the same time, educationists who write about 'educational development' are unwilling or unable to relate this to the movement of the society as a whole. The inclusion of the topic in this series of seminars attests to its fundamental importance to the political, economic and cultural changes taking place in Africa over the past eight or nine decades.

A 'balance sheet' approach to the colonial period in Africa invariably fastens on to the building of schools as a decisive element in favour of colonial benevolence. No attempt is made to explain how this benefited or developed Africa and the Africans, but the argument carries great force because of the universalized assumption that Western education per se is good. Africans came to believe it and the vast majority still do believe it. After all, someone with a school education on the continent is distinctly better off than someone who has not gone to the kind of school set up by Europeans. It is also obvious that the leadership of the political parties that strove for independence was drawn mainly from the educated elite. In this sense, European education of the colonized may appear to have been a crucial factor in political development. Yet, there is perhaps no subject on which conscious Africans can be so roused as that of colonial education. The path to political awareness in Africa more often than not leads to a denunciation of missionaries, colonial schools, Shakespeare and cultural imperialism. When prodded, any African educated under the colonial system can point to numerous incongruities from individual experience of the curricula, teachers and procedures of the schools he or she attended. Indeed, within the same individuals there is often the ambivalence of pride in scholastic achievement on the one hand and self-flagellation on the other, because they had acquiesced to the racist colonialist educational programme.

Education in Africa was not approached systematically by the colonial powers until the 1920s.[1] By that time, colonial administrations had been set up throughout the continent and a range of economic activities were placed in motion with the aim of providing surplus for the metropoles.

A small fraction of that surplus was redeployed to ensure that Africans would fill certain jobs in the lowest echelons of the economic and administrative sectors. Primary schooling was all that was essential for these positions as messengers, clerks, police constables, and so forth; but it was also necessary to train African teachers and a handful of Africans who were sufficiently initiated into the European way of life to pass the experience on to their brothers and to act within church, state and private firms as middlemen between the European hierarchy and the African masses. Hence, the growth of a modicum of secondary schooling, teacher training and eventually the rare experience of university education.

Functionally, colonial education was developing the 'modern' sector in Africa – mining, cash-crop agriculture and trade with Europe. In effect, that meant the development of Europe and the underdevelopment of the African economy. It must not be forgotten that Africa had its own Indigenous system of education to the European impact.[2] This system did not simply disappear, but it suffered the same contraction and diminution of vitality as did the 'traditional' economy. The disappearance of craft skill is nothing else but the disappearance of the education that had previously caused those skills to flourish. Indigenous African education lost its leading role in the society just as the traditional economy was displaced by the money economy. Those who entered the money economy saw European education as the element which might lead to upward mobility. Thus, the son of an agriculturalist was no longer apprenticed to him on the land but was sent off (wherever possible) to a school which would fit him for a part in the money economy – preferably in the administrative services where prestige was highest.

Education, even at the most revolutionary periods, highlights continuity in those aspects of the society which are cherished by the masses or by the dominant class. Education at its best seeks to bring out the potential of individuals to serve their own society and master their own environment. Colonial education interrupted the patterns of education which performed these functions and substituted instead learning associated with the advancement of an alien society and which usually had little to do with increasing African mastery of their own environment. Curriculum development in Africa over the past decade has everywhere had to face up to the problem of irrelevance in the colonial school system. The examples which cropped up throughout the school day were alien and irrelevant to the African child. Rather than building upon what existed, colonial schooling destroyed what existed, which made it easier in the long run to subscribe to the great lie that no education was previously available. One is concerned here with an African's basic awareness of his environment. Before the European or in a context of freedom from European education, a cattle-keeping people observed their animals with such attention that European languages have no words to describe the seventy or eighty varieties of cattle that, say, a Zulu or a Fulani felt it necessary to distinguish.[3] In a similar vein, it was noted that African children in the forests would normally know the names of dozens of trees at an early age and would confound the European visitor who could not tell one leaf from another.[4] The point here is that a European-educated African was just such a stranger and ignoramus in his own land.[5] It is this break in the continuity of the historical movement in Africa that I am consistently referring to as 'underdevelopment' in an active sense, and it embraces economic, political and cultural fields.

Presumably, if African education had been replaced by something of greater value to the African people, it would still have been possible to claim that Africa benefited and developed. Indeed, it could be argued that they had jumped to a higher stage which would have been long in coming if the process of uninterrupted evolution had gone on. However, the new education was severely lacking in many ways. To begin with, it was education for a tiny minority, replacing a system of education for all that had previously existed. The quantitative limitations of colonial education need to be stressed both as a corrective to the colonialist claim that they brought education to Africa and as a means of understanding that the present situation in Africa is profoundly influenced by the fact that the school system inherited from colonialism cannot possibly cater to the majority of the population.[6] Masses of figures could be brought to show how few were the Africans who were allowed schooling by the colonial powers. A large proportion of the few were primary school dropouts while an insignificant minority made it to secondary school. After all, it has to be noted that Africa today still has appalling figures of illiteracy and inadequate schooling in spite of the fact that the independent governments have often done more in ten years than the colonists did in seventy-five. That is what a truly African education policy will not merely have to extend the colonial school system, but it will also have to break with the basic rationale that has guided it so far: of training a minority to aid in the work of administration.

Producing Africans to aid in the task of colonial administration was of course not simply a matter of functional skills but also of ideology. Always learning is presented within a given ideological framework. Europeans could not do otherwise but instruct Africans within the bourgeois framework which was brought from Europe. However, winning over Africans was not left to chance. Policymakers for colonial education deliberately and carefully worked out the kinds of programmes designed to create the 'loyal' African servant. The French referred to them as 'cadres' and emphasized that they should not merely serve as clerks, translators and the like but as active agents of French cultural imperialism among the African masses.[7] Occasionally, a far-seeing colonialist thought in terms of training Africans who would continue to run the continent in the interests of Europe after Europeans had relinquished direct political control. But for the most part the educated elite was viewed as being permanently available for aiding their white masters, since scarcely any colonialist contemplated the end of European rule in Africa within this century.

One extremely interesting example of the way the colonial powers saw education as buttressing colonial rule ideologically and practically lies in the treatment of African rulers and their sons. African rulers had been deprived of power in the process of imposing European rule, but they still retained varying degrees of authority in the eyes of their own people; and all colonial powers used what they called 'chiefs' as agents within their administrative systems. To the French, this was so important that they made it mandatory for chiefs to send their sons to school, in order that this stratum within African society should develop the same perspectives as educated Africans from different backgrounds. The French were being perfectly logical in expecting that all who aided them in the work of administering African territory on behalf of France should have an ideological perspective determined by the French themselves. The English, too, at some points felt the education of their 'indirect rule' chiefs to be a priority; and schools for African rulers were opened at Bo in Sierra Leone and Tabora in Tanganyika. Although the experiment of special schools was not carried very far, it did translate that the sons of the 'traditional' rulers allied to the British did rise to the top of the educational ladder. In the Gold Coast colony and Nigeria, clashes between the educated elite and the 'illiterate' chiefs used to be common in the 1930s, but they disappeared in the post-war epoch as education and other factors cemented the privileged into a class whose interests were more readily reconcilable with those of the colonialists than they were with the interests of the African masses.[8]

When the German and English ruling classes of the nineteenth century decided to give more education to their workers, they did so out of the realization that they were enhancing the value of labour. Similarly, European policymakers for African colonies perceived that education was one aspect of the maximization of the continent's resources – the policy of the *mise en valeur* as French colonial minister, Albert Sarrault, put it. Inevitably in such a case the oppressor tries to re-create the oppressed in the image which is most suitable for persisting with the relationship of domination and subordination. In the case of Africans, the education system was doubly dangerous because it also fostered white racism and destroyed the African sense of identity to the point of self-hate. The kind of studies done on the impact of white education on the blacks of the US and the sort of conclusions taught by Fanon of the 'white masks' of the black West Indians are all highly relevant to the educational situation of colonial Africa. The system produced individuals like the Senegalese Blaise Diange, who vigorously proclaimed that he was the most 'French' and would always be French. Those who were most qualified were understandably the most alienated. The highly trained black lawyers of West Africa performed the role of black Englishmen so fastidiously as to outdo the models they were imitating. The picture they present is both droll and tragic. Colonial education in this respect was a tragi-comedy.

Some colonists recognized how distorted and destructive were the images produced by colonial education in Africa. One high-ranking French official was distressed to hear that black Africans were made to recite that 'the Gauls, our ancestors, had blue eyes'.[9] Others expressed dissatisfaction with educational standards in the more conventional sense, because the colonial education given to Africans was hopelessly inferior by the criteria of contemporary Europe, and it became relatively more backward as the colonial period advanced. The widening gap between the African and European sectors of the world imperialist economy was matched by a widening gap between the standards and achievements of the European-type education available in both sectors.

While teaching methods were evolving in Europe, those in Africa remained fixed in a Victorian mould. While some freedom was being created in the atmosphere of a European classroom, the authoritarianism of colonialism reinforced the authoritarianism of backward scholasticism. Racism added to this mess, so that even the African head teacher ran the risk of being publicly disciplined within his school by some twitter of a white school inspector. Europeans were quite aware that they were giving Africans an inferior education by European standards, quite apart from the contradictions that sprung from offering a European-oriented schooling to African children. Wherever there were white settlers, their children went to schools whose curricula and standards were more or less equivalent to the best metropolitan schools of the time, so as to allow such white children to return and fit into their home society when they so decided. This discrimination was most marked where settler societies had come into existence, notably in Algeria, Kenya, South Africa and the Rhodesias.[10] But everywhere on the continent the education offered to Africans was quantitatively and qualitatively as inferior as it could be and still remains consistent with the European objective of training Africans who would be effective auxiliaries in the work of colonization.

Perhaps the most striking aspect of the backwardness of colonial education in Africa was its adherence to a so-called literary model producing 'white collar' types at its highest points. This model persisted in spite of the reorientation towards science which was taking place in the metropoles themselves. But of course, once one understands that Africa had a fixed role to provide unskilled labour for the international capitalist system, it is not surprising that scientific and technical education was never a marked feature of colonial education. Such a development would have contradicted the very purposes of colonial rule. Only in a place like the Congo did industrial activity force education into a technological channel so as to provide semi-skilled labour. The same potential existed throughout Southern Africa, but it was denied by the avowedly racist policies designed to keep Africans from rising into the skilled and semi-skilled employment grades of the mining economy.

Africans as well as Europeans made requests for reform and radicalization of the colonial educational system. There were demands for more school places for girls, for more technical colleges and for curricula that were generally more relevant to the ecology and to the African people. None of these demands could get very far, because the parameters of the educational system were set by the phenomenon of colonialism as such. Capitalism in Europe had hardly done much to liberate the woman and in a colonial context it actually undermined the position of the African woman. To recommend more education for girls was to fail to take account of the fact that the constricted money economy had no employment opportunities for women. A demand for more technical colleges was usually met by the answer that there was not enough finance in the coffers of the colonial administration. Of course, there was a vast difference in the amount of surplus expatriated to Europe and the amount of money raised by taxing Africans to meet the daily expenses of subordinating the said Africans. Colonialists were naturally loath to forgo any of the surplus unless it went into the infrastructure for future profits and for maintaining the system as it was. Technical education was ruled out because it actually ran counter to the international division of labour that was part of colonialism. And the same was true of high-level agricultural education. It must not be imagined that Africa's role was agricultural and Europe's industrial, scientific agriculture was also monopolized by Europe. Therefore, the superficially attractive idea of agricultural education for Africans was put into effect by colonialists in a degenerate racist form, which had as its rationale the training of Africans to take their 'national' place as manual workers on the land.

A complete catalogue of the evils of the colonial educational process in Africa would be long indeed. It was no less decisive than the economic factor in bringing about the underdevelopment of Africa. Indeed, in examining the concept of dependency as a crucial aspect of underdevelopment, one cannot fail to realize the major contribution of the educational system in producing the individuals with all the syndromes of psychological dependence and with the lifestyles that derive from serving as European puppets in Africa. Yet, it is equally vital to understand the contradictions that were set in train because of the colonial school system. Those contradictions arose in spite of the intentions of the colonial masters, and they have already served in undermining the foreign domination of Africa.

Education elicited a very positive response from large numbers of Africans. A great deal of force in one form or another was employed in getting the money economy in

motion; and education was one of the very few positive induce-
ments that motivated people both to join the money economy
and to increase their participation in ways such as extended
acreage of cash crops. Colonized Africans not only pressured
the colonial governments to build more schools, but they
themselves made tremendous efforts, including thirty-mile
walks to the school, local financing of schools and teachers,
and community programmes for educating students in Africa
and even abroad.

To some extent, these efforts aided the colonial enterprise.
More Africans were thereby having access to European-type
education without the colonialist having to release as much of
their profits as they might otherwise have had to do. However,
the African drive for more education defeated the purposes
of the colonialists in a number of ways. The principal consequence is that particularly in British colonies there were more
Africans with primary education than the colonialists really
required for their own tasks. The colonial regimes were unable
to provide such individuals either with secondary schooling or
with the jobs that fitted the expectations created by the years
of schooling. It is clear that in many colonies the crisis of the
primary school leavers was a serious factor lending dynamism
to the African independence movement.[11]

The African search for 'modern' education also had a
marked mobilizational and organizational effect. The act of
getting together to finance a school was a political act. The
sponsorship of a scholarship scheme tied to palm oil or to
cotton cultivation was also a political response on the part
of the oppressed. The form of welfare organizations which
catered to educational objectives during the 1930s and 1940s
was later subsumed by the mass political parties. As Africans
broke beyond the bounds of colonial educational opportunities, individuals as well as collective opposition to colonial
rule was engendered. At the individual level, it has been
noted how significant were the roles played in independence

struggles by West Africans educated in the United States. Those individuals were part of the process of seeking out Western education wherever it could be found. Coming from places like Nigeria, their normal outlets for limited higher education was in Britain; but they sought new frontiers in the United States when they found no openings in Britain.[12] Africans who never received higher education or any education at all were part of the movement to change certain vicious racist trends of the colonial educational system in which they placed hope for their children. In French West Africa, the major issue over which there was popular protest was the French attempt to create 'Bush Schools' that were supposedly more relevant to African needs but were fundamentally aimed at creating an inferior educational environment for 'the natives'. The struggle against these schools was a victorious one, and it formed part of the national independence struggles in French West Africa and French Equatorial Africa in the post-war era. The same is true of the African movement against agricultural education in British East and Central Africa.

The powerful African independent Church movement had a somewhat less powerful counterpart in the independent schools that sprung up on African initiative. In Kenya, they had a Christian background; in North Africa, they had a Muslim background; while elsewhere, as in the Sudan, no particular religious preference was expressed. In all these situations, however, the independent spirit went far beyond the classrooms, and the colonial powers were themselves quick to see the generally 'subversive' implications of Africans controlling their education in this way. In any event, contradictions arose within what the colonists would have considered as the most advanced institutions espousing European value systems. With very few exceptions, the leaders of African independence movements were products of an educational programme that was aimed at keeping them as colonial subjects. The opposition to the colonial intellectual formation took place at two levels. A few individuals actually rejected the entire value system of capitalism, individualism, racism and exploitation. These were the few who uncompromisingly continued to strike out against imperialism after gaining the tokens of constitutional independence. The second level of protest was generated by the contradiction between the value system and the personal aspirations of educated Africans. They had been taught about freedom, liberty and a career open to the talents, and instead found that colonial rule offered the educated elite none of these things. Taken together with all the other contractions of colonial society, the antagonism between the colonizers and the African educated elite was a notable contribution to the emergence of national political parties, and to the gaining of constitutional independence as a step on Africa's march towards reconquering the political power lost through the imposition of Europe's colonial rule.

Everywhere on the African continent, education originating with the colonialists was meant to ensure mental and physical enslavement. To a large extent it did carry out this function. But every aspect of Africa's subjugation also contained the seeds of revolution since capitalism in its colonial guise could not satisfy even the minimal aspirations of the African people. The more cash crop farming there was the more likely it became that there would be peasant revolts. The larger the wage-earning sector, the more likely it was that there would be the revolt of organized labour. Dissatisfaction with education and with the opportunities for education was at the forefront of colonial grievances and it helped to weld together the vast majority of the population to address themselves to the principal contradiction between themselves as the colonized and the Europeans as colonizers. No other facet of the African experience so clearly illustrates the dialectic of oppression and resistance. Historical underdevelopment is a key aspect of the story, while the rebirth of freedom is the other.

12

Education in Africa and Contemporary Tanzania

I. Education in Africa

In discussing education in Africa, we should first contrast the independent educational system as it existed before the arrival of Europeans with the colonial education system established after 1885, which is the conventional date for the beginning of African colonization. The differences between the two are critical to any real evaluation of contemporary education in Africa.

Communal and universal vs particular and elitist societies

Education in independent pre-colonial Africa was universal. Everyone received either a formal or informal education designed to give him or her a role within the society. Mothers passed on values to their children and the elders acted as models of behaviour for the youth. That was informal education. It went on all the time and could not be stopped.

Formal education in independent Africa occurred throughout teaching one's skills to apprentices. For example, if a man were a hunter, a miner or a cloth-maker, he would educate his children or other family members or other persons in the society, in order to preserve his particular craft. In addition to vocational skills, social values were specifically transmitted to the young at puberty during the rites of initiation. Many societies also had formal training schools for those preparing for the equivalent of the priesthood. So this, very briefly, was the African educational system. It provided education for everybody. It had a role for everybody.[1]

Colonial education, or European education in colonial Africa, stood in contrast to the above. It was doled out to a minority. Colonial education was elitist, because it was based upon elitist philosophical and ideological assumptions derived from European class society, as distinct from African society which was communal and relatively unstratified. In a stratified sociological system, education serves the interest of the dominant class, caste, race or geographical unit, irrespective of pretensions to the country. Such an education is for the few, whether they be the actual children of the ruling class, or children of the exploited and oppressed classes who are co-opted into the services of that system.

When the European education system was transported to Africa, it became even more limited and elitist, because the purpose of the colonizers within Africa was to select only a very small number of Africans to aid in the work of colonization. The point was made very clearly by the colonizers: 'Why do we want to educate the blacks? Because we are running the country, but we cannot do it all on our own. We need some African messengers and translators. We need African clerks in the railways, the civil service and the trading companies. We need teachers to train those messengers and clerks.' That is why it became necessary for the colonialists to establish some form of school education in Africa.

The African vs the European personality

Another set of distinctions exist between indigenous African education and colonial education. African education was designed to develop what I call the 'African personality', a term which has been used by Kwame Nkrumah, Sekou Touré and a number of other prominent African spokesmen. It often carries vague mystical overtones, but what I have in mind is simply that a society, both consciously and unconsciously, develops individuals to sustain its mores and values. In unfettered African society, Africans were part of the extended family. They developed a consciousness of their relationship to their kin, their land and their ancestors. All these factors made up the 'African personality'.

Any educational system, so long as it is independent, develops people for purposes which the society internally and independently chooses for itself, notwithstanding the fact that a particular sector may be more influential than another in exercising that choice.[2] In the colonial system, it was not the people themselves, not the colonized, who set the terms and goals of their education. The colonizer did so. When he educated a few Africans, he did so not to develop them within their African context, as Africans, but rather to alienate them from their society from which they came. His purpose was to create or recreate them in his own image, to mutilate and transform the very sense of their African identity.

A dramatic illustration of this is found in French West Africa, where African school children were told to recite, 'The Gauls, our ancestors, had blue eyes.' When a French school child says this, it is a means of identifying himself with his past, and this is normal in any educational system. But when a colonized Senegalese or Dahomean is told that the Gauls, his ancestors, had blue eyes, and he knows he has black eyes and a black skin, he experiences a tremendous sense of alienation.[3] His sense of who he is, his sense of being an African, is in danger of collapsing. He becomes instead a black European, which was, in fact, the purpose of French as well as British, Belgian and Portuguese colonial education. It was designed to alienate the few who received it from the mass of the people as a whole, not to reinforce the connection between those educated in the formal system and the rest of the population.

Interdependence vs individualism

A third set of contrasts is related to the communal nature of African education which stressed the interdependence of individuals within the society. Work and social effort had to be collective if they were to be meaningful. This collective emphasis sprang from the structure of the society, which was non-stratified or relatively undifferentiated. Suth class contradictions that did exist were, by and large, non-antagonistic class contradictions, except in a few areas where feudal or quasi-feudal social forms had come into being.

An antagonistic contradiction penetrates to the basic means of production. When the existence of members of one class depends upon exploiting members of another class, race or nation, then their interests are antagonistic. In African societies, there were non-antagonistic contradictions based on the division of labour. Such, for instance, was the opposition between pastoralists and cultivators, between whom there was at the same time a considerable degree of interdependence. Also, there was a division of labour in which some individuals became priests, while others wielded political authority. When the division of the social product is relatively egalitarian, a major contradiction does not arise between the priest and ruler, on the one hand, and the rest of the subjects on the other.[4]

In the African situation, it was possible to teach that labour is a collective activity, since this was in accordance with social reality. Colonial education, deriving from bourgeois values, portrayed labour and even social existence to be competitive. Not only was this idea extolled within the classroom, but in the arena of real life such progress as was possible within colonial society was granted to Africans because of their personal achievements, thus further separating the individual from the mass of his fellows.

The colonial educational system was competitive in the

metropoles, but it was more so in Africa, because only a tiny handful – far less than in Europe or North America – became, as it were, the chosen few. A tiny handful went to school, and it was made clear to them that: 'Here it is! Here is your avenue to progress. You have to compete with others to get there. And once you make it within the system, you will establish yourself as a superior individual, not as some small part of a collective.' Ideological values were buttressed by material changes which further differentiated African society.

For example, where land used to be the property of the whole community, it became commercialized. Under colonialism, land was bought and sold in Africa, a concept almost unknown previously. Once it was bought and sold, a few individuals got the land. And others had to do without. They became sellers of labour to those who owned land. The individualist approach struck at the roots of the land tenure tradition, and the educational system reinforced that individualism as well derived its rationale from it.

Orientation to, or away from, the 'life environment'

A final set of contrasts suggests that the original African education was carrying forward what may be called the principle of praxis – the unity of theory and practice. One was learning about life. The individual was instructed about the life of the community in order to fulfil his own role within the community and simultaneously understand and complement the roles of others. African education was specifically oriented towards the practice of day-to-day life. It must be reiterated that educational systems are both formal and informal. We should not hold to the idea that education takes place only if there is a classroom – and only if people remain outside of the process of production for months or years. That is the narrow Western conception of education that evolved out of feudalistic and capitalist times. But Africans were educated differently.

Consider, as an example, the African pastoralists. When Masai youth, aged five or six, deal with cattle, they are at school. By the time they reach the age of ten they can distinguish dozens of species of cattle – their shape, the color of their skins, their particular markings, the shape of their horns, and so on. The Masai can even identify the species of ticks that come and rest on their cattle. They have gone to school with their cattle because it is essential for their survival and the survival of their community that they should know about cattle, for that is how the community makes its living. Therefore, whether they get that education by formal or informal means, it is at all points linked to the question of practice, of doing, as distinct from a purely abstract appreciation.

Colonial education in Africa was hostile to the principle of praxis, partly because of unconscious and ill-considered European premises about education. Consider a subject as basic as geography. A European schoolteacher in a tropical schoolroom in Africa or in the West Indies would teach about spring, summer, autumn and winter, which relatively few Africans or West Indians would ever have seen.

Brought from Europe, the educators too often taught the same things they would have taught in Europe. But more than that, they insisted that education in Africa be essentially 'white-collar' education. They promoted what they considered to be the values of Christianity, and values connected with doing certain types of low-level bureaucratic work. It was a non-specific, non-technical education, unrelated to the actual physical environment of Africa.

In Europe, a scientific and technological bias had been imparted to education in the late nineteenth century and even more so in the twentieth century, because such a bias was necessary to the development of capitalist society in Europe. However, because Africa had been allocated the role of primary producer within the imperialist international division of labour, it was not only unnecessary, but undesirable and antithetical to the interests of capitalism that African education should take a scientific and technological direction. The colonizers did not want Africans to do anything more than supply labour in its cheapest and crudest forms. When, for example, rural Africans in South Africa did manage to get skilled or semi-skilled jobs, the whole racist society galvanized itself to hold back African development, because an African was considered even more of a threat if he had an education and a skill. He was then either not given a job or given it at a wage as much as ten times less than that which a European received.

The African schoolchild who did receive a colonial education very often was removed physically to a primary or secondary boarding school. Many Africans who experienced this kind of education found that they could no longer relate to their own home communities, or that they had tremendous difficulty in doing so.[5]

The church too was responsible for outdated forms of African education. By the nineteenth century, churches in Europe had ceased to play the hegemonistic role in education which they had played in previous centuries. Europeans had come to an awareness that the church should be separated from the state and from civil education, because the metaphysical approach of Christianity was hostile to the full elaboration of European knowledge, especially in science. For the most part, Europeans very calmly separated the church from their school system.

But, at the same time that the Europeans were separating the church from *their* educational system, they were bringing the church into Africa. They found it useful, one presumes, to create irrelevant and mystifying approaches to knowledge, because all they wanted the African to learn was the fear of God. The missionaries said this very clearly: 'We want to teach them the fear of God.'

II. Education in Tanzania

Qualitative gains

Against the background of colonial and pre-colonial education in Africa, it may be helpful to take the narrower example of Tanzania today to pinpoint some of the things that Tanzania has achieved, and some of the things that it has tried to achieve, in the educational sphere.

The legacy of colonial rule was an extremely high rate of illiteracy throughout the continent. The number of children going to school very seldom went above one out of ten, and in some cases it was less than that.[6] In the United States one talks about high school dropouts and college dropouts, but in Africa one talks about *primary-school dropouts*. Fifty per cent of the children in Africa had to contend with an enormous quantitative problem in the area of education. Heretofore, colonial education had only been made available to a very small percentage of the African population. But the government planners of the new African educational systems were charged with providing a *formal* school education for everybody. They had to start thinking in terms of universalizing education, pushed by the demand of the working classes.

In my opinion most African countries which attained independence with a few secondary schools and with almost non-existent facilities for technical and university education, have done more in ten years of independence than the colonialist did in seventy-five years of colonial rule, as far as expanding the physical educational facilities are concerned. I have many reservations about some independent African governments, but it is simply an indication of how shabby the colonial regimes were, that in seventy-five years they did not manage to give to Africans, quantitatively, even the primary education which governments in Ghana, Nigeria, Uganda, Kenya, Tanzania and elsewhere are giving to their people today. Very seldom does the new education arrive, however, at anything near universal school education. Not even in Tanzania.

The Tanzanian government projected the year 1980 as the date when it hoped to arrive at universal primary education. This wait is justified by policymakers in terms of a lack of finances. Education is a huge financial investment which does not bring immediate returns. It is a long-term investment. Many governments spend 25 per cent, perhaps thirty per cent of their budget on education, and of course this is not as productive an investment as a farm or a factory, which will conceivably show returns in one to five years.

In spite of this, many young Tanzanians have not been very happy about the idea of accepting incomplete primary education for a number of years. Their imagination has been caught by the kind of experiment which went on in Cuba and which provided the Cuban people with universal literacy. While coming nowhere close to the Cuban 'Year of Education' strategy, Tanzania has stepped up its adult education programme. President Julius Nyere argued that because so many of the present adult population had been denied the opportunity of education during the colonial period, adult literacy campaigns should become a matter of the highest priority, and Tanzania has had one of the more successful adult education programmes in Africa. Altogether, it cannot be denied that ten years of independence has shown a tremendous development, in purely quantitative terms, in the number of children going to school, and in the number of people in the society who received a formal education of the same schoolroom type as had been established under colonial rule. That is the first achievement.[7]

The elimination of racism

Another early achievement in post-colonial Tanzania was the elimination of the racist structure of colonial education, which reflected the racism of the colonial and capitalist world.

There were white settlers in Tanzania, although their Kenyan counterparts were more numerous and more notorious. These white settlers received, by far, the largest proportion of the educational budget. Arabs and Asians received the next largest slice, and finally, the majority, the people of the land, the Africans themselves, received the scrapings. This racist school structure was promptly attacked and destroyed.

Teacher training

The idea of teacher training had to be seriously reconsidered, because part of the process of African alienation resulted from the physical presence of white teachers in African schools who, whether or not they consciously subscribed to all the goals of colonial rule, reflected the biases and individualism of the metropoles and the racism inherent throughout the capitalist world.

Since Tanzania had been one of the more 'backward' colonies, few Africans were trained to be teachers at the time of independence. Its leaders wanted to expand their school system, but the teachers who were already entrenched there were primarily white expatriates and Asians who did not always opt for national status. The university opened its first college of arts, social sciences and natural sciences in 1965, and it was used virtually as a teacher-training institution. A programme was devised by which an undergraduate could emerge at the end of his studies as a teacher in two subjects. Normally within the British system, one earns a Bachelor's degree before proceeding to study for a year, or two years, to acquire teaching certification considered appropriate for secondary school teachers. Tanzania had to break with that practice and integrate teacher training within the undergraduate programme. About 80 per cent of all the early graduates went straight from the university into the secondary schools to meet the priority of 'Tanzanization'.

A small example of the consequences of 'Tanzanization' can be seen in the return to traditional dance (*ngoma*) within the school system at both primary and secondary levels. Music and dance have always been dominant African art forms, and they were relevant to culture in ways that were far more fundamental than mere recreation. Not only has *ngomo* been revived in the schools but the traditional forms have been given a new content, a new thrust. The words the students sing and the scenes they act out in *ngoma* might today be related to *Ujamaa*, the collective, for example. Or they may even be concerned with the question of defence against the Portuguese. So there is a merger of new political content with old African form.

The National Service programme

Beyond the quantitative changes and the more obvious transformations of the school structure, one confronts much more complicated questions. Tanzania has had to struggle to retrieve its education from a colonial to a distinctly African path. At the same time, these African values had to be set in the forward-looking context of socialist reconstruction. A key problem is that colonialism (like any other social system) has means of self-perpetuation. 'Africanization' per se could not break the continuity of colonial education, given that African teachers had been taught by Europeans within a European value framework. In effect, the African teacher was often a 'programmed' European: making Fanon's phrase 'Black Skins, White Masks' even more apt than it initially appears, since the mask in indigenous African practice symbolized a complete change of identity on the part of the wearer. Higher institutions of learning in Africa were particularly prone to emphasize colonial continuity, often under the guise of maintaining 'international standards'. Any African teacher who had access to higher education, either before or after independence, was likely to be as elitist as the European who had preceded him; alienated from his African roots, and as individualist as though he had been socialized in Britain or the US. The National Service was perceived as a device to induce change of a practical and normative kind in Tanzania. It was instituted as a means of bringing a number of youth into more active participation in the life of their community. One of its principal aspects was the provision of the rudiments of military training for self-defence. Colonialism disarmed the African people, except for those who served the master in the colonial army. One of the first things which the National Service did was to revive the normal practice whereby the youth are entrusted with the physical defence of the society. At the same time, the National Service revived the principle that education should provide real skills, practical skills, as distinct from 'while-collar' education. So, the National Service offered agricultural and craft skills regarded as relevant to the question of economic development. Its first recruits were youth with primary and lower secondary education.

The National Service also rested on the premise that young people should be educated to serve rather than to command peasants and workers. University graduates represented the pinnacle of the old elitism. They had to learn to reintegrate themselves with the rest of the population. Therefore, in 1966, the National Service Act was extended to cover secondary and university students previously exempt from its provisions. Tanzanian university students completing their training that year were required to enter National Service. Like everybody else, they were to live in a National Service camp for six months and were to be trained by instructors who often had only primary school education. At the camp, servicemen received an allowance. For a subsequent eighteen months they were to make a contribution of 60 per cent of their salary to the national budget. University students promptly demonstrated to signify their non-acceptance of these terms. This was confrontation of the people versus the elite; and being an elite without power, university students were disciplined to perform National Service in order to complete their education. Now secondary school graduates proceed immediately to National Service camps for some months before joining the university.

The National Service programme succeeded to a limited extent. After setting out on the difficult task of re-fashioning people's values, it has, not surprisingly, ended up with a degree of formalism. In other words, students will go to the National Service and they will do what they are told. But they will not necessarily accept the idea that they are there to serve the people and merge with the community of producers. No one in Tanzania would be so naive as to say that the National Service works perfectly, or to suggest that months of work on nation-building projects will create a new sense of identity for servicemen. One of the excruciating problems is that the National Service is shot through with hierarchization and commandism, which is antithetical to its own goal of maximum participation along socialist and democratic lines. While given a highly political task to perform, its direction at various levels is manifestly 'apolitical', which means in effect petty bourgeois. A political education wing was incorporated in the National Service at an early date, but it appears to have been swamped rather than to have expanded in a manner that would allow the institution to be considered a cadre-forming one. For the moment, the most positive thing that can be said about the National Service is that structures have been set up and that meaningful goals have been defined which go far beyond the structures and goals of the colonial educational system.[8]

A national language

Tanzania has been fortunate in being one of the few African countries with an authentic national language. There are dozens of linguistic units in Tanzania, but, with few exceptions, everybody can communicate in Swahili. Most observers have commented on this phenomenon as evidence of Tanzania's national and territorial integrity. In addition, the existence of Swahili as a lingua franca has implications with regard to transcending both stratification and external orientation. English, which was the teaching medium in the colonial secondary schools, was one of the mechanisms of alienation. The continued use of English and French in post-colonial Africa helps keep the African petty bourgeois attached to their masters. With the introduction of Swahili as a language of national education, those who entered the secondary schools were offered the opportunity of defining their visions of the world in a language which grew out of their own environment. There also emerged the possibility of using an idiom which could bind together the peasantry and the upper classes, in contrast to the European language, the use of which previously divided them.

English is still the language of instruction at the university and in the higher reaches of the secondary schools because it takes time to make the transition to Swahili. Textbooks have to be developed and new concepts have to be incorporated into the language. Some foot-dragging in the practical implementation of the national language policy is evident. It is probably due, in part, to the lack of self-confidence of most of the petty bourgeoisie and their wish to continue the English language identification with the metropolis. However, debate in local circles has produced a consensus that Swahili can – and must – take precedence at all levels of communication – including the university.

Education for self-reliance

In the wake of the famous Arusha Declaration of 1967, *Mwalimu*[9] Nyerere made public a major policy document on education, entitled *Education for Self-Reliance*.[10] It should be borne in mind that the subtitle of the Arusha Declaration was 'TANU's Policy of Socialism and Self-Reliance'.[11] The emphasis on self-reliance thereafter became the principal theoretical premise for educational reconstruction. *Education for Self-Reliance* starts with an awareness that the colonized were educated to be dependent upon the colonizers: an education for dependence. In contrast, the goal for Tanzanians in the conceptualized socialist, self-reliant Tanzania was that they should be dependent on their own efforts, their own skills, their own creativity. Education under colonialism was mainly supported by the state or church. That is to say, Africans paid taxes and generated surplus out of which the colonial administration or the church allocated funds for education. Those who went through the formal educational systems were removed from production and kept as specifically privileged persons for the duration of their secondary education. Patterns such as these were challenged in *Education for Self-Reliance*.

The colonial education system was a pyramid, starting off with a narrow base of primary education, becoming extremely narrow at the secondary level and tapering off sharply at the point of higher education. *Education for Self-Reliance* insisted that a national educational system could not have as its goal the well-being of a few at the top. A change of priorities was required so that the edifice could be built around the well-being of the majority. Under the colonial system, primary school was not an end in itself, for it meant nothing to emerge after six years of primary school. The primary school graduate was considered by the colonialist a potentially better labourer or cultivator. But the African who was to help in administration needed to proceed further. Given the 'white-collar' orientation of colonial society, Africans also accepted that the purpose of education could only be achieved by climbing the pyramid.

The new approach in Tanzania was based on the contention that it is absurd to spend millions of shillings on an educational system whose end product is a handful of trained people – especially since the only thing they can do is administer the country rather than spearhead production. If only a handful still continued to reach the top of the educational pyramid in independent Tanzania, that would constitute a secondary achievement. The major focus was to be on primary education, because only in this sphere could the policymakers conceive of giving everybody an education in the near future. All primary school graduates had to be fitted for service in the society, rather than as misfits with no meaningful jobs – as happened in colonial Africa and as happens in neo-colonial Africa.

The goal of a self-reliant education led to a re-evaluation of the age at which children should start school. Generally, the starting age is six years, and at twelve the child is finished with primary schooling. The logic behind the TANU decision to start school at a later age was that a primary school graduate of twelve years or less is neither physically nor mentally equipped to assume the role of producer in the society. Consequently, in 1963, the starting age was pushed upwards to seven years and the school leaving age to fourteen years. Interestingly enough, in pre-colonial African society, a child became an adult at the time of puberty; the initiatory 'rites of passage' meant that a girl became a woman, and a boy, a man. The European conception of a teenager – someone who is unproductive for four or five years – was totally unheard of.

The policy of education for self-reliance placed a lot of emphasis on agricultural work, because the vast majority of people in the country earn their living from subsistence. The colonial educational approach was designed to downgrade and degrade manual work, particularly as it related to agriculture. That is why the educated African elite despised (and still despises) the peasants. When the colonialist did introduce agricultural education, as happened in several areas, it did not allow for improvisation or innovation. It was agricultural instruction of the crudest form, based on the premise that hoeing the land through the expenditure of sheer physical energy was the natural lot of Africans. Education for self-reliance, on the other hand, asserts the dignity of African labour, and aims at strengthening the connections between theory and practice, so that schoolchildren can be involved creatively with their environment. Labour in the field was not to be a punishment, as it was in the colonial era, but an exercise in the scientific utilization of natural resources.

In this framework, school farms have become very important to the development of the *Education for Self-Reliance* movement in Tanzania. The farm is useful in that it can provide revenue for the school. But that, I think, is a secondary purpose. Much more relevant are the attitudes connected with agricultural labour, the possibilities of innovation, and the experience of study and work. Within a self-reliant educational environment, the whole school community of teachers and students act as a democratic entity. The student and their teacher are supposed to set priorities – determining what is to be planted and what is not, how it is to be done, how it is to be marketed, and to what use funds will be put. The school, like an *Ujamaa* community, is to be an exercise in self-government, whereas colonialism was the negation of that self-government.

Some observers have belittled the significance of self-reliant education by pointing out that this idea and many others are not at all new, having been mooted and experimented upon during the colonial period.[12] What they fail to recognize is the limiting and distinguishing factor of the colonial political economy and the fact that the same policies can assume radically different meanings within a new social order. It would have been unrealistic to the point of infantilism to expect even the most honest of colonial agricultural-educational programmes to convince Africans of the merits of agriculture, when the colonial value structure, deriving from the mode of production, pointed to the success of those who abandoned direct participation in agriculture and engaged instead in more 'civilized' pursuits. These observers fail to address themselves to fundamental issues, such as who wields power and in whose interests. The policy of education for self-reliance opens up revolutionary possibilities because it is the decision of people in their own interests. To suggest that the colonialists had the same vision of African well-being is an exercise in apologetics – and not a subtle one at that.

Other commentators have lined up for or against *Education for Self-Reliance* in terms of their assessment of its class content and significance for socialism. Thus, the pan-Africanist Marxist, *Mzee* C.L.R. James[13] waves ecstatically about the document. He affirms that 'the simplicity with which Dr. Nyere states what his government proposes to do disguises the fact that not in Plato or in Aristotle, Rousseau or Karl Marx will you find such radical, such revolutionary departures from the established educational order.'[14] *Mzee* C.L.R. James is as much influenced by what is within the document as by the creation of *Ujamaa* socialism, which he regards as a revolutionary response to the objective conditions of Tanzania and Africa. On the other hand, a negative assessment has been offered by an American educationist, Philip Foster, which is filled with bourgeois assumptions. He expresses a firm commitment to class society in Africa, on the grounds that there are 'conflict objectives of equality and efficiency'. He is convinced that future progress in Tanzania and Africa must mean further class stratification. His real quarrel with *Education for Self-Reliance* is that not only does it hark back to traditional African communalism, but it also points forward to a new socialism, starting with the countryside.[15]

Of course, five years after the promulgation of the policy, the more rewarding activity is not to contemplate it as theory, but rather to focus on its implementation to date. The Brazilian educationist, Paulo Freiere, when asked to comment on education for self-reliance in Tanzania replied that it looked liberating on paper, but that the answer would only be found in *praxis*, because 'the question is not *is* it but *do* it.'[16] Studies on the practical meaning of self-reliance programmes in Tanzanian schools are in their infancy, but even a casual awareness of the Tanzanian contemporary scene suggests that education for self-reliance has not been working according to plan – far from it. Inevitably, with such a complex manner, people grasp the formal and superficial aspects first. Many schoolteachers think that education for self-reliance means having a farm. They decide to have a farm, and 'self-reliance' is placed on a timetable just like physics, mathematics or history. At a given time, the students go out, they work and they come back in, but no serious attempts are made to integrate the different aspects of the curriculum so that it points in a given direction. Teachers may seldom make any attempts to involve students in determining what constitutes self-reliant activity in their respective regions. They still use the authoritarian, bureaucratic approach, although they might boast of self-reliance in their schools. In this connection, their class allegiances and ideological outlook are factors of great importance.

Education and liberation

Ultimately, the success of the schoolroom revolution is itself dependent on the development of structures and patterns within the society as a whole. Tanzanian education is trying to create new norms, but at the same time the total society must be moving in a given direction. These two things are mutually supportive. In Tanzania, serious attempts have been made to create new structures and establish new norms in many aspects of the political economy. They all have a bearing on the attempted revolution in education. During the early 1960s, students scoffed when they were told to limit their aspirations for the future and regard themselves as servants of the people. They asked, 'How can these politicians, driving in their Mercedes-Benzes, accumulating real estate, joining capitalist companies, tell us to be socialist?' When university students demonstrated against the National Service in 1966, one of the things they said was that if they were to have a 60 per cent cut in their salaries for the time spent in National Service, then something should be done about the cabinet ministers, principal secretaries and other top civil servants. Although President Nyerere disciplined them and sent them home for a year, it is significant that this student revolt sparked the Arusha Declaration. Nyerere agreed that the political leadership should discipline itself. He cut his salary by 20 per cent, and other cabinet ministers followed suit. For those who did not initiate this sacrifice voluntarily, a law was passed reducing the salaries of top civil servants. Much of the Arusha Declaration was in fact devoted to outlining a code of behaviour for the top echelons of the society – outside of the private business sector. That leadership code was something of a self-denying ordinance, which has since been used as a yardstick to measure observance or non-observance of socialist ethics in the lifestyles of the nation's politico-bureaucratic leadership.

The TANU leadership code achieved some correlation with values in the educational system. One cannot have a constant contradiction between practice in the political and educational arenas. Children will follow certain models, and the most important models actualized within the society cannot be flagrantly out of step with those idealized in the classroom. Similarly, as far as agriculture is concerned, a lot of small-scale capitalist ventures were encouraged in Tanzania in the early 1960s; but, in the most recent period, collective *Ujamaa* agriculture has been given the greater sanction. It makes sense to have notions of *Ujamaa* given structural form in an agricultural community at the same time that they are being extolled in school. Furthermore, when children leave the school where they have been taught the value of communal and collective efforts, they have before them the possibility of joining an *Ujamaa* village and thereby becoming a permanent part of the movement for the construction of socialism, as shaped and conditioned by their history and environment. How far this possibility is realized and how effective the *Ujamaa* villages are themselves, are of course questions which immediately arise and demand an answer.

The transformation of the colonial education system in Tanzania and Africa as a whole is part of a much broader front of combat against imperialism and neo-colonialism, internally and externally. Although it is a critically important aspect, educational transformation alone will never lead to the total liberation of society. Indeed, it is dialectically impossible for profound change to take place in the old educational system within antecedent and concomitant transformations of all aspects of the political economy. The prognosis for change in Tanzania and African education processes is therefore the same as the evaluation of the prospects of socialist revolution and total liberation from colonialism and neo-colonialism. In the long run, this evaluation must be based on the multifold contradictions of imperialism, which are tearing it apart and which have transformed it into a moribund part of the world order. In the short run, the dynamic of change within Africa is determined mainly by the configuration of emergent class society and by the rate at which the mass of direct producers acquire the consciousness of and capacity to act in their own interests – with the support of intellectuals drawn from all strata. For these reasons, our discussion of education must rest suspended, since an examination of the above short- and long-run trends is beyond the modest scope of this analysis.

IV

Building Socialism

13

Tanzanian *Ujamaa* and Scientific Socialism

This chapter attempts to identify Tanzanian *Ujamaa* with Scientific Socialism in certain ideological essentials. It is an exercise in theory, bearing in mind that historically the theory of socialism preceded the establishment of socialism as a system in any part of the globe. Scientific Socialism (or Marxism, if you like) is an explicit worldview which contemplates every conceivable phenomenon from protein to literature, in terms of a methodology applicable to nature and society. Therefore, the comparison with Tanzanian *Ujamaa* is not completely analogous, since the latter is neither explicit nor all-embracing. However, the same kind of reservation could probably be expressed for any ideological variant other than Scientific Socialism. One must, in most cases, seek ideology in human actions, combined to greater or lesser extent with statements of principle or policy. The Tanzanian political process has produced over the last decade several noteworthy declarations of principle and sufficient actions which give meaning to the said declarations. The word '*Ujamaa*' has already been popularized in two contexts: first, as referring to the extended family of African communalism; and second, with reference to the creation of agricultural collectives known as *Ujamaa* villages. The relation between the two is that the *Ujamaa* villages seek to recapture the principles of joint production, egalitarian distribution and the universal obligation to work which were found within African communalism. In the present discussion the world *Ujamaa* incorporates both of these meanings, and includes also the implications of several policy documents and public plans.

A necessary piece of ground-clearing must be performed by advancing the negative proposition that Tanzanian *Ujamaa* is not 'African Socialism'. Such a disclaimer may appear curious and even presumptuous in view of the fact that in 1962 *Mwalimu* Nyerere referred to *Ujamaa* as 'the basis of African Socialism'. But, there are several reasons for keeping the two concepts widely apart. When 'African Socialism' was in vogue early in the 1960s, it comprised a variety of interpretations ranging from a wish to see a socialist society in Africa to a desire to maintain the status quo of neo-colonialism. Since then, the term has come to be identified with its most consistent and least revolutionary ideologue, Leopold Senghor, and with the late Tom Mboya. As such, 'African Socialism' is generally taken to mean a set of relations which leave capitalism and imperialism unchallenged. It is therefore essential to disassociate the anti-capitalist and anti-imperialist stance in Tanzania from a caption that has been pre-empted by non-revolutionary African leaders. Furthermore, when *Ujamaa* was presented as an option shortly after the independence of Tanganyika, it was (knowingly) defined as an abstract set of values without reference to the social forms necessary for their realization.[1] Much has now been done in the way of policy decisions to indicate and build the relevant social structures, thereby further differentiating *Ujamaa* from its erstwhile counterparts of 'African Socialism' in so far as the latter never advanced from the ideal to the real. Above all, one must take note of the progressive evolution of Tanzanian theory and practice over the period of nearly a decade, as a positive response to national, African and international developments.[2]

Conversely, to associate *Ujamaa* with the category of 'Scientific Socialism' seems to be flying in the face of assertions to the contrary by Tanzanian policymakers. Scientific Socialism is held to be synonymous with Marxism, Communism and the like, which have been held at arm's length by Tanzanians who propound *Ujamaa*. The contradiction is more apparent than real. In part, it disappears when one takes into account the above-mentioned factor of significant politico-ideological advance from the Arusha Declaration to *Mwongozo*. In addition, and more decisively, the difference is largely based on a caricature of Scientific Socialism (Marxism), which proposes that socialism must come through proletarian revolution within an already developed capitalist state. Such a definition would automatically exclude Tanzanian *Ujamaa*, which looks towards the socialist organization of peasants and seeks to revive and perpetuate the collective principle of production and the equalitarian nature of distribution which characterized communalism. As carried out both by some self-professed Marxists and by bourgeois analysts, the transformation of Marxism into a barren, dogmatic, mechanistic and uni-dimensional theory has understandably led many creative individuals to reject what purports to be Scientific Socialism. To reopen the issue, one must go back to first principles and rescue the essence of Scientific Socialism.

Socialism emerged as an ideology within capitalist society. All of its exponents saw the viciousness of capitalism and agreed on the need for replacing the prevailing production for private profit with a system which met the needs of all. However, they did not agree on either the precise content of socialist society or the means by which it was to be instituted. It is in these areas that the necessity arose for distinguishing between unrealistic socialist hopes and a more rigorous analysis that could claim to meet the canons of scientific method and which by its correctness guaranteed meaningful action for the realization of socialism. For Marx, 'Scientific Socialism' is quite simply socialism that is scientific.

Saint-Simon, Owen, Fourier and other pioneer socialists of the early nineteenth century were dubbed 'utopian' by Marx and Engels for a variety of reasons, notably because they failed to appreciate that human social development proceeded through certain stages and because their model socialist societies did not take cognizance of the reality of class struggle.[3] On the other hand, the rubric 'Scientific Socialism' still attaches to the mode of perception which predicts the emergence of socialism as a product of the dialectic movement of all previous history and as a consequence of the triumph of the working class. Utopian socialism, or at least utopian elements in socialist thought, have persisted and reappeared from time to time. 'African Socialism' is utopian in its refusal to come to grips with the class relations in which Africans are enmeshed and in its romanticized ignorance of the stages of African historical development. It is the contention of the author that, in contrast, Tanzanian *Ujamaa* is correct in its perception of the principal motion of its own society.

The assertion that 'there are no classes in Africa' is often used to justify capitalist investment in the continent, and in recent times it has come under criticism from progressive African thinkers.[4] First, it must be noted that the international character of capitalist production in the era of imperialism has placed the propertied class in the metropoles while the greater portion of their working force resides in the colonial or semi-colonial areas. Second, the colonial sectors show varying degrees of stratification and class formation as a consequence of their integration in the international capitalist economy. Both of these features are recognized in the Tanzanian policy documents which elaborate on the theory of *Ujamaa*: TANU's[5] Arusha Declaration and *Mwalimu* Nyerere's *Socialism and Rural Development* being the most relevant.

The Arusha Declaration had little to say about the development of socialism in the countryside beyond expressing the opinion that concern for the peasant farmer must be a priority. However, this document set the stage for the policy of constructing *Ujamaa* villages by expropriating the foreign capitalist class who until then were owners of the major means of production within Tanzania. It stated unequivocally that the major means of production are under the control and ownership of the peasants and the workers themselves through their government and their cooperatives. Nationalization and the acquisition of part ownership of several companies were steps in the direction of severing the links between the local working classes and the international bourgeoisie. The Arusha Declaration also stated that socialism was incompatible with the presence of capitalist elements, in contrast with 'African Socialism', which has as one of its major tenets the advocacy of coexistence of private and public ownership.

Utopian socialists promoted models in which capitalists cooperated with their workers in the new society. They sometimes assigned a major initiatory role to the bankers. Senghor's proposal was to socialize agriculture, to establish public utilities as a mixed sector and to leave banks, commerce and industry to capitalist enterprise.[6] The sum total of these arrangements would be 'African Socialism'. In so far as contemporary theory and practice of *Ujamaa* in Tanzania does allow for private enterprise, this is well understood to be transitional, an entirely different concept from that of the permanent coexistence of capitalist and supposedly socialist relations within the same society, and one that has been implemented in every socialist revolution from 1917 onwards.

Both feudalists and capitalists are cited by the Arusha Declaration as enemies of socialism. The former had their place in the scheme of things in Africa before the coming of the Europeans, while the latter came into being as part of the process by which metropolitan capitalist society was remodelling colonial society (wittingly and unwittingly) along lines of stratification and exploitation. The Indian businessmen in East Africa were the closest representation of a locally resident bourgeoisie, and it is no accident that they were the most affected by the measures of expropriation behind the nationalization of foreign-owned property – that is, by the Acquisition of Buildings Act, 1971. Thus, both ideological statements and government policy pinpointed that within Tanzania there were capitalists and feudalists standing in opposition to the workers and peasants. The Arusha Declaration does, in the same breath, make a rather unsatisfactory distinction between urban and rural Tanzania as representing exploiters and exploited, respectively.[7] It is in *Socialism and Rural Development* that stratification in the countryside is also acknowledged and a realistic assessment is made of African communal society, as it was and as it is becoming.

Having extolled the virtues of 'traditional' African living in Africa, *Socialism and Rural Development* proceeds to identify both its inadequacies and the fact that communalism as a way of life and a value system has been constantly eroded under the pressure of African involvement in capitalism. Because of cash-crop farming in particular 'the old traditions of living together, working together and sharing the proceeds, have often been abandoned'. In place of the old *Ujamaa* patterns, there was a growing gap between those who owned and hired labour and the landless who offered their labour for hire in order to survive. In this context, *Mwalimu* Nyerere predicted that, unchecked, such a development raised the spectre of most of the peasantry becoming a 'rural proletariat' working for the minority landed class.[8] This observation attests to the fact that the theory underlying the modern version of Tanzanian *Ujamaa* identifies contradictory forces within the nation as well as the direction for change that must result from the interplay of such forces. Marx and Engels attacked 'Proudhonism' because, among other things, Proudhon saw socialism as being based on independent petty producers of the artisan class.[9] But changes in technology by the mid-nineteenth century had convincingly demonstrated that the artisans were doomed to extinction by machine production and the universalization of capitalist relations. Of course, the

peasant is also a petty producer and has actually been eliminated in large parts of Western Europe. The question as to
whether there is a possibility of using peasant production as
the basis for a socialist state has been raised in many debates,
and its resolution depends upon the local and international
political economy of the time. Before tackling this issue in the
specific context of Tanzania, it is enlightening to pursue briefly
the debate on 'Peasant Socialism' as it was conducted in the
rather similar context of late nineteenth-century Russia.

Like contemporary Tanzania, nineteenth-century Russia
was an exploited semi-colonial sector of the international
imperialist economy. Unlike Tanzania, Russia had experienced fully matured feudal relations and was becoming
capitalist and industrialized from its own internal dynamic,
quite apart from the intrusion of Western European capitalism. Nevertheless, there had persisted under feudalism and
embryo capitalism certain communal forms of organization
among the peasantry – namely, the *obshchina* or *mir* (village
communes) and *artel* (artisans' cooperatives). Russians of a
socialist or anti-capitalist bias contemplated a socialist society
that was qualitatively different from that envisaged by their
counterparts in industrialized Western Europe. They argued
that Russia could avoid the maturing of capitalist relations
within its national boundaries and move directly to a brand of
socialism where the dominant social class was not the industrial proletariat but rural peasants, living a life that was not
far removed from the communalism that preceded enserfment
and capitalism.[10] Obviously, there is a great deal in Tanzanian *Ujamaa* that is analogous to the preoccupations of the
Russians in question, who are known to posterity as Populists.

In the 1870s and early 1880s, late in their veteran careers,
Marx and Engels were asked to comment on the possibility of
Russia avoiding capitalism. In a letter to K. Kablukova, a Pop-
ulist, Engels viewed favourably the opportunity presented in
Russia 'to be able to appeal to the people's thousand-year-old

natural urge to associate, before this urge is wholly extinguished'. Marx expressed the opinion that the rural community was the mainspring of Russia's social regeneration, but that in order that it might function as such, one would first have to eliminate the deleterious influences which then assailed it from every quarter.[11] The vital condition for the successful building of socialism in Russia on the old communal base was speed to forestall further inroads on surviving collectiveness. In addition, it was essential that revolution in Russia be preceded by or immediately followed by the outbreak of a workers' revolution in an industrialized part of Europe. This point is made in the introduction to the first Russian edition of the *Communist Manifesto* published in 1877 and again at some length in Engels' statement *On Social Relations in Russia* (1882). Some years later, Engels reaffirmed the contention as follows:

> I would say that no more in Russia than anywhere else would it have been possible to develop a higher social form out of primitive agrarian communism unless – that higher form was already in existence in another country, so as to serve as a model. That higher form being, wherever it is historically possible, the necessary consequences of the capitalist form of production and of the social dualistic antagonisms created by it, it could not be developed directly out of the agrarian commune, unless in imitation of an example already in existence somewhere else.[12]

As seen in the above extract, Marx and Engels dealt with the stages of human social development in a much more flexible manner than they are usually given credit for. They are, of course, insisting that the movement from communalism to feudalism to capitalism to socialism is a movement from lower to higher forms, with implications for the volume and efficiency of production and the satisfying of human needs. But they are not implying a single mechanical line of historical progression, and they actually deny this in the course of the discussion. In a comradely letter to Vera Zasulich in 1881, Marx explained that his description of the historical inevitability of the foundation of the capitalist system was expressly limited to the countries of Western Europe.[13] Four years earlier, he had made the same point with rather greater asperity in reply to a detractor, Mikhailovsky, who insisted on misreading Marx. Firstly, Marx reminded his readers that the chapter on primitive accumulation in *Das Kapital* does not pretend to do more than trace the path by which, in Western Europe, the capitalist order of economy emerged from the womb of the feudal order of economy. He then proceeded to show that the given historical sketch of Western Europe might be applicable to Russia if Russia continued to move in the same capitalist direction as Western European countries; for in that case Russia could not succeed without first transforming a sizeable number of peasants into proletarians. However, Marx vigorously disavowed any intention of using his model of Western Europe to provide a historical-philosophical theory of the general path every people is fated to tread, whatever the historical circumstances in which it finds itself.[14]

Although Marx completely disowned the proposition that a people must move to socialism via capitalism, it is understandable that bourgeois academics ignore this and interpret Marx to mean exactly what he said he did not mean.[15] But even self-styled Marxists have also made it appear that Scientific Socialism can be arrived at only on the basis of an advanced proletariat within a given country and hence only after capitalism has held in sway that country for a lengthy epoch, in precisely the same manner as Western Europe.

As far as Russia was concerned, the discussion by Populists and Marxists about avoiding capitalism turned out to be one about a non-realizable hypothesis. Marx and Engels feared that the process of stratification in the countryside would continue unchecked. Information reaching them from the late 1870s suggested that Russian communal forms were becoming shells which only hid the new exploitative relations of capitalist society. Towards the end of his life, Engels regretfully concluded that the *obshchina* should be treated as a dream of the past. A fine chance had been missed, but reality had to be faced, for capitalism was being built in Russia on the labour of landless peasantry turned proletariat.[16] A few years later, when Lenin made his in-depth analysis of *The Development of Capitalism in Russia*, he convincingly demonstrated that the capitalist process was far too advanced to think in terms of by-passing that stage. In other words, the creation of a rural proletariat and of landlord farmers which *Socialism and Rural Development* was interested in avoiding in Tanzania had already occurred in Russia by the turn of the present century among the peasants themselves – in addition to the continued existence of feudal and bourgeois landowners.[17]

Even after it became clear that internal and external factors were hastening the final decomposition of Russian communal forms, some theorists still clung to the idea that Russia could build socialism on the model of an old commune. Only at this point were they eschewed by Scientific Socialists as propagating Populist Utopianism. For instance, in 1890 Engels declared that the Populist, Danielson, was beyond hope, in spite of prolonged ideological exchange and correspondence to clarify the conditions under which Russian communalism could be revived.[18] For purposes of an analogy with Tanzania and Africa, what is crucial is that the founders of Scientific Socialism seriously and enthusiastically contemplated a variant of socialism very much akin to *Ujamaa*, and they indicated the conditions under which it might be realized. The most important requirements were: first, that the 'traditional' forms should exist in real life and have some social vitality; and second, that international conditions should be favourable owing to a socialist breakthrough in some part of the world. For Africa, the fulfilment or non-fulfilment of these conditions needs to be examined.

An effort has already been made to underscore the idea that for Marx different paths to socialism did exist, precisely because of varied experience of movement from one social phase to another. It is of some value to the history of philosophy to keep the record straight on this issue; although one is primarily concerned not with establishing Marx's correctness but rather with confirming the truth of the observation that the movement of different peoples through history has had significant variations. This could be illustrated within Europe with regard to the contrast between Eastern and Western Europe. As far as Asia is concerned the social stage parallel to that of feudalism in Europe bore sufficient peculiarities to be categorized separately as 'the Asian Mode of Production'.[19] Most relevant to the African continent is the debate on a possible 'African Mode of Production'.[20] With the exception of parts of the Middle East and Egypt, neither Asia nor Africa had slavery as a distinct social system, and African societies had very little servitude outside of the context of capture for export. From African communalism, the evolution was in a feudal or quasi-feudal direction, and communal forms persisted even in the most stratified societies. Ruling elites in empires as large as those of the western Sahara still maintained their authority through the heads of communities rather than through contractual relations with individual peasants.

It is in the pre-European era that Senghor seeks his model of pristine 'Socialism' in Africa. But, to begin with, communalism was not socialism. Collective production was narrowly restricted on an ethnic, clan and geographical basis, and the egalitarian principle of distribution was limited by the low level of production so that societies came nowhere close to fulfilling the needs of all their citizens – hence Marx's description of this stage as 'Primitive Communism'.[21] Socialism is inconceivable prior to the emancipation of man from such elementary forces as drought, flood and disease. Besides, in determining whether African communalism has any relevance in the present time, one must identify it as still persisting – that is, the thousand-year-old urge to associate must not have been extinguished. In many parts of Africa, communal forms lost their primacy centuries ago with the emergence of feudal and quasi-feudal forms of exploiting labour, including household servitude. Large parts of Africa were integrated within the capitalist economy since the fifteenth century because of the European quest for slave labour. Finally, there was the period of colonial rule which introduced capitalist exploitation of labour in every part of the continent. It certainly is not enough for Senghor to sound a warning of possible class formation in the present period, when it is obvious that Senegal has already passed through a lengthy and intense historical experience incompatible with the maintenance of communal forms or the practice of egalitarianism.

Admittedly, in 'Ujamaa – the Basis of African Socialism' *Mwalimu* Nyerere sounded a note rather similar to that of the standard version of 'African Socialism', when he asserted that 'We, in Africa, have no more need of being "converted" to socialism than we have to being "taught" democracy.' However, taking the continent as a whole, Tanzania is exceptional in that even at the end of the colonial period the communal forms were still recognizable. This is a consequence of its people having been relatively little involved in the capitalist money economy of mining, settler plantations and cash-crop production. The low degree of internal stratification at the time of constitutional independence was reflected in national cohesion and the solidarity of a single mass party. Between 1961 and 1967 there was increasing differentiation, so that *Socialism and Rural Development* dealt with the core of the problem by determining that socialism could only be built in Tanzania by halting stratification and the creation of a rural proletariat. This was the first of the conditions that Marx and Engels laid down when discussing how socialism might have been built on the basis of the Russian commune.

The possibility of regenerating traditional communalism also depends upon factors outside of the national political economy. This model for *Ujamaa* is as much in the present as in the past. If certain socialist values can be recovered from communalism, then equally there is the possibility of importing (and modifying) values and concrete attributes of socialism in any part of the globe. When *Mwalimu* Nyerere referred to the weakness of traditional African communalism, he mentioned technological inadequacy.[22] This factor should be given greater emphasis because it was technological inadequacy that meant scarcity and led to stratification and the internal evolution of classes in parts of Africa before contact with Europe. It was also technological weakness that led to loss of independence when Africa was confronted by European societies. Movement to a higher stage means massive strengthening of productive and defence capacity. But, with true political independence, any African society can resume its interrupted socio-economic and technological development at a higher level by utilizing the fund of scientific knowledge now available to mankind. Some of this knowledge is already in the hands of the first socialist states; and even if it is still the property of capitalists, it can be expropriated.

In effect, the skipping of stages involved in the jump from communalism to socialism is only possible in a given society because elsewhere the intervening stages have existed or are still existing, and because, as Engels postulated, modern industrial socialism has broken the stranglehold which capitalism previously maintained on the world at large. The first condition opens up the technological possibility of building socialism, while the second provides a model and profoundly influences the international political situation. Amilcar Cabral put his finger on these points and explains lucidly that 'the possibility of such a jump in the historical process arises mainly, in the economic field, from the power of the means available to man at the time for dominating nature, and, in the political field, from the new event which has radically changed the face of the world and the development of history, the creation of socialist states.'[23]

Potekhin, the well-known Soviet specialist on Africa, a few years ago expressed his agreement with those versions of 'African Socialism' which aimed essentially at building socialism in Africa and using African paths to socialism. In his opinion, colonized Africa could move directly and uniquely to socialism largely because of the Soviet Union. The latter was available as a source of help and a power transforming the global political balance in such a way as to restrain the large capitalist nations in their exploitation and oppression of small would-be socialist states.[24] The unstinted aid supposedly available from the Soviet Union would be regarded as illusory by most progressive Africans who are learning that self-reliance is definitely a superior alternative to any 'Big Brother'. However, it is true that the socialist sector of the world (divisions notwithstanding) offers a set of models, a set of alternative partners for trade and a more accessible source of technical aid. Tanzanian external political and economic relations have already gone a long way towards maximizing the advantage created by the existence of socialism in various parts of the world. It is one of the key ways of seizing what Marx considered a golden opportunity for moving to socialism on the basis of communalism and without having to experience the full development of classes characteristic of capitalism. It can further be argued that a colony or semi-colony within the imperialist framework can never develop to full capitalist maturity. Africa has experienced almost as many years of capitalist development as Europe, but in our case the unfolding of capitalism has meant historical arrest and backwardness. The accompanying stratification never approximated the dynamic of capitalism in the metropoles. Thus, one could never expect capitalism to perform in Africa the historically progressive role it played in Western Europe.

This is yet another fact of a more refined theory concerning the states of human social advance. Such a theory must cease assuming that development is self-contained for any given group or society, and this line of reasoning also reinforces the conclusion that for Africa a different path to socialism is not only possible but is unavoidable.[25] An ideology such as *Ujamaa* is scientific in so far as logically and scientifically it charts this new path.

The fact that the path of *Ujamaa* in broad outline is so reminiscent of one perceived by Marx is a salutary coincidence in so far as this particular discussion is concerned. Since so much of Marx's time was spent applying his scientific method to a critique of capitalism in Western Europe, any debate outside that geographical area cannot be tied merely to what Marx said, as though Scientific Socialism were entirely comprised within the pages of Marx's writings. 'Marxism' when considered as synonymous with Scientific Socialism means the application of scientific method (of which Marx was a founder) to the study of any given situation. This is a task of such complexity that Marx and Engels often issued warnings that the chances of incorrect conclusions were high.[26] However, the argument that *Ujamaa* is consistent with Scientific Socialism is made easier to substantiate because of Marx's conclusions with regard to an obviously analogous situation. The Marxist who considers the stress on 'traditional' African communalism as theoretically incompatible with a Scientific Socialist approach must bear the onus of proving that Marx's brief application of his own theory was unscientific in the Russian case. At the same time, the non-Marxist seeking to isolate *Ujamaa* from what he imagines to be Scientific Socialism must at least be brought up short in light of evidence that Marx himself explicitly countenanced the possibility of a development towards socialism that integrated peasant collectives from the communal epoch.

After Marx's time, new (Scientific) Socialist ideas have been elaborated out of revolutionary experience. Their accuracy and relevance have been tested by nothing less than the experience of building socialism in economically backward countries in the teeth of imperialist opposition. *Ujamaa* has not yet been fully tested in this sense and there are a wide range of 'social engineering' problems which have still to be tackled in the creation of new structures, new values and ultimately a new socialist man. If agriculture in Africa were already somehow mystically socialist, then there would not have arisen all the travail of physical transposition and social readjustment that is actually going on in Tanzania. Resettlement and collectivization proves how many aspects of the prevailing system were at odds with modern socialism: notably, the isolated production units, low-level technology, stratification and narrow vertical divisions. 'African Socialists' formulated 'socialist agriculture' as an existing reality rather than a goal to be achieved by rescuing communal elements; so, it follows that they had no socialist programme. Under Senghor, nothing has been done to relieve the exploitation of peasants producing cash crops and to remove rural exploitation; while in Kenya the only practical change in the agricultural sector as envisaged by Tom Mboya was the introduction of advanced agricultural machinery for the individual capitalist farmer.[27] Even the more progressive African political and ideological leadership long neglected the countryside, and opted for a one-sided industrialization strategy. Tanzanian *Ujamaa* is a unique contribution to the African socialist revolution and to socialist theory as a whole because of its solid connections with the observable data in the Tanzanian countryside. This is the characteristic which causes 'Leninism' or 'Maoism' to be considered as having enriched the Scientific Socialism of which Marx and Engels were the founders.

Undoubtedly, a much greater gap emerges when one compares implementation of Tanzanian *Ujamaa* with the implementation of Scientific Socialism in the particular countries where this has been attempted. Here is where the disavowal of Scientific Socialism makes a real difference because it encourages an attitude of mind that masks contradictions and even throws overboard theory as such behind the guise of being 'practical'. It can be argued that measures taken to implement socialism in Tanzania run the risk of being defeated for lack of a rigorous theory that comprehends the antagonistic and non-antagonistic contradictions of the world scene. The issue of nationalization is a case in point.[28] However, this does not mean that *Ujamaa* and Scientific Socialism are on two divergent paths. One should distinguish between an awareness of the fundamental movement of society and history, on the one hand, and adjustments to that movement in terms of struggle and construction, on the other hand. The latter is always very problematic but the first is more fundamental, requiring an understanding of which classes are on the ascendant and which social systems are moribund. Tanzanian *Ujamaa* can claim to be correctly focused in this regard. This being so, there is no insuperable barrier to the development of scientific strategies and tactics.

The above argument may be considered further in relation to the rural sector. It cannot be said that the construction of *Ujamaa* villages has followed a scientific line of identifying points of weakness and strength as advocated by Engels and Lenin and as practised by Mao Zedong and Kim Il Sung. But the theory and policy of *Ujamaa* has logically determined that the key role in Socialist construction has to be played by the Tanzanian peasants. This is in accord with the present stage of the development of productive forces within Tanzania and with the present international conjuncture, and such an insight gives *Ujamaa* its chances of success and ample scope for evolution, which it would have lacked if the theory had backed the wrong class or the disintegrating capitalist social system. The actual building of *Ujamaa* villages is a task requiring definite expertise. From a sociological viewpoint, practical implementation must take into account both the varying socio-economic formations found in Tanzania as well as the phenomenon of stratification.[29] Any sociologist might deal with some of the problems of collectivization but ultimately it is only a Scientific Socialist approach that can guarantee success. By way of illustration one could turn to Vietnam, where bourgeois social scientists lent their skills to the US government in the creation of 'strategic hamlets'.[30] Their technical expertise ran counter to the movement of the society and the hamlets were dashed aside by the conscious and organized peasants of Vietnam. At the same time, collectivized agriculture in the liberated parts of the country has been moving forward steadily.

One searching test of the scientific nature of any version of socialism is its reflection of the interests of the most exploited and oppressed classes. Marx regarded Utopians as having advanced towards a more defensible position to the extent that individuals like Owen and Fourier grasped the fact that socialism was the ideology of the working class and that it must therefore uncompromisingly serve this class.[31] Significantly too, the later Social Democratic deviation from scientific and revolutionary socialism reflected bourgeoisification of intellectuals and worker leaders in the epoch of imperialism. By way of rounding out a working understanding of Scientific Socialism, it should be made clear that socialist theory must voice the interests of the most exploited of the producers – this being perfectly possible alongside the phenomenon of class desertion by individuals from propertied or privileged strata, and alongside the assumption of leadership roles by these individuals. In Africa (as in Europe, Asia and the Americas) it is from within the ranks of an educated elite that leadership is drawn for movements claiming to be socialist. But there is a vast difference in the fundamental class loyalties of those espousing 'African Socialism' as compared to Tanzanian advocates of *Ujamaa*; a difference between a parodied mischievous use of the term 'socialism' and the de facto elaboration of the theory to which a Marxist could readily subscribe in terms of its potential for realizing a socialist society along scientific lines. Fanon called for the self-liquidation of the African petty bourgeoisie and their regeneration as a revolutionary intelligentsia, but of course this is far from being the case within the continent as a whole. 'African Socialism' is the inflection which the African petty bourgeoisie have given to bourgeois ideology in an attempt to camouflage from the masses the deepening capitalist exploitation of the neo-colonial era. In sharp contrast, Tanzanian *Ujamaa* has begun to make the decisive break with capitalism. The evidence lies in the Arusha Declaration, in the *Mwongozo*, in the Tan-Zam railway, in the nationalization of certain buildings and in virtually every act of Tanzanian foreign policy. Tanzania *Ujamaa*, limited as it is in actual achievement, can substantiate the claim to be the ideology of the majority of Tanzanian producers in the countryside and the towns.

In the final analysis, simple honesty is a vital ingredient in Scientific Socialism – honesty in the cause of man, the workers and dedication to his emancipation. Subjective as this may initially appear, it is very much part of the scientifically determinable process of social change, because consciousness is a principal factor in this process. This is precisely why Marxist theory is not mechanistic. Wherever it makes a projection into the future, the calculation includes human will and consciousness as a variable, because knowledge, self-awareness and organized activity by the exploited are all tied together. Tanzanian *Ujamaa* has broken with the crude manipulative dishonesty of 'African Socialism'. For instance, Tanzanian political leadership does ask for the 'traditional' communal virtue of hard work, but not in a context where local exploitation and class formation is allowed to proceed unchecked and is indeed promoted by the very theorists of 'socialism'. Therefore, *Ujamaa* can appeal to and deepen the consciousness of peasants and workers which imparts greater momentum to the people's struggle to build socialism.

From the viewpoint of social theory, it is not satisfactory that writings propounding *Ujamaa* never indicate awareness of the universality of communal forms. Examples broadly similar to African communal organization can be drawn not only from Russia before enserfment, but from every part of Europe and Australasia at one time or another. One of the first tasks of the scientist is to place things in the same category. Reluctance to do so in this case is probably due to the hankering after uniqueness among progressive Africans – something which occasionally leads into blind alleys, but which on the whole is essential for the liberation of the colonized.

The insistence on an African identity is a worthwhile corrective not only to bourgeois cultural imperialism but also to dogmatic expositions by self-styled Marxists or Scientific Socialists. Identification with the particularity of experience in Africa is as essential as appreciating the universality of scientific method. When the doctrine of *Ujamaa* postulates an African path to socialism it affirms the validity of Scientific Socialism, in spite of the lack of any declaration to this effect by Tanzanian leadership and in spite of deliberate efforts to distort both *Ujamaa* and Scientific Socialism so as to present them as fundamentally contradictory.

Serious political considerations make it necessary to undertake this kind of abstract enquiry from the viewpoint of one committed to the African Revolution. When the task of evaluating African social thought and practice is left to bourgeois theoreticians, they find it convenient to place all ideological strands into one amorphous mystifying whole, which includes utterances by Tubman as well as Nkrumah, by Mboya as well as Sekou Touré, by Senghor as well as Nyerere. Indeed, some go so far as to assert that 'in substance Nyerere and the Senegalese are closer than he is to Sekou Touré or Nkrumah'.[32] At the same time, progressive European friends often display a penchant for armchair Marxist perfection, so that for them Nyerere and Senghor are indeed in the same bag, because the former has not come forward to declare for Marxism.[33] The superficial and confused nature of such a conclusion is a consequence of the authors not being involved in making revolution, for whoever is involved in the actuality of revolutionary transformation will not fail to perceive the differences between form and substance. The substance of *Ujamaa* is its stand against capitalism, against imperialism, against racism and against exploitation of all kinds; and (to put it affirmatively) its stand for the emancipation of the working population of Africa and for the remodelling of the society along lines of socialist equality and socialist democracy.

Curiously enough, progressive Europeans are the ones who display the hegemonic tendencies characteristic of the imperialist metropoles, in so far as they have no time for insights that seem in any way to depart from models originating in Western Europe. The former imperialist masters, knowing the force of African nationalism which ousted them from the politico-constitutional sphere, do not ignore the search for an African identity, but rather take care to foster its most negative aspects; namely, the alienation from revolutionary features of European thought. To remedy both defects, theory for the African Revolution must spring from those who have had the historical experience of and socialization under slavery, colonialism, de-culturalization, racism and super-exploitation which has been the peculiar lot of Africans. Within that context, it will then rapidly become clear who is supporting an anti-people line, such as 'African Socialism', and who is advocating genuine liberation as envisaged by Tanzanian *Ujamaa*.

A more rigorous assessment of current ideologies in Africa is also a political necessity on account of the possible dialogue between Scientific Socialists and nationalists. The former are a mere handful, and in most African countries today can scarcely hope to cooperate with the existing regimes. To do so would

be to repudiate socialist principles, as well as to risk sense-
less liquidation at the hands of the 'African Socialists', 'Arab
Socialists' and other denominations who are more concerned
with fighting religious wars against 'Communism' than with
emancipating the African people. But, the contention here is
that Tanzanian *Ujamaa* offers a radically different framework
for political action on the part of the self-conscious Marxist.
Whatever verbal affinities *Ujamaa* has with anti-Marxist doc-
trines, it has placed the common struggle against capitalism
and imperialism on a much higher plane. Scientific Socialism
has been attacked time and time again. Whenever the attack
is based on overt or covert hostility to the working masses, it
has been accompanied by a policy of alliance with the bourgeoisie against the most resolute worker elements. The history
of Fabianism, Social Democracy and the like illustrates this
clearly, and helps further to distinguish Tanzanian *Ujamaa* as
being compatible with the precepts of Scientific Socialism and
with the construction of a genuine socialist society.

Presumably, it could be documented that Tanzanian
Ujamaa as it now stands is the product of a series of 'prag-
matic' adjustments to difficult situations, comprising things
such as the crisis of school leavers, the coup in Uganda and
the problem of foreign exchange.[34] However, the inference of
most of the foregoing arguments is that the response has been
suggestive of a commitment to the masses. If this were not so,
why then have other African regimes reacted differently to the
same stimuli and pressures as have manifested in Tanzania?
The progressive strengthening of a revolutionary stand in
Tanzania (to which attention was drawn at the outset) is a
factor of the greatest significance. It suggests movement on
the road to socialism, both in practical terms and as an aspect
of ideological development. Of course, there is a major difference between historical tendency and accomplished fact, but
consciousness and political behaviour form part of the bridge
between the two. This is not to be overlooked by anyone

attempting the rigorous task of applying scientific method to social reality with the view of aiding the birth of African and International Socialism. Theory that is non-Marxist must be evaluated in terms of whether or not it is substantively anti-worker or anti-scientific. Invariably, socialist revolutions have their roots not only in Scientific Socialism as a body of thought but also in the formulas independently and correctly arrived at by precursors who did not use Scientific Socialism as their point of departure.[35]

African nationalists are certainly involved in the African revolution in the two types of front represented in Mozambique and Tanzania respectively: namely, the fighting front and that of 'peaceful' transformation. Leaders of these two related struggles will at some point have to come to terms with a consistent theory for 'appreciating' their situation and taking action. Russia, China, Vietnam, Korea, Cuba – that is, every successful socialist revolution has borne out the truth of Engels's observation that Scientific Socialism is the fundamental condition of all reasoned and consistent revolutionary tactics. The mobilization of the producers, the defence of revolutionary gains and the advance of the struggle against modern monopoly capitalism are not tasks that can be accomplished by good intentions alone. Masses of people have to enter into an epistemology and a methodology different from those to which they have been accustomed. In China, they call it 'Mao Zedong thought' – a blend of specific insights and pre-existing theory. There is nothing inherently improbable in Tanzanian *Ujamaa* continuing to advance to reach that position. But, in the light of the claim that certain intellectuals have become so enamoured of Tanzania as to relinquish their critical function, let it be clear that this is no paean of praise. It is an assessment of a possibility that can be realized only through an ideological and political struggle to transcend the alienation from that part of the heritage of man which is called 'Scientific Socialism'.

14

Class Contradictions in Tanzania

Samir Amin, who is today one of the leading Marxist theo-reticians on the African continent, wrote an article in 1964 entitled 'Class Struggle in Africa', and it was anonymous. This was very significant, demonstrating that at that time it was not even safe for someone to write an article on class struggle in Africa. Those were the days when Leopold Senghor and others were parading their theses which gathered or attracted worldwide attention – theses to the effect that there were no classes in Africa. Today, eleven years later, changes have taken place both on the level of popular perception as well as in the academic sphere concerning the question of class and its relevance to an understanding of the analysis of Africa at the present and in the recent past – and indeed, using the broader scientific framework, in the more distant past.

Even at the very outset when the debate was raised in the early sixties, it was not true that there were no classes in African society. What was probably true is that the main manifestations of class contradiction within Africa then was still in the form of the extension of the class contradictions of the dominant capitalist metropolitan society. So that for all practical purposes, it was the capitalist class of Europe or Euro-America which was the exploiting class of the African continent, and any intermediaries between them were rela-tively unimportant and did not manifest real political presence. Consequently, when Marxists attempted to look at the inter-val evolution of class problems, they were seen to be or held to be not just alien but irrelevant concepts into the discussions of

African society. Today, it has become sufficiently generalized that one does not need to be defensive about adopting this particular posture. For Tanzania, it is striking because here is probably one of the territories where class formation is least developed on the African continent, and yet it would excite no controversy at first sight to raise the questions of class contradictions in Tanzania. This indicates how well entrenched the position has become on the African continent today.

The Concept of Class

I will begin by trying to explain the concept of class formation before I look at class contradictions, because I think that the classes in Africa are embryonic; that is, they are still very much in process of formation. Perhaps one could say that no class is ever completed. In any society classes are continually undergoing change. But there are periods when it is more difficult to utilize the tool of class because the individual's social groups that comprise the class are themselves moving towards an awareness of themselves, and do not necessarily have the organizational apparatus to express themselves as a class. By way of comparison, one may think of the eighteenth century in France. In writing about that period, Marx had to make the point that the bourgeoisie was not in existence at the time of the French Revolution – however much it may be called the bourgeois revolution. Elements which went into the making of the bourgeoisie were certainly present in eighteenth-century France, and over the period of the late eighteenth and early nineteenth centuries that class matured into the form which it came to take in the middle of the nineteenth century. The same applies to Africa. But here one must be careful; one must be able to understand that strands and strata are coming together to produce what could definitely be called classes.

The Process of Class Formation

While this process clearly began in the colonial period, for Tanzania my argument will be that class formation post-1960 has been as important, if not more important, than class formation before 1960 – or before 1961, if you want to take the exact date of independence. It is a very recent phenomenon, and it has been accelerated by the process of national independence. The low profile of classes in Tanzania before independence accounts, to my mind, for a number of the unique features of political and social development in that country. One of these features is political unity.

Political unity can only be explained in part at any rate as a function of the non-emergence of strong sectors of the petty bourgeoisie in pre-independence colonial Tanzania. By looking at the historical experience of a number of other places – for instance Ghana, the earliest and still in many ways the best studied of the African states moving towards nationhood – we find that there had been a considerable proliferation of embryonic petty bourgeois elements of different types. Some had their matrix in the old traditional society: they had been chiefs, or sons of chiefs, or they had been incorporated into the structure of the British so called native-authority rule; they had developed a base in the land and of course, in primary cash-crop production of cocoa; they had professional classes that date back to the late nineteenth century in West Africa; they had a certain number of indigenous traders including the very important market women, and so on; they had fractions of a petty bourgeoisie in Ghana. I think that the development of these factions was such that the British were able to manipulate elements and create intraclass contradictions long before the bourgeoisie, the petty bourgeoisie, had really matured. Already at this very embryonic stage, it was struggling within itself, and again that is not historically new. Sectors of classes, mercantile as opposed to industrial sectors, or of the capitalist class have always had their internal contradictions. And those contradictions became politically important because of the deliberate policies of colonial powers. Britain, in this case, tried to withdraw from Ghana – as from Nigeria, as from the Sudan and Uganda – in such a way that the state machinery was left in the hands of different elements of the petty bourgeoisie.

In Tanzania, because the class – or perhaps we should say it was still a stratum, or several strata at that time – was not well developed, the attempt to play one section off against another was not very successful. Attempts to get what we may call conservative African nationalists to organize a political party to oppose TANU[1] had far less success than similar attempts in Ghana to oppose the CPP.[2] The first consequence of this low profile was the move towards national unity; and even after independence, again taking as a point of reference what has occurred in a number of other territories – notably Kenya, Nigeria, Uganda – we find that the petty bourgeoisie politicizes ethnic differences in its search for state hegemony. Ethnic differences exist and, of course, they exist on the African continent. They are not necessarily political differences, however. They don't necessarily cause people to kill each other. They become so-called 'tribalism' when they are politicized in a particular framework. And in post-independence Africa they have been politicized largely by sections of the so-called African elite. (I refer to them as the African petty bourgeoisie, in the search for bases for their own maintenance in power.)

In Tanzania again we see that this is rather unique. Occasionally one hears in internal discussions in Tanzania some reference to so-called ethnic or tribal loyalties, but it has never reared its head within the state as a determinant of the direction of political change. Clearly this is not a function of the absence of ethnic groups, because Tanzania has as many or more ethnic groups as other areas. Nor is it the function of dominant ethnic groups, because if we broke Tanzania down, we could pick out two or three very dominant ethnic groups. The pattern in Tanzania is not all that dissimilar from, say, the pattern in what is now Zaire, where ethnic politics have become important. So the lack of politicization is mainly not due to ethnic differences but due to the rather weak development of the petty bourgeoisie as a class. They didn't have the chance to get involved in jockeying among each other, utilizing their own ethnic bases for that purpose.

A third point, and perhaps the most important point concerning the process of class formation in Tanzania, is that the weakness of the petty bourgeoisie allowed the specific development which we see in Tanzania, which is the development towards what is called *Ujamaa*, or Tanzanian socialism. It seems to me we must try to explain historically why it is that this particular African country made that option. It's not merely a choice, a political choice, which any African state could have made. I think we should look for the conditions which made it possible for Tanzania in 1967 to declare so-called socialism, to announce the Arusha Declaration. I would suggest the weakness of the particular class who stood initially to lose from such a declaration is the prominent reason.

In other parts of Africa where the petty bourgeoisie or some of its elements were already sufficiently entrenched, it would have been difficult to envisage an Arusha Declaration being made, and these elements simply retreating to their shells and offering no opposition.

I was fortunate to have been in Tanzania at that particular time; in seeing members of the leadership of TANU then, in 1967, one got a distinct impression of the discomfort on their part. Many elements, people that you could look up as individuals – ministers, members of the hierarchy and the civil service – were applauding the Arusha Declaration very painfully. One could see that it did not exactly fall in line with their conception of where the country should have been going. And one must therefore say that in a certain sense they were coerced, or at least constrained, to move in that direction. And one could see the constraint: the constraint was a class struggle, it was between themselves and the mass of the people. The mass of the people, workers and peasantry, came out in such tremendous force behind the document that I don't think that the small, fragile petty bourgeoisie could ever have had the confidence, or that anyone in that class could get up and say, 'We stand opposed to this option.' It would almost have been equivalent to committing suicide. They had no power base to confront the mass of the population at that time. Consequently, we will see of course that they retreated and devised a number of stratagems to avoid a head-on confrontation, but a refusal of that position was just not possible, given the balance of class forces in 1967.

The same thing occurred in 1971 when TANU produced another important document, the TANU guidelines or *Mwongozo*, as it is called. In many ways this is an even harder hitting document than the Arusha Declaration. One could perceive that in a sense the wording of the document, the elaboration of the document, was due to only a small number of individuals within the hierarchy of the party who took a particular position. But the others were not prepared to come out openly against it, again for the same reasons. It was too obvious that the vast majority of Tanzanian people stood in that framework, and that anyone who wanted to oppose it had to do so surreptitiously. Opposition had to be done in devious underhanded ways and not by coming forward and saying 'we are against the policy of socialism and self-reliance', or 'we are against the policy of worker control', or 'we are against an anti-imperialist line'. Except for a small handful, everyone felt constrained to at least mouth the slogans. There was a tiny handful who, after the Arusha Declaration, said, 'Well, it's time for us to cut and run; we prefer property to socialist jargon and we will leave.' But quite a number decided that the best strategy was to say what they felt needed to be said, and then to try to vitiate it, try to trivialize and denude the concepts of their real meaning.

Of course, I'm talking about a relative situation – Tanzania relative to the rest of Africa, not relative to the rest of the world. To the rest of the world, it is obvious that class formation in Africa has not produced the same sharp differentiation it has historically in other parts of the world. But relative even to the rest of Africa, in a significant number of African territories there has arisen a small landed class, a landed petty bourgeoisie, a kulak class to use the familiar Russian term. In Tanzania, analysts who have been looking around the countryside have also discerned what they call an emergent kulak class, but I think very often they are straining at the evidence. One kulak doesn't make a kulak class. What one could discern in Tanzania is that when you take the size of the country and the development of cash-crop farming in certain isolated pockets of the country, you could go into a given community and you could find one or two kulaks, but it cannot be said that they began to operate in a way comparable to Ghana, or the Ivory Coast, or Western Nigeria or Senegal. This was because quantitatively and qualitatively it was a different phenomenon. There was no real kulak class in Tanzania, no landed class comparable to either Uganda or Kenya in the East African countries. Of course, there were no industrialists; very few African countries had industrialists. But there were in a number of African countries a few African capitalists, timber traders or people having timber concessions, merchants of course, other than industrialists – the merchant class in West Africa or Central Africa, for example. But in Tanzania, as in the rest of East Africa, the presence of the Asians as the comprador class, as the merchant bourgeoisie, has meant that very few Africans entered that pattern of trade, or acquired wealth through trade. And there were even very few professionals, less than in West Africa, and certainly less than in Uganda, Kenya and Tanzania. Kenya had less for different reasons, partly because of the white settler economy which had allowed very few African professionals. What we find, therefore, is that the petty bourgeoisie in Tanzania was small. And not only was it small, but it also had a second important characteristic: it was limited to certain sectors of production or sectors of social activity, particularly the civil service, and as an extension of that, the other coercive apparatus – the police and the army. This is where African petty bourgeoisie found itself. I think this is as important to understanding the subsequent evolution as is the fact that it was a small petty bourgeoisie. It was small but its character was also circumscribed and limited to particular sectors. It was not mercantile. It was not involved professionally to any great degree. It did not have land. It was concentrated in effect in the area of the state, either the civil service or the police–army apparatus. I believe that this established a certain determination, a certain predilection, for state or status solutions to their particular problems – a predilection that was not present in either Uganda or in Kenya, to use the East African neighbouring territories as a way of comparing and contrasting the Tanzanian development. In Kenya there is still a definite commitment to the landed bourgeoisie or the landed petty bourgeoisie, and the same applies to Uganda. In Tanzania, the emergent elites never had any real commitment to the land in the form of private ownership. Therefore, in a real sense, it wasn't too surprising that they began to pursue policies which immediately returned the land or confirmed that the ownership of the land should be in the hands of the population. Had there already been a substantial development of anything approaching latifundia, then it would not have been an option that could so simply have been put into effect, but because of the lack of development of a private landed class, it seems to me there was no barrier towards a development in this direction.

The Structure of the Working Class

Let us take a brief look at the working class before returning to the petty bourgeoisie, who are really going to be the focus of the analysis. In Tanzania (as in so many of the African countries) the working class was small. It was a transient working class with a high proportion of migrant labour, although there has been a fair degree of stabilization of migrant labour in the post-war years. But the working class remained essentially rural, the larger proportion being on the sites of plantations, largely unskilled either in the same rural occupation or in other spheres such as the docks where they remained unorganized. The Tanzanian working class never achieved a significant measure of independent organization. And it is independent organization which ultimately makes a class. The workers of Tanzania engaged briefly in the struggle for their own organization in the late 1950s and early 1960s in the period between colonialism and independence. The trade unions that had evolved by 1961–62 were still continuing the same trajectory as they had in the anti-colonial struggle; that is, a trajectory designed to ensure that workers were represented and that workers built an independent organ of expression. But by 1964 this was completely halted by an attempted army mutiny in which some of the trade union leaders were involved. The government acted to virtually put an end to independent trade union organization – independent meaning independent of the state, independent of the leading party. This was in contrast to Kenya for instance, where there is a lesser degree of trade union independence in any real organizational sense.

Consequently, the working class has also been competing for power through the dominant party, TANU, and through the state. If the workers had retained an independent trade union organization, it is conceivable that we would have seen them as the instrument of their own struggle. But that organization post 1964 was incorporated into the governmental party machinery. Consequently, to whatever extent there is worker power in Tanzania, it is expressed through the party, TANU, or through the state which is, in some sense, the instrument of the ruling party. And, therefore, we have both the petty bourgeoisie and the workers concentrating their energies on the same social organization, on the same mechanism – the political party and the state becomes the arena in which the contradictions between the workers and the petty bourgeoisie still resolve themselves. That is what I would like to look at. How does the state serve? In whose hands does it rest? What derives from state policy?

The Workers, the Petty Bourgeoisie and the State

The Arusha Declaration is a starting point of modern Tanzania development. This was a response to internal crisis, a response to the stagnation of the neo-colonial economy in Tanzania, and it really marked the failure of the hopes of the petty bourgeoisie that international capital would have entered their situation to strengthen the class in a particular kind of way. The petty bourgeoisie had assumed that after independence, if they took the attitude of welcoming foreign capital and welcoming foreign aid, international foreign capital would be forthcoming. This was really the assumption: they imagined that there was some process of growth within the neo-colonial picture, within the post-colonial imperialist framework, which would allow them to develop as a class. But this was not in fact forthcoming. Any study of the period for Tanzania and for a number of other African countries shows very clearly the unfulfilled hopes of foreign investment and aid. Unfulfilled in many senses, particularly because (in many instances) it just did not come. Even when it came, it did not necessarily come when and where the government expected it to come. And when it was available, it was available with a number of other complications, political and economic, which the government of Tanzania found hard to accept. Therefore, by the mid-1960s, the Tanzanian economy was definitely stagnant in the face of declining world prices for major products (like sisal and cotton). The option it seems to me was taken by the petty bourgeoisie under pressure from the working masses in the sense that the stagnation and decline of real standards were bound to raise their own current from the working people. That pressure had to be responded to, and the response came in the form of the Arusha Declaration. This declaration was positive in the sense that it went along with popular aspirations and popular hopes that the producers would be able to control the product of their own labour and to control the shaping of the society to cut down the alienations which stem from the primary alienation of the product of a man's labour. It was positive, but at the same time the petty bourgeoisie were able to work out the strategy in which they would use this new intervention as a means of entrenching their control over the state.

Whatever the objective of the exercise of transformation, one thing was certain: the petty bourgeoisie intended to maintain their hegemony over the state apparatus. Indeed after 1967 they used the new policies as a means of reproducing themselves as a class. In a way this was almost axiomatic; since they were essentially a bureaucratic formation, the moment that they nationalized and began to engage in some forms of control over economic production, the bourgeoisie expanded itself, or extended itself into those sectors of economic operations. They built huge complexes like the National Development Corporation (NDC) and the State Trading Corporation (STC), which became known in Tanzania as, in effect, extensions of the state, extensions of the old civil service. The people who benefited most from this were the young petty bourgeoisie.

In Kenya there was a different line because the Kenyans

always had one advantage from their class perspective: Kenya was and still is a sub-imperialist centre in East Africa. It is the point of entry for foreign capital into the whole of the East African community, not just into Kenya alone. Consequently, the opportunities for 'pickings', if you like, were always higher in Kenya. The presence of the multinational corporations, partially determined by the presence of settlers in the colonial period, meant that Kenyans could actually think in terms of becoming directors of various multinational corporations. For Tanzanians, it was not feasible on ideological grounds. Besides, there were very practical reasons why the petty bourgeoisie could not hope for very much in this direction. Tanzania was not that type of economy. The rate of expansion of multinational capital in Tanzania before 1967 was relatively small. Consequently, it was through the state intervention that they could increase the possibilities of holding jobs equivalent to directorship. They wouldn't be directors of a foreign company; they would be directors of branches of the NDC or STC, or they would be managers of particular plants. In effect they were extending themselves as a class.

At the same time the African petty bourgeoisie in Tanzania, as in the rest of East Africa, had an old opponent: the Asian commercial comprador element. This group had been foisted on the African people in many respects; they had been deliberately promoted by the British government as a layer between foreign capital and Africans. They were allowed access to credit; most of them based their operations on the ninety-day credit system. They were in effect sponsored by the banks and the large import-export houses – the same banks which refused to give credit to Africans. The British government and the colonial states had sanctioned this by issuing credit restriction ordinances which made it impossible for Africans to advance as middlemen. So, the experience of the so-called Asians, that is those from the Indian subcontinent, was linked with British policies in East Africa. As so often happens, the comprador or the middleman often attracts the ire of different indigenous classes much more so than the metropolitan ruling class. In Tanzania and in Uganda there were what were called Asian riots or anti-Asian riots in the 1920s, '30s and '40s. For some people they may be classified as racial riots; but they were not racial riots, they were manifestations of class struggle, since you find the same kind of thing in Jamaica where you would find anti-Chinese riots simply because the Chinese happen to be the middlemen in that particular context. The ordinary peasants in the countryside, the working people in the sisal estates and in the towns found that their immediate enemy was the so-called duka walla – the Indian who controlled the duka, or the shop – because that Indian bought their product, he cheated them in weighing their product, he cheated them in reselling to them what he imported from abroad. Although this was petty in relation to the fundamental exploitation of the market which was being established in Mining Lane in London, the peasant and the worker had to react to his immediate enemy. And so there has been a considerable anti-Indian sentiment which is class-based. The African petty bourgeoisie too, as he began to move forward and to have certain aspirations for advancement felt that the Indian was the first obstacle. He couldn't see Barclays Bank as the immediate enemy, because that was too distant, too powerful, and in his own horizons he didn't really aspire to become a competitor to Barclays Bank, but he could aspire to become a competitor to an Asian merchant or an Asian professional or an Asian civil servant. So, for the petty bourgeoisie too, the Asians were very often the immediate enemy. In the post–Arusha Declaration period in Tanzania, the Asians as a comprador class have begun to disintegrate. This is true in East Africa as a whole.

In Uganda the people are of course aware of the dramatic turn of events after Amin came to power. People may be less aware of what's going on in Kenya, but in Kenya there's also been a constant pressure and harassment of the Asian petty bourgeoisie by a would-be African commercial petty bourgeoisie. In Tanzania it did not take the same form. It did not take the form of individual Africans seeking to take over Asian shops. What has happened is that the state has encroached upon areas in which the Asian petty bourgeoisie were dominant, and since the African petty bourgeoisie controls that state it means the expansion of the bureaucratic class or the bureaucratic sector of the petty bourgeoisie as against the commercial petty bourgeoisie. The State Trading Corporation, for instance, took over a large number of the functions initially carried out by a host of private importers among whom Asians were predominant. Buying and selling abroad was initially taken over. Then slowly the STC has also attempted to establish itself with certain retail outlets. It has also meant that questions as to what is to be purchased, in what quantities, at what prices, and how it is to be sold are questions now being determined by the state, by the African bureaucratic bourgeoisie, and not by the Indian merchant class – except in so far as they can react defensively and try to break out by certain stratagems which they do indeed adopt. But, by and large, initiative in these regards has passed into the hands of the African petty bourgeoisie, the bureaucratic African petty bourgeoisie.

The impact of the Arusha Declaration and the move towards social and state controls over production and distribution has been to sharpen that contradiction between the commercial petty bourgeoisie, which was a particular ethnic grouping, and the bureaucratic petty bourgeoisie. It has been resolved in their favour in the sense that the Asians, for the most part, seem to have decided that there is no further stake in East Africa; their main concern has been to try to liquidate their capital, to try to get it out of the country, which they have done in an infinite variety of ways. In Tanzania it is extremely difficult to get money out of the country. Usually what happens, however, is that whenever there is a new edict concerning foreign exchange control, it has come at least a year if not two years after the Asians have been using that loophole. Therefore, the amounts of money already sent to London and to Canada and the US are quite fantastic. At the same time, the Asians do interact by attempting to form liaisons with members of the African petty bourgeoisie, utilizing the straightforward cash nexus just to bribe them into an acceptance of the Asian position. So they are a declining class, but they can at the same time exercise influence based on the fact that they do have some liquid funds, and this is used to increase the amount of bribery and corruption that is present in the system.

Nevertheless, I would say that one could conclude at this point – even before the Asians are completely finished as a class – that there is no longer any future for them in the old roles which they had in East Africa and Tanzania. In Tanzania this has been done through the instrumentality of the state, in Uganda through the instrumentality of the army and other private African entrepreneurs, and in Kenya through the instrumentality of private entrepreneurs. Most important to the people of Tanzania have been those contradictions manifested between the petty bourgeoisie and what I will call the producer class – the peasantry of the countryside, excluding the very few kulak owners. There is also a contradiction between the petty bourgeoisie and the workers of the towns and the countryside. This contradiction – which is a much sharper contradiction, a much more antagonistic contradiction than the earlier one between the commercial element and the bureau element – manifests itself at all levels in a variety of ways.

Ideology and class contradictions

In the education sphere, for instance, and having taught in the country I hope I am sensitive to what went on in that area, I would say that the class struggle was reflected in ideo-logical terms and conducted in very sharp ideological terms in Tanzania, more so than in any other African countries with which I am familiar, with the possible exception of Ethiopia. There it was conducted in a rather different way, primarily by Ethiopian students as a part of a whole underground. In Tanzania it was conducted out in the open, inside the education institutions, particularly within the university – a young university which had been established like so many of the Third World universities as just another factory being put into the Third World by the metropolitan countries. It was established in 1961 as a typical institution of bourgeois learning and functioned in that way, in terms of its curricula, its staffing, its programmes, its structure, and everything else in the mid-1960s when it was formed. But because of the move towards socialism – even at the level of rhetoric since much of it wasn't put into practice – the move towards socialism itself had behind it the power of producing classes in Tanzania, and this could not be kept out of the development of the University of Dar es Salaam. Therefore, one found there a tremendous con-flict taking place between bourgeois knowledge and scientific analysis, which derived from looking at the actual practice of the producer classes in Tanzania and in the world at large at this particular point in time. Some of the questions were of theory; they had to address themselves to the whole plethora of bourgeois knowledge and understand its methodology, its perceptions, to understand the struggle between idealism and materialism. I presume it would not be necessary for me to go into that kind of detail. Those of us who took part in this in one way or another related to the students and related to the population outside of the university, so that it was a genuine reflection of changes taking place in the society as a whole. There were, of course, broad debates about the organization of the university, about how one organizes academic disci-plines, and so on. But there were also a number of debates that were very pertinent to the immediate policy choices of the Tanzanian government. The question of development, for example, was not evolved as an academic debate per se. It evolved from a perception of real choices in the policy sphere: what was to be done at the particular point in time in specific areas of economic, political and social development. It arose out of the formation of the solutions to the so-called problem of underdevelopment. People began to question the kinds of theoretical framework and paradigms that bolstered particular kinds of solutions. If the solutions proved to be false in practice, their theoretical justifications were exposed to much more critical analysis, and ultimately to an onslaught in that institution from which they have not recovered. So the debate was linked to the ongoing struggle within Tanzania.

From time to time, students themselves would take the initiative. This was extremely useful because the students were not only students of the university but they were at the same time members of the TANU Youth League. Therefore, it was ensured that this was a struggle that was at all times relevant to the immediate needs of Tanzanians.

That is one level. Within the university and within all other educational institutions, such as the secondary schools, the same kind of struggle went on to try to clarify theory and to recognize that the ideas which existed in that society were not simply free-floating ideas. They had historical roots. They had social class origins, and one had to pin down these social origins if some progress were to be made in clarifying these ideas.

Economic policy and class contradictions

More immediate – and more critical, from a political viewpoint – were the contradictions taking place at the level of economic policy that were also partly tied up in some ways with the contradictions in the educational system. But major debates were also taking place on specific aspects of policy – for instance, tourism. There was a whole year at least in which the question of whether Tanzania should promote tourism or not was an issue of national importance that people were battling back and forth on this option. In some ways you may look at it and imagine: 'Tourism, are you for it or are you against it?' This is a free decision. We express a position, we analyse the situation, we subject the data to some scrutiny and we come up with a position for or against. But it is not as simple as that. When one looks carefully at the way in which the debate was conducted – who stood for the tourism option, who opposed it – one sees there were class roots in taking up a position for tourism or against it. Fanon, in his usual manner, remarked quite a long time ago in 1960–61, that tourism is a very important vehicle: a way in which the petty bourgeoisie organizes relaxation for the metropolitan bourgeoisie and uses that opportunity also to reinforce their class ties. It was very clear in Tanzania that, in spite of the protestations for socialism, this tremendous need to push tourism and to rationalize what after all, in purely economic terms, is one of the most meaningless so-called industries, was linked with the necessity – this perceived need on the part of the Tanzanian bourgeoisie to keep in touch with their metropolitan masters. In effect it wasn't particularly different from what was going on in Kenya; Kenya just did it openly and pursued their tourism in the name of capitalism. Tanzania was trying to do their tourism in the name of socialism. In fact, it is already in shambles, but the need was to rationalize this position, which was a class position, and the petty bourgeoisie conceptualized development along certain lines. They had a vision of what needed to be consumed, of what needed to be built, of the kinds of societies that derive from bourgeois metropolitan society. The hotels, the airports, the transit facilities: these were things which fitted the class perspective of the petty bourgeoisie in Tanzania.

On the other side were members of the same class, naturally enough, engaged in a debate which required articulation in certain ways. Essentially this involved young Tanzanians who were of the same social class origins, but who were responding to different class loyalties and who were expressing different class loyalties. They were saying that our workers and our peasants are not concerned with those who want to come and watch the lions and gazelles and to watch the Masai and so on, and call themselves tourists: that this will not do anything for the mass of our population. On the contrary, it will inhibit a development of serious economic options which could lead to real integrated development. It will introduce and reinforce cultural backwardness and cultural penetration and place our people continually in the position of servitors of Euro-America. This was an argument that was lost in the first instance by the anti-tourism elements. It was won by those who wanted to promote international tourism; but in the year that followed, tourism has been proved to be simply economically unprofitable – quite apart from everything else. It was pointed out that deploying such a large proportion of finances into this sector was bound to be disastrous and it has already proved to be that way. A huge modern automated airport was built between Kilimanjaro and Arusha where the game reserves are located only ten minutes flight from Nairobi. This was completely unjustifiable in any terms, but it was claimed that an airport would enable more visitors to come to watch the animals. When the visitors did not come to watch the animals and this huge airport lay empty, the same petty bourgeoisie began to suggest that possibly they might do some market gardening around this airport. They might therefore export fresh vegetables and make some profit. The order of priority was not just due to lack of vision but due to a particular straightjacketing in which this class found itself. So they thought first of tourism, and only subsequently when the tourism was in shambles did they begin to think about

CLASS CONTRADICTIONS IN TANZANIA

production; even then, of course, the production will have to be tied to the existing infrastructure, which is a meaningless infrastructure because it is pointless to engage in production simply for export to Europe. But that is another question. The same clash of views came out, not always as clearly as the tourism debate, with regards to questions concerning irrigation, choice of crops, and the general conduct of agricultural policy. The tourism debate was very sharply focused, and people took sides. It may not be clear with regard to other aspects of economic policy such as cash crops, general crop selection, and whether or not the country should engage in irrigation, and other questions. But looking at it even at least with hindsight, one can perceive that there was a tendency on the part of the petty bourgeoisie to treat agriculture mainly as an intensification of that which had gone before. There was no conception of a break. To take sisal or cotton as examples, when the prices declined the tendency was to imagine that one could grow more. Certainly for cotton and sisal specific areas had to be abandoned, because they were not profitable. There was no new conceptualization of breaking with the international division of labour in which they as a class had emerged. Consequently, we find today significant sectors of Africa are suffering from famine. In suffering from this famine, each one, depending upon their religious affiliations, will appeal to Allah or God or the ancestors of whoever it is – or the rain gods, who are supposedly responsible for there being no rain. So it becomes a mixture of natural phenomena and the solution is a metaphysical or religious intervention. Of course, famine is neither natural nor metaphysical. It is a social phenomenon. Drought and famine are not just 'natural'. I don't know in what sense one can just describe them as 'natural', when the society has the capacity technically and organizationally to plan, first, to eliminate or at least reduce the incidence of drought and famine, and second, to reduce the consequences of drought and famine. So we see that these societies had continued their colonial policies of failing to deal with the critical question of food first, and being preoccupied with what they call 'foreign exchange', they have been growing coffee, cotton and sisal, and what have you.

That must be put as part of the historical explanation of why the famine and drought are so widespread throughout Africa at the present time. It is a reflection of the incapacity of neo-colonial societies to even feed themselves or to protect their populations from the vicissitudes that lie outside the immediate control of each individual, but do not lie outside the control of the society as a whole, if that society is geared towards resolving the problem. So these are aspects of bourgeois thought, of petty bourgeois policy, and the fact that they were pursued when there were at least some individuals in the society arguing to the contrary is an indication that they were pursued in spite of the contradictions or by way of contradictions. They were not simply steamrollered; it was not that the whole society was blissfully unaware of other alternatives. Alternatives were discussed and the petty bourgeoisie chose their own road, which in most cases have led to disaster.

To conclude briefly on the point about the Tanzania economic policy, there still is an ongoing debate about factors such as economic advisors, about the questions of economic agreements, so called 'managerial agreements' by which nationalized or partially nationalized companies are placed in the hands of foreign management consultants. That debate about consultants and experts and advisors still goes on. In part it was attacked from a nationalist perspective. Some Tanzanians said, 'well, we need to nationalize or Africanize, so we can't have all these sensitive positions.' But nationalization has not been enough. In fact, the nationalists themselves, the petty bourgeois nationalists, stopped short at a particular point, because of a lack of confidence in themselves. To understand the petty bourgeoisie again go back to Fanon and look at the pitfalls of the national consciousness in *The*

Wretched of the Earth. He captured that very well: the lack of confidence in a class that is an outgrowth of another historical experience that never controlled anything in its own right. It didn't control production. It didn't control property. It is derived from the colonial system. It hasn't the confidence to challenge that system fundamentally. It is culturally dependent as well as economically and politically dependent. Consequently, they find it very difficult to break with this conception of foreign advisors, foreign management, and so on; and having no confidence to break with these concepts, they therefore rationalize it by saying, 'Well, McKinsey isn't really advising us how to be socialists. McKinsey is merely giving us the technological expertise. We will account for the political inputs.' The capitalist firm comes in and goes through all our records and the Harvard advisory team and all those various paraphernalia of bourgeois individuals still trample around in and out of Dar es Salaam and the countryside. This is rationalized by saying, 'We are taking from them a technical expertise and this is all. We will account for the political inputs.' One of the most fundamental bourgeois fallacies is that you can separate technology from ideology, that you can separate the mechanics of a process from the fundamental direction in which you are going, from the class content of the kinds of advice that you get about organizational structures, and so on.

Production of class contradictions

For Tanzania, outside the economic sphere, the most decisive contradictions – the ones on which the real earthy manifestations of the class struggle are based – have come directly out of production, either in the countryside or in the towns. In the countryside, there have been contradictions arising out of the policy of *Ujamaa* and its implementation: in the towns these are seen in the clash between bureaucratic management and the workers at the point of production. The policy of

Ujamaa itself has a great deal to commend it. It is not merely a form of social organization and of economic production; it is meant to be a social whole, a cultural whole. It is meant to be an environment in which the rural producers resume control over their own lives by participating in running their day-to-day lives, and by making choices about fundamental things in their day-to-day lives. It intended to put a halt, as Nyerere made clear, to the incipient penetration of the money economy and the class formation in the countryside. It was intended to put a halt to the rise of any kulak elements, and to the accompanying rise of a landless proletariat. What has in effect occurred is that only a very few of the functions of this operation have been successfully concluded. In large measure there have been concluded a certain regrouping of forces, particularly in areas of the country that had been sparsely settled or where the pattern of spatial distribution of population and economic activity was such as to warrant a grouping of forces. This regrouping took place, for instance, in central Tanzania where there is a low density of population, and in western Tanzania where the homesteads were also scattered. This is useful because it allows people to come together where one can provide them – or the government can provide them – with medical services, schools and a number of other things. It means that a government proclaiming itself to be socialist has had to carry out an historical task, which in other societies had been carried out in a previous epoch. Capitalism, and feudalism for that matter, had helped in the grouping of populations; certainly capitalism very ruthlessly enclosed land and brought farms together. It also concentrated populations in urban centres.

In Tanzania, this programme of grouping rural populations has had some serious setbacks in recent years. Evidence of this came late in 1973 and 1974 when the programme for creating *Ujamaa* villages seemed to have become bogged down. It had not reached the quantitative dimensions that had previously been planned, because a number of areas apparently had not moved into the villages as they were expected to. On some examination it does not appear as though there were serious political inputs into getting these individuals to move. To ask people to move, to ask them to make a new life, to participate in a whole new form of production would obviously require a considerable politicization. This was the premise upon which regrouping was based in China – mutual-aid teams through the brigades right up to the communes. It was a political process first and foremost, but to the bureaucrats they could only reduce it to a bureaucratic process, not one of entering in and with the mass of the population to effect transformation, but one in which they see it as a question of logistics and figures and maps with little pins stuck in to show where the *Ujamaa* villages are and what is growing where. They can conceptualize a problem which says, 'we need to move X number of people from this point to another and we need so many lorries, so you get the lorries, you go to the area, you get the police to come with you, and you break up people's villages, and tell them it will be much better you for. Possibly it will work out; possibly those people will decide it is better for them.' But the world has had a great deal of practice of certain individuals telling other individuals what is good for them and telling them they will kill them for their own good if necessary. We see the end product of that in South East Asia today. Certainly from a socialist perspective, it is always dangerous that bureaucratization should parade in the name of socialism. It happened of course under Stalin, and it did put a certain blight upon socialism for quite a long time. Therefore, one does look with some concern at this same manifestation.

The high incidence of bureaucratic activity, of bureaucratic decision-making within the context of the *Ujamaa* villages, created a real contradiction because those peasants are fully aware of what is going on. Inside the villages, once they are formed, there is a struggle over controlling the day-to-day policy. The peasants don't give up. They are quite tenacious. They have a way of bringing their perspectives to bear on the problems also. So it is not one-sided, but because the petty bourgeoisie are more in control of the state apparatus, it becomes rather difficult for the peasantry to win significant victories at this time.

And then, finally, there are the workers themselves: a small class, judged in comparison with Europe, an insignificant class. A very tiny percentage of the total producing force can be regarded in any way as a proletariat. But, as so often happens in this type of economy, the proletariat is strategically situated. It is situated in the capital town and other urban areas and in sensitive sectors of production and therefore what it says and does simply cannot be ignored. It strikes me that the contradictions between workers and the bureaucrats have really come out in a very sharp form as the working class itself has advanced in its own clarity, partially as a result of the same policies which have been pursued by the government. You see the ambivalence of policies: the elements within the petty bourgeoisie have allowed for the elaboration of a certain theory of certain ideas within the Tanzanian environment, which have further strengthened the Tanzanian working class. And the Tanzanian working class makes demands on the system in very enlightened terms. Not merely demands concerning increased wages (those have been made and they are necessary to defend living standards of the population), but going beyond that, workers have in the last several years in Tanzania been making a number of very advanced demands concerning their role in the productive process and in the control of the productive process.

Once the factories were nationalized, once an institution fell under the National Development Corporation and was either government-owned or partially government-owned, the petty bourgeoisie imagined that was the end of the process. It was now a Tanzanian enterprise and, as a Tanzanian enterprise run by Tanzanian managers, it was enough for the workers to fall in line and behave more or less as they had behaved previously. But this did not turn out to be the case. Workers began to raise demands that the nationalization of those industries meant that they had to be run by Tanzanians in a new kind of way consonant with the interests, the self-images, and so on, of the Tanzanian working people. One of the consequences of this was that the party agreed to issue the party guidelines of *Mwongozo*, which in effect addressed itself to the whole problem of bureaucratic management. The party was saying, 'Well, bureaucrats cannot behave in the same fashion as the colonialists or the imperialists used to', or they said that the nationalization implies a whole new way of organizing production and change, a qualitative change in the relationship between the workers and the management during the period immediately following the proclamation of *Mwongozo* in 1971. But an interesting thing which occurred after the acceptance of the guidelines was that the petty bourgeoisie themselves recognized that this was too dangerous a weapon. The workers used to move around with a very small version of the guidelines, a document printed up into a very tiny booklet, which could be stuffed into any pocket. Workers had a habit of moving around with the *Mwongozo* and taking it out – as we understand the Chinese consult their little red book[3] – and opening it to the appropriate page, and confronting bureaucrats and saying, 'Well, look, according to paragraph 14 so and so; this is what it says and now what you are saying there and doing is quite different from what is going on here.' And then they would move on to paragraph 15 and so on, and this was becoming very dangerous. Workers were presuming to educate the educated. In other words, it was threatening to become a revolution.

Interestingly enough, when this class contradiction manifested itself, the petty bourgeoisie began to withdraw from the issue of *Mwongozo*. They began to say, 'Well, each one in his own institution would come up with an exception why *Mwongozo* didn't apply there.' The doctors started to say, 'Well, look at this hospital. We are the doctors. After us come nurses and cleaners and so on. I mean this hospital has to be run by doctors. We have the expertise. You can't have *Mwongozo* and self-management and things like that in a hospital. People will die.' What they need to do, of course, is to go and look at the Chinese experience, to look at a book such as that by Joshua Horn, *Away with All Pests*, and they will understand that in a truly democratic society the hospitals are run by all, including the patients themselves. But they felt they were making a valid case for exceptions. The youngsters in schools began to flash *Mwongozo* and argue against the missionary-type education – the pattern of hierarchy and the authoritarianism that prevailed in a large number of boarding schools in Tanzania – and of course the headmasters and the schoolteachers said, 'Well, you are too young to know about *Mwongozo*. *Mwongozo* was written for adults, not for children. As children you are under our care.' And so they seized all copies of *Mwongozo* which might be circulating among the student population.

Then in the banking institutions the bankers and the chief bankers would say, 'This is a lot of money we have here. We can't be joking with this financial question. These workers don't understand accounts. They don't understand questions like: "What is the current rate of the Tanzanian shilling as compared with dollars?" So how can we have *Mwongozo* operating in our institution?' So, in a variety of ways, one saw the petty bourgeoisie retracting from the position into which they had been forced initially on the question of the *Mwongozo*, and one found the workers advancing by raising the level of their demands, so that they constantly talked about various issues on the basis of principles. They constantly talked about incorrect behaviour in the factories. They talked about favouritism, firing in accordance with the kinds of ethnic loyalties of the manager. They exposed any ways of victimizing or exploiting the women in the factories, sexually or otherwise. Things of this sort began to increase considerably in 1971 and 1972, reaching a high point when in one factory, a rubber factory, the workers decided to lock out the management and run the factory themselves for a certain period of time (not a very long period of time; actually until the police came). The workers ran the factory because of the things that had been raised against the workers when they went on strike: that because they were striking now that Tanzania has national property, any strike was therefore against the national interest, and not the interest of capital as used to be the case before the factories were nationalized. So the workers in that factory were answering that argument. They were saying, 'We are not going on strike. We are not putting an end to production in the country. We will increase production when we are running the factory.' So they were posing a more fundamental question: the question of who controls production; who is the boss in so-called socialist society. But for the time being, of course, the petty bourgeoisie is still essentially in control of the state, and it could not allow the working class to exercise this type of initiative, so those workers had to be rounded up and scattered.

Conclusion

Many times when I speak about Tanzania, I find that I fall into the difficulty of trying to justify it against reactionaries and to clarify the realities against those who are romanticizing such realities. Each one is a different kind of operation. There are enemies of Tanzania who do not like the socialist content, so for them whatever is going on wherever it fails, that is so much the better. Against such an assault one has to be careful to be critical of the reality, and the transition, but to be critical of it from the viewpoint of its failure to live up to certain types of expectations, and the fact that the contradictions have not yet resulted in the positive benefits for the working masses. And then, on the other hand, when one is talking with the romanticizers – those people who essentially have a sympathy with what is going on in Tanzania, but have not been exposed to it in day-to-day reality – then it is necessary to understand or to point out that social contradictions do not cease because a government issued a document.

The Arusha Declaration is very nice. Another document is issued which says that socialism is for self-realization or education for self-reliance and *Mwongozo*. All these are very positive – certainly better than neighbouring territories like Kenya and Uganda which either have no document or have some policy statements that are really absurd. But that is not an answer to reality or a substitute for reality. The position was a position in part won by progressive elements and by the pressure of the workers and the peasants, but it can only be worked out in practice depending upon the balance of class forces. And at the present time, the petty bourgeoisie, although small in number, is in control of the state. It is reproducing itself. It still retains certain kinds of links with the international monopoly capitalist world.

It would be difficult at this time to make a prognosis about the immediate resolution of the contradictions outlined above – whether progressive tendencies or more reactionary tendencies will win out. I have a certain confidence – perhaps a confidence tinged with hope – that the trend will in fact lead, even in the short run, towards the resolution of these contradictions in favour of the progressive elements among the working peoples. Clearly, I can not be quite certain. But that is not as important as the long-run trends. Over the long run, there is no doubt about it: I think that the masses of the population are being brought into a politics of participation and that they have in these first five years, starting in 1970, entered into struggles in a way that is much more meaningful than for most other neo-colonial African territories. Therefore, whatever happens in the short run, one can see the towns, serving their best interests in terms of the access to power, because these historical changes will not take place by themselves. History is, of course, made by people. Marx and his followers clearly understood this. There is a tendency on the part of bourgeois detractors to suggest that somehow a Marxist formulation is talking about things and about abstractions, and reification, whereas in fact we are talking about people in society, and certainly history is made by people depending upon their particular level of consciousness. In this sense, the contradictions are sharpening the consciousness of the most exploited and oppressed classes, heightening their consciousness – and this must be in the long run a very positive fact.

15

Transition

The term 'transition' has already appeared in scholarly works dealing with contemporary countries in the process of development. It has been attributed precise – although sometimes conflicting – meanings within this growing body of scholarship, concerning both the concept of collateral ideas such as the transfer of technology, the economics of transition, the dynamics of cultural change and the state's own role in development. Each one of these facets would obviously demand the keenest of attention and their examination can take place effectively only through comparative study of different objective situations. The present analysis sets itself a more modest task: namely to explore the parameters of the concept of transition as it might plausibly appear from a general perspective. Transition and development are already part of a popular vocabulary. One needs to bridge the gap between academic specializations and the wider informed community, which is committed to seeking both the understanding and the positive action inherent in the notion of transition in this era and in this part of the world.

Neither the rate of change nor the duration of change are immediately established with the use of the word transition. Mankind was in transition over hundreds of millennia while using stone tools. The neolithic portion of the Stone Age itself lasted for several thousands of years; but it is possible to affirm that the beginning of agriculture in that period constitutes the most important 'revolution' in the history of human society. To speak of transition from one mode of production to another allows for somewhat greater precision: yet one is still confronted with timescales of several centuries which mark the passages from antiquity to feudalism and from feudalism to capitalism. In the history of Guyana, the end of chattel slavery in 1838 provides an opportunity to treat the first post-emancipation decade as an experience with free labour; and yet it was not until 1921 that direct legal coercion of labour gave way to more conventional relations between wage labour and capital. One can therefore argue that the transition from slave labour to free labour in Guyana lasted from 1838 to 1921. (The last indentured labourers arrived from India in 1917; all indentures expired in 1921.)

In each of the contexts above, the term transition is legitimately employed, and yet there is the disconcerting possibility that approached in this way all history may be characterized as transition from one stage to another. To avoid tautology and trivialization, it is clearly essential to assign a narrow timespan to the concept as it relates to contemporary social change. Further, limiting the duration of transformation implies an accelerated rate of change.

Whatever the context, the state of transition can only be established by inference. It is a link between two historical epochs, and it incorporates elements of both the old and the new. By definition, the state of transition lacks unique, classical or sharply outlined features. All of this is being conceded in the present analysis, without prejudice to the premise that it is meaningful to utilize the term with regard to modem developing societies (each of which possesses its own specificity) only if transition is a brief interlocking rather than an amorphous and protracted phase. Transition, then, constitutes a transitory phase between two epochs.

The moment of transition is determined by contradictions in the preceding era. The presumption is that the contradictions have reached a point of maturity and their resolution necessarily implies a qualitatively different situation. It is for this reason that transition is a brief period of intensified activity when new social forms triumph over the old in a context of sharp struggle. Transition is analogous to the older Marxist philosophical term 'leap,' as the point at which evolution and quantitative change gives face to revolution and qualitative change. Thereafter, the evolutionary rate of change once again applies. Contemporary transition implies a leap or (better still) a series of leaps, in material production, social relations and consciousness all taking place within a circumscribed period of time and acting in a self-reinforcing manner.

It is the contention here that Marxism provides the single consistent worldview for a resolution of the problems of transition. Long-term and relentless social forces have made transitional monopolies the characteristic and dominant form of capitalism. Transnational capital (which is of course imperialist) has socialized the means of production far beyond the point identified by Lenin in the early part of the twentieth century. Simultaneously, transitional capital has concentrated the control of surplus into fewer and fewer (private) hands, and it has set up an international division of labour that is inherently unstable and crisis-ridden. Meanwhile, proletarian and peasant alliances have affected socialist revolutions in several countries. However incomplete and distorted these socialist revolutions may be, the countries concerned have made the leap from theory to practice as far as socialism is concerned, and they are enmeshed in a set of social contradictions different from those prevailing in the capitalist/imperialist world. Within the underdeveloped sections of the capitalist world, certain social forces operate in a manner that sustains capitalist/ imperialist production relations, while others favour the resumption of material production at a higher level under the aegis of the working class guided by socialist ideology. The latter option provides the setting for that moment of historical change that will usher in a new society. In this connection, transition in the contemporary Third World should be unambiguously identified as 'the transition to socialism'.

In practice, the transition to socialism has always been attempted under inherited conditions of material and social backwardness and powerful external constraints. Socialist revolutions have been initiated with poor technology, they have been conducted where the proletariat has barely crystallized, they have carried the load of transforming pre-capitalist social formations, and they have been faced with the alliance between local propertied classes and the bourgeoisie of the epicentres of imperialism. This was true of the Soviet Union and China; it holds true in greater measure for Cuba, Vietnam, Kampuchea (Cambodia), Mozambique and any other ex-colony where internal contradictions place socialism on the agenda, both as the ultimate goal and as the means of transformation.

The anti-colonial movement as a whole (most of which was non-socialist) must be given credit for reopening the discussion on development and transition – a discussion which first appeared in explicit fashion with the emergence of the Soviet Union after the First World War. Interestingly enough, the heightened consciousness of change in the post-colonial world gave rise to an African journal with the name *Transition*, which was once extremely popular among the intelligentsia on that continent. The reoccurrence of the title in Guyana is more than just coincidence. It attests to similarity of objective and subjective conditions, for the rapid dissolution of aspects of the old order of colonialism forces consideration of the possibilities of qualitatively changed societies. Throughout the 1960s and 1970s, the debate on social transformation has been extended to virtually every part of the globe, but it has not necessarily been made more penetrating. On the contrary, transition and development have been given the vaguest of definitions, and the urgency of revolution has been muted until indistinguishable from the timelessness of evolution. In part, these tendencies have to do with lack of clarity in defining the stage of advanced imperialism that has come to prevail; while above all they stem from bourgeois and petty bourgeois class interpretations of the historical stages which lie ahead.

All classes and strata within the anti-colonial nationalist movements identified alien domination as a negative feature within the world society which was in the process of dissolution. Nationalist class alliances have virtually demolished the old political superstructure of global imperialism. Beyond this point, there can be no unanimity at the national level. The presence of conflicting classes in Third World countries means that there can be no agreement on identifying capitalism and imperialism as the sustaining elements of the Old World Order. Vested interests therefore inevitably deny that transition and development necessitate the demise of capitalism and imperialism. It is the contention here that exploitative classes propose pseudo-solutions to the problems of development. There is no real *problematic* of transition outside the framework of the transition to socialism. A working-class solution offers a revolutionized society; all other proposals modify or extend to greater or lesser degree the system of production and reproduction based on the commoditization of labour power and the alienation of surplus labour.

The post-colonial world is too differentiated to be reduced to any single neo-colonial stereotype. Nevertheless, at one end of the spectrum, there is the classic neo-colonialism of states which have barely altered their politico-military dependence on the former colonizing powers and which have strengthened their ties with international capitalism on the conventional basis of private ownership of the means of production. In such instances – for example Malaysia, Zaire, Trinidad and Tobago – the departure of the colonial administrations has been followed by rapid reconstitution of the local bourgeois and petty bourgeois into transnational capitalist production. Technology transfers, moderate shifts in the international division of labour and the increasing hegemony of the US and Japan are some of the novel features of the classical neo-colonial tendency; but of course the result is the intensification of something which is centuries old: namely, capitalist accumulation on a global scale. For the rest of this analysis, attention will be focused only on those conditions and strategies which at least offer the appearance that they mark the beginning of a new social era.

In several Third World countries, the idea of a 'mixed economy' has been presented in a very attractive format. A private sector, a state-owned sector and a sector of joint ventures would ensure the best of both worlds and would itself constitute a new entity defined as socialism of a special type – see the works of Leopold Senghor, for instance. The fact that these ideas have been most ardently propounded by the ruling class in countries such as Senegal and Singapore is far from reassuring, given that these two states function integrally and comfortably within the imperialist framework. Whether the political leadership of Senegal or Singapore had any intention of building socialism is highly debatable; but, conscious intention apart, the transition to socialism could not have been affected by a few piddling measures of government participation in an economy that remained firmly located within the international capitalist system. The 'mixed economy' is at best a logical fallacy when it is not a deliberate smokescreen for bourgeois and petty bourgeois class interests. Transition must necessarily have mixed features of capitalist relics and embryonic socialism, but the latter would exist in a position of dominance. Transformation would therefore involve the inexorable displacement of the last legacies of capitalism.

A number of Third World countries have declared themselves adherents or discoverers of one species of socialism or another. Where there is a verbal commitment to the transition to socialism, it requires greater scrupulousness to see whether what is proposed is indeed transition. Tanzania's *Ujamaa* socialism is one of the more revealing experiences.

The socialist Arusha Declaration was announced some twelve years ago, in 1967; the implementation has been carried out by a government which commands respect in the Third World, and a significant body of literature has accumulated on *Ujamaa* socialism. One of the most recent and carefully documented studies of the *Ujamaa* village collectives in Tanzania casts serious doubt on whether the process of socialist transition has yet been initiated within the countryside. The principal reasons for this adverse judgement are as follows:

- the low level of production and productivity of the agricultural co-operatives (that is, *Ujamaa* farms);
- the stagnation and regression of the co-operative sector in attracting labour;
- the failure of the co-ops to provide a basis for improved agricultural technology; and
- the bureaucratization rather than democratization of decision-making in the villages.

The researchers Mapolu and Philipson located the fundamental problem not within the villages themselves but in the political framework, which is not firmly based on those classes with the greatest objective interest in transformation: that is, the peasantry and working class. The questions of productive forces, social organization, ideology, state and class were all touched upon in an attempt to explain why socialist development/transition had failed to get under way in the Tanzanian instance. The premises of the assessment were made explicit:

> Since the development of the productive forces specifically includes the development of the general abilities of the producers themselves, co-operation should enable progressive ideas to take root more firmly in all aspects of peasant life; and through co-operative self-management and decision-making, give the direct producers more control over the state apparatus at the

local level, thus enhancing their participation in running the economy at a national level.

Co-operation ... takes on its class characteristics from the general strategy of development in which it is inserted, which is in turn an expression of the interests of the ruling class (or alliance of classes) in each particular social formation.

The low level of production and the rate of progress in rural Tanzania cannot be explained outside an analysis of the existing social structure and of the manner in which the economy is linked to the international capitalist economy. Hence the fact that this particular policy has not proved to be a substantial basis upon which improvement in rural production could be generated arises from the failure of the policy to address itself to the fundamental problems of social structure and economic integration. In essence, therefore, the issue is really political: to be able to sufficiently mobilise and organise the masses in a manner which would extricate the economy from its domination and exploitation by international capitalism, requires a class base and an ideological perspective which hardly a single African government can be credited with at present.

The cogent formulation above allows us to advance the understanding of transition, with particular reference to its political facets. The necessity for social change in the Third World arises out of a conjuncture of contradictions in the system of capitalist/imperialist production. But the appreciation of this necessity and its historical implementation requires the political organization of those social classes with an objective interest in the overthrow of capitalism and the creation of a society freed from the exploitation of labour. The leap from evolution within capitalism to evolution within socialism is no mere spontaneous process. It involves changing levels of consciousness, building working-class organization and self-discipline, and above all the revolutionizing of the state and hence the character of all subsequent social and political intervention.

The struggle for national independence often nurtured euphoric hopes that in the post-independence period national development would virtually take care of itself. 'Seek ye first the political kingdom and all things else will be added thereunto' was a famous dictum of Kwame Nkrumah's. It presupposed that the contradictions which undermined colonialism, and which therefore forced imperialism to alter its political form, would also force an alteration of its social, cultural and economic substance. However, imperialism has proved itself far more powerful and resilient in the periphery than had been suggested in interpretations of 'moribund capitalism'. The local petty bourgeois, comprador classes became more and more marginalized after independence. Such a context was hardly propitious for initiating transition; and the Third World states aimed at modifying the international division of labour so as to promote the indigenous bourgeoisie. An examination of the development plans of the great majority of independent African and Caribbean states discloses almost identical provisions for nurturing domestic private capital; and the growth of indigenous capital has been registered in all Third World countries, alongside of the pauperization of workers, peasants and lumpenproletariat. The emergence of the indigenous bourgeoisie may create tensions with respect to the established multinational capitalists; yet the new class in the periphery contributes to the reproduction of capital and of capitalist social relations on a global scale. The coming into being of such a class has been welcomed by institutions such as the World Bank, and one has grave difficulties in identifying the strategy of indigenous capitalist growth with any variant of socialism whatsoever.

Non-Marxian versions of socialism often deny the existence of classes or at any rate deny the central dynamic imparted to society by antagonistic class contradictions. Even seemingly anti-imperialist leadership – as in Ghana and Tanzania – has espoused this position. Meanwhile, the reality has been that the petty bourgeoisie has consolidated itself as a class. A programme of development which denies the independent existence of the working class and the peasantry is unable to mobilize these classes in their own interests or to make them the leading classes within the state. Conversely, the same denial of class formation enables the petty bourgeoisie and the comprador bourgeoisie to take state control – first surreptitiously and then brazenly – on the abscess of their greater sense of organization during the nationalist phase of anticolonial struggle.

The options which the petty bourgeoisie and allied strata may pursue in relation to international capital vary from joint ventures to the nationalization of foreign and domestic capital. Obviously, there is a difference between the uninhibited private enterprise in Trinidad or Morocco and the attempted state ownership in Guyana and Algeria. However, it is quite remarkable how the instances of state intervention have failed to produce any substantial improvements in living patterns as far as the mass of direct producers are concerned. Even more remarkable is the tendency towards instant reversal of such progressive objectives as might have been secured by the nationalist mass base at an earlier period. A progressive foreign policy, for instance, has been known to change into its opposite virtually overnight. Transition is movement in a given direction – it is not a shuttle service. Yet, ownership of the means of production has been transferred from private hands to the state and then back again to private hands – in Indonesia, in Egypt, in Ghana. One could say that, objectively, the period of state ownership merely served to guarantee that some section of the indigenous population would be better prepared to undertake the role of small and medium-sized private capitalists in the era of the multinational giants.

There is one particularly troubling question in evaluating those 'progressive' countries that differ in some respects from the classic neo-colonial states. Have they begun to chart a new course which is anti-imperialist and non-capitalist or is it that they represent socio-political formations which capitalism can accommodate and welcome? Advanced sectors of French capitalism are quite reconciled to the Algerian 'experiment'; the World Bank finds it useful to associate with the Tanzanian petty bourgeoisie; North American mining capital has given the stamp of approval to the Guinean regime; and with respect to Guyana, the American state ignores the application of its own recently designed 'human rights' criteria. The implication is that imperialism has not yet been stretched to the limit of its potential. It will accommodate states that have taken steps against foreign private property in response to internal and external forces, provided the new juridical property relations affect neither the long-term contribution of the country to global capitalist accumulation and provided the state continues to guarantee class differentiation. The crucial variable is the composition of the state. Any given Third World country is at least arguably transitional when the classes and strata which were pre-eminent in the colonial period begin to lose their control over the means of production and the state. To put it another way, the movement towards socialism demands a prior constitution of the working class into the state so that the state would increasingly reflect the role of the working class in production.

States with different class bases may concur with respect to some policies of national development. Changes in the international economy, for instance, are being advocated by all Third World nations. The accumulating petty bourgeoisie concurs with realists among the leading bourgeois spokesmen, who admit that the old international order cannot survive with the same form and content; hence the calls for a new international economic order and for the initiating of a so-called North/South dialogue. In effect, the strains of imperialism in its present stage demand partial change if there is to be a new lease of life. Marxists and working-class intellectuals have long called for revamping the international economic order. They can claim to have been more resolute and consistent in working for such changes, and have realistically pressed for the best of the short-term arrangements even within the strictures set up by agreements such as the Lomé Convention.[1] However, working-class objectives are more far reaching than those adjustments that give breathing space to accumulating classes on the periphery of capitalism. After all, it is from the perspective of alienated labour in the Third World that the operations of the old international order are most intolerable. It is only a working-class state that will revolutionize social reproduction within its own boundaries and simultaneously contribute to the final dismantling of global imperialism.

By implication, the leap towards socialism is inseparable from the conscious intentions of working-class leadership made manifest through the state. All historical leaps have not been consciously directed. On the contrary, passages from one mode of production to another previous to socialism have been the result of forces that were improperly understood even by the main classes in the drama. The bourgeois class could hardly have been said to have directed the early formation of capitalist society. Socialism is unique because of the highly developed consciousness of the two combatant classes – the bourgeoisie and the proletariat. Social relations in Third World countries today cannot be changed independently of men's will. Conscious decisions have to be taken to change the forces of production (including the size, skill and composition of the working class), the relations of production and the mediation of those relations by the state. Of course, 'conscious intentions' mean much more than mere statements or ideological declamations. Verbal adherence to Marxism in Congo-Brazzaville, Guinea, Somalia and Ethiopia has accompanied social developments indistinguishable from those in states where there has been an explicit rejection of the theory of class contradictions: that is to say, Marxist intellectuals have been silenced, workers' representatives have been eliminated and the working class as a whole excluded from democratic participation in social reconstruction. For transition to have validity, it must include the widespread promotion of socialist education without caricature, and it must rest firmly on workers' democracy.

The contradictions within the imperialist system and between imperialism and socialism provide the objective basis for the passage to socialism in dependent capitalist countries. This has to be reiterated and then qualified by the equally important variable of action by class-conscious elements. Transition therefore equates with guided transformation; it means social policy directed by the working class in its own interest. Broad and challenging possibilities are opened up by the notion of workers' democracy, which has relevance both at the point of production and within the several levels and branches of the state. It should also be clear that such transition would allocate meaningful roles to strata which are closely or potentially allied to the working class: above all, the peasantry as well as independent craftsmen, shopkeepers, the lower salariat, students, technocrats and other intellectuals. The scope of the present discourse does not permit elaboration of the complex interrelated problems that have to be resolved once the process of transition is under way. In the final analysis, comprehensive answers will be forthcoming through social practice and attempted transformation.

16

Decolonization

When dealing with such a broad topic in a short time, one automatically runs the risk of being extremely superficial. Consequently, I will concentrate my attention on one particular hypothesis, attempting to draw certain correlations between colonialism and neo-colonialism, and will illustrate the hypothesis with reference primarily to Southern Africa.

If we look at the UN Committee on Decolonization, we find that the committee is concerned at the present time with countries such as the Republic of South Africa, Zimbabwe, Namibia, the French and the Cameroon Islands and the French territories of the Afars and the Issas of Africa.[1] They are concerned, in other words, with the remnants of formal colonialism. That is what decolonization means in that particular context, to terminate the formal, colonial rule of Africa.

Many Africans and non-Africans would perhaps say that the subject is passé, for certainly that subject is less important and less pressing than the question of what one does with those states that are nominally independent on the African continent. In other words, for many people living in the African continent, the issue is not nearly or perhaps not principally freedom from formal colonial rule, but the enlargement of freedom within the states which are juridically independent. And that means, of course, confronting the neo-colonial providence that has been established in the wake of colonialism.

My proposition is that those African states which are yet to win their independence – which are yet to be decolonized in the manner in which the UN Committee on Decolonization approaches the subject – are carrying through their struggle for independence at a time when other Africans and other peoples elsewhere are carrying through a struggle against neo-colonialism. And this overlap, this interpenetration of the existence of colonialism with the existence of neo-colonialism clearly affects the character of decolonization in a number of ways.

It affects the character of the decolonization of those states which are still formally non-independent, which are still formally colonies, and it affects the character of decolonization in those areas which are normally colonies. It is this particular interrelationship of contemporary Africa that I would like to examine briefly.

My starting point would be the so-called territories of Portuguese Africa in the 1960s, now the independent countries of Mozambique, Angola and Guinea-Bissau. But in the late 1960s and the early 1970s the independence movements were developing in all three of these territories one of the characteristics discernable in the writings of leaders such as Amilcar Cabral in Guinea-Bissau before his assassination, Samora Machel in Mozambique and Agostinho Neto in Angola. One of the characteristics was a concern with looking at those states in Africa which were already nominally independent. But the programme for decolonization or liberation of Angola, Mozambique and Guinea-Bissau, respectively, was, in part, dependent upon a pattern already set by independent African countries. There was a yardstick. Angola could look to Zaire, Mozambique could look to Zambia, Guinea-Bissau could look to Guinea and it could look to Senegal and ask itself what was happening in these supposedly independent African countries and whether the pattern of change represented the type of goals, the type of society that they in Guinea-Bissau, Angola and Mozambique should be struggling for. There was a pattern; there was a blueprint. There was an actual objective, historical situation with which they could compare, which did not exist, of course, in the earlier period of decolonization.

Then, my argument is that what was programmed in Angola and in Guinea-Bissau was, in fact, determined by the prior access to independence by a number of other African countries, and the illustration of what independence could mean in an African country. You may easily test this for yourself in the writings of the aforementioned political leaders. They would say time and again our struggle is not merely to replace the Portuguese; our struggle is not merely to stain the structures of exploitation and replace white maintainers or white supervisors of that structure with black maintainers of the same structure. They would continually indicate that it is more than the need to raise a glass and celebrate a national anthem that the people of Angola and Mozambique and Guinea-Bissau were struggling for, and it seems to me that it is a very important dimension of the evolution of thought and action and organization within the liberated territories of what used to be Portuguese Africa.

Of course, there are people engaged in armed struggle who are making, very often, the maximum sacrifice of life, making the sacrifice of limbs, making the sacrifice of being uprooted from their homes. Such people had to be more careful in defining goals that would be considered the goals of decolonization. In a previous era, it was permissible and understandable that people merely said we are struggling for independence, which means freedom from the white man's rule. It was permissible, but at a later stage, when this freedom was supposedly achieved in a number of African countries, then the material conditions of life did not radically alter. And then the cultural conditions were not radically transformed. And then the social structure, the political structure was merely transformed only insofar as it allowed a new possessing class to take control. Then, people in other parts of Africa began to wonder whether this was the kind of state and society for which they were making these tremendous sacrifices. And by and large their answer was no. No one in Angola and Mozambique and Guinea-Bissau could be mobilized to sustain that tremendous people's war on the basis of simply saying we want to be like the other African states which have gained their independence.

And the deepening of the appreciation that undoubtedly took place in Portuguese Africa was in part dictated by the logic of the armed struggle, but it was also partially influenced by what decolonization supposedly meant in these other parts of Africa. I believe in Zimbabwe the situation is bound to be the same thing; that if for the sake of argument in 1964 when Smith unilaterally declared independence on behalf of the white settlers of Rhodesia, if, at that date, the British had had the power and will to organize the transition and the handover to black rule, they would have given the government over to Zanu and Zapu. They would have given the government over to the masses in Matabeleland and Harare. And the pattern which would have emerged in Zimbabwe from 1964 until now could not have been radically different from the pattern that has evolved in Zambia from independence until the present date because the leadership is from the same social structure; the leadership did not indicate that it had any other ideological presence other than that which others had in Zambia. And the vast majority of the population – the peasantry, the workers, the transient workers and permanent workers in the farms and mines – were not yet involved as participants in that movement for national independence. And therefore, to my mind, in 1964 a transition to independence which we may call decolonization, would have meant something radically different from what decolonization means today in the era of neo-colonialism? The existence of neo-colonialism is there as a guide which transforms the character of the demands and the expectations of those involved as far as decolonization is concerned.

Today in Zimbabwe the masses of the population have already been involved in part in carrying through a political struggle which had to be sustained while it was illegal, and in carrying through a political struggle that has a very significant armed component, having been raised to the level of an armed people's war; it means that there are so many dimensions which have been enlarged, including primarily the political dimension and the dimension of popular participation. So, for Zimbabwe to be decolonized today, it requires, of course, the removal of Smith as it would have required in 1964, but it requires more than that. It requires that the Zimbabwean people should make certain kinds of choices about the options which are being presented by the leadership – and if, as seems to be the case, most of the leadership which survives the original, earlier era, has lost touch with the sensibilities and the demands of the Zimbabwean people in this process of learning, then that leadership automatically becomes outdated. And there will have to be new leadership, new structures, new demands which reflect the contemporary period. So this is the change that is being wrought, in part, by the interpretation of the stages of colonialism and neo-colonialism.

More than that, to the peoples of Zimbabwe we can add Namibia and the Republic of South Africa, who are all colonized in the old, traditional sense, and are also in a position to witness certain changes taking place on the African continent which indicate that, after all, the political rule characteristic of colonialism was only one facet – and at that, a rather superficial element within the pattern of imperialism – and that colonial rule as a political phenomenon was, of course, reflective of much deeper forces of penetration into the African continent – forces which actually intervened in transforming the mode of production within Africa and in transforming the social relations within Africa, forces which went beyond the mere political boundaries as established by the British, the French, the Belgians, Italians, and so on. And today I believe these forces can be seen more clearly because the facade of political rule has been removed in many territories, and the reality of economic exploitation exposed for all to see. One can see, for example, that not only with the end of colonialism has there been a clear rise of the forces such as the multinational corporations acting now as the new links, as the new forms for guaranteeing the export of surplus; but one can see that there has always been an underlying, economic partition and a continuing economic repartition which has gone on during the colonial period and is even more marked today. And this again, I believe, gives some new dimensions to what decolonization must mean because decolonization in the early epoch meant dealing with the political power which had formal control over one's political system. The British at Westminster controlled the territory, then decolonization meant going to the British and demanding that such political rule be withdrawn.

But decolonization today means going to these economic command centres of the capitalist world-system and recognizing that one has to break the particular character of the connections that exist with those command centres, and therefore enter the United States of America. The US has never been a colonial power on the African continent, but always lying somewhat in the shadow, lying somewhat in the background behind French, British and Belgian colonialism. American capital has emerged in various parts of Africa but particularly in the southern section from Zaire southwards to the Cape behind the cover provided by the Portuguese, the Belgians, the British in Rhodesia and the South African government in Namibia and the Republic of South Africa.

There was a continual process of economic repartition in so far as the United States was constantly gaining at the expense of other colonial powers, in their share of the African trade, in this share of the investment in Africa and of the profits which were being repatriated from Africa. This process was highlighted by the development of the Anglo-American corporation in the inter-war years and in the full galaxy of multinational corporations in the post-war years. The United States has clearly come in a crooked position where it is now hegemonic within this economic partition of Southern Africa. It has quite clearly taken over from the Portuguese; quite a while ago it took over the leadership from the Belgians and the French in the old Congo, the Republic of Zaire, and it has for long time been bolstering and supporting the British in the Republic of South Africa, and has clearly taken the lead from the British in South African investments. So that economic repartition is a very significant element because the peoples of Southern Africa today in speaking about decolonization have not merely to look to their colonial power or the white settler minority which is resident; it has to look beyond that and ask what forces sustain the particular mode of production, what sources sustain the mine labour and the farm labour, what forces sustain the particular ways in which Southern Africa is integrated into the capitalist world-system. And the principal forces which sustain this happen to reside within the most developed capitalist sectors of this economy, the multinational or transnational sector.

The entry of the United States into the diplomatic realm and the political manoeuvrings around Zimbabwe and around Angola and the Republic of South Africa is ample testimony to the fact that the United States has been forced to assume this hegemony, taking over the political role of policing Southern Africa from the British who are no longer capable of so doing.

It seems to me then if we're going to enlarge the meaning of decolonization, one of the most useful ways of doing so is precisely to lay side by side these two modalities of colonialism and neo-colonialism and recognize that in the process of carrying through a struggle for decolonization in the formal territories, one is automatically guided by the transition taking place in the continent as a whole – which includes, of course, those areas that are supposed to be independent. I would go further; it works the other way. The reverse is also true, that in a territory which is supposedly independent, looking at the total configuration inside of Southern Africa where the Africans of Southern Africa are fighting against apartheid, seemingly against apartheid alone, where the people of Zimbabwe are fighting for independence. Those in the rest of Africa can well ask themselves what are the principal contradictions manifested on our continent today, and they will know those contradictions go far beyond the old formulations of mere political rule. Someone looking at the configuration in Southern Africa from territories such as Tanzania, Kenya, Uganda and Nigeria and the like, such an individual must be able to recognize that the confrontation and the contradictions are much broader, much deeper than the confrontation which they themselves in the independent African states might have considered to be the most important during the 1960s.

One takes a look at the economic structures to recognize that there is no way to speak about decolonization without talking about the recovery of the national resources, for instance. Yet, the question of recovering the national resources has really only been posed in the period subsequent to political independence, and it still remains a legitimate concern for decolonization. So, we have to be careful with the use of language here, or we will wrap ourselves in some knots. We now, therefore, have to recognize the continuum of change and recognize that political independence was merely a moment, and perhaps not necessarily a very important moment in a totality of transformation which we might call decolonization, and that the territory which has achieved political independence, if not necessarily perhaps to lose the terminology of the colony, at the very least we must retain the title of neo-colonial until we can see more fundamental changes taking place. And if those changes are going to take place at the level of the economic structure, there are those of us who would argue that they must automatically take place also within the class structures because economies of formally colonial or neo-colonial territories must be sustained by some social mechanisms. They don't operate in a vacuum. There are specific social classes which represent, first of all, the links between external capital and the indigenous labour, and there are local classes that are emerging which are consolidating their own strength vis-à-vis other sectors of the African people, usually by consolidating around the state apparatus and securing a large portion of the goods and services that are being produced within the economy. And, therefore again because of the conjunction of stages, one is forced to ask more profound questions than a nationalist or a decolonizer might have asked a decade ago. One has to give a social content, an ideological content to the programme for decolonization. Whereas decolonization was, some years ago understood as Africanization, one now has to talk about socialism as an integral part – not a later stage – of the very process of decolonization itself. Without speaking about reorganizing the class relations within Africa, one is not in fact addressing oneself to cutting the reproduction of capitalism as it has reproduced itself in Africa over the last five decades or more.

It seems then that when Cabral, who was writing within the period of struggle when he had not yet got rid of formal colonial rule, said, 'we regard it as indispensable, as an indispensable prerequisite for national independence that we should have recovery of our national resources', he had reached a level of analysis which is only now being reached by many Africans within independent Africa who had postponed the question of the recovery of economic resources as though it were not relevant to the phase of decolonization. But to someone like Amilcar Cabral, and to Samora Machel and to Agostinho Neto, and hopefully we would see to some of the Zimbabwe nationalists such as Mugabe, the question of recovery of the national resources is one of the items that has to be placed on the agenda in the present phase of the achievement of political independence. They have to organize political movements which are in themselves more participatory, more representative of the mass of the common people in their own territories, and therefore at the moment of the conquest of state power these systems will incorporate an element of participation that will allow the mass of these mobilized cadres to operate in a situation where at least there will be layers of grassroots leadership prepared with both political education as well as the arms which may be necessary to combat the deformation that takes place under neo-colonial domination.

To be concrete, let's look at the example of FRELIMO.[2] This was a system which did not initially conquer the state power of the Portuguese. Rather it began to create and initiate systems of political participation and political organization and civilian administration in the liberated areas which at least represent a counter to the alienation which one would find when you inherit the state structure that was left by the colonialists, so that I can assure that when one inherits the state structure of colonialism, one merely becomes a tool of that colonialism. It is not that such a structure can become the tool of independent Africans, but rather the structure becomes the determinant and the African rulers become mere participants in the same type of capitalist and authoritarian structure. And it seems to me that in those parts of Africa which are still struggling for independence, they have the opportunity – given these lessons from so-called independent Africa, from neo-colonial Africa – to deal with issues which have not at all been posed in the earlier phase.

And I conclude with a look at the independent states which are aiding the liberation movements of Southern Africa. One rough yardstick that indicates the level or extent to which an African state has been decolonized in any profound way is the extent to which that African state is capable of entering into meaningful relations with the liberation movements. That is to say, outside of Southern Africa it is not an accident that the most conservative, the most reactionary states are the ones which have consistently failed to give any meaningful support to the liberation movements. They all start from the premise of national liberation. Yet, they are incapable of and unwilling to give support to the liberation movements. They are the ones who always drag their feet with regard to contributions to the OAU Liberation Committee.[3] They are the ones that always put obstacles in the way of any of the more progressive sectors of the liberation movements. They are the ones, who around Angola, prevaricated and delayed and manipulated to try and avoid the recognition of the MPLA,[4] and instead, to introduce the government which incorporated UNITA[5] and the FNLA[6] as spokesman of the imperialism interest so that one can use this almost as a touchtone, the formal independent African state. What attitude does it take towards the independent states that are struggling for formal colonialism? To them, if Southern Africa were to become independent in exactly the same way as Zambia or Kenya is independent, then that is good enough.

I spoke, for example, with a representative of the OAU Liberation Committee who said at the time – when it was clear that the Portuguese were about to be defeated – that as far as they were concerned in Mozambique, the task of the Liberation Committee was at an end. They couldn't care less to whom the Portuguese gave independence because the Portuguese were manoeuvring to try and give independence to some other organizations in Mozambique, in Guinea-Bissau and in Angola too. And this official was saying that it was okay with him. He said, 'we are not concerned with who is going to rule and how they are going to rule. We are only concerned with freedom; that is decolonization.' Such officials and such elements of the African ruling class in independent African countries would prefer to see an independence that is merely nominal, because the Mozambique that FRELIMO is striving for is something more than merely nominal independence and threatens not just the Republic of South Africa but threatens the elites of independent Zambia too. And it threatens Malawi by virtue of the fact that there are some sorts of social confirmations taking place in this state but not in their own.

Let us sharpen our awareness of what is to be done in Southern Africa, as well as what is to be done in independent Africa, by recognizing that the definition of decolonization is itself undergoing transformation – that it is becoming richer and deeper because of people's struggles, because of the life experience of Africans in various parts of the continent; and by recognizing that, in effect, decolonization is going to be inseparable from a total strategy for liberation that encompasses a control of the material resources, which encompasses a restructuring of the society so that those who produce have the principal say in how their wealth is going to be distributed. These essentials would have to be taken into account when we consider decolonization in any part of the African continent, and indeed outside, although that is not our concern at the present time.

Notes

2. Masses in Action

1 For an exception to this pattern, see *New World Quarterly*, 1: 1, 1963.

2 This chapter is largely based on the newspaper reports for the period, as contained in the *Chronicle* and the *Argosy*.

3 G. Pendle, *A History of Latin America* (Penguin, 1963).

4 C. Jayawardena, *Conflict and Solidarity in a Guianese Plantation* (Routledge, 1963), p. 12.

5 Raymond Smith suggests that this was because the East Indian 'middle class' was not accepted by the already established 'coloured' and Portuguese 'middle class'. See R.T. Smith, *British Guiana* (Oxford University Press, 1962).

6 Smith, *British Guiana*.

7 See P. Ruhomon, *Centennary History of the East Indians of British Guiana* (Daily Chronicle, 1938), in which he gives the credit for founding the association to his brother, Joseph Ruhomon, who started an East Indian Association in Berbice in 1916. However, this association was virtually defunct in 1919, when the Georgetown effort was made.

8 *Editors' note:* James Crosby was the Immigration Agent-General in British Guiana from 1858–80 who took frequent legal action against plantation owners on behalf of immigrant laborers.

9 A.R. Webber, *Centenary History and Handbook of British Guiana* (Guyana Heritage Society, 1931).

10 I have been unable to ascertain the exact terms of the concession, but the matter was by no means satisfactorily dealt with, and further measures had to be taken in more recent times.

3. Marxism and African Liberation

1 Consciencism is a syncretic and controversial political philosophy developed by Kwame Nkrumah in the course of establishing an

independent Ghana. For an in-depth elaboration from its founder, see K. Nkrumah, *Conscienciism: Philosophy and Ideology for Decolonization* (Monthly Review Press, 2009; originally published 1964).

4. Marxism as a Third World Ideology

1 Leopold Senghor was a celebrated poet, the first president of Senegal (1960–80), a prominent theoretician of Négritude, and a politician that looked to both develop an 'indigenous socialism' opposed to Marxism and preserve post-colonial Senegal's special relationship with France.

5. Labour as a Conceptual Framework for Pan-African Studies

1 In 1975, Dahomey changed its name to the People's Republic of Benin.

7. The Historical Roots of African Underdevelopment

1 *Editors' note:* Present-day Benin.

8. Problems of Third World Development

1 Obote was overthrown as president in a military coup led by Idi Amin in 1971.

9. Slavery and Underdevelopment

1 Useful bibliographies are to be found in the following: F. Bonilla and R. Girlng (eds.), *Structures of Dependency* (Stanford University, 1973); N. Girvan (ed.), 'Dependence in the Old World and the New', *Social and Economic Studies*, Special issue, 1973; P.

Gutkind and I. Wallerstein, *The Political Economy of Contemporary Africa* (Sage Publications, 1976).

2 S. Amin, *Accumulation on a World Scale: A Critique of the Theory of Underdevelopment*, 2 vols., (Monthly Review Press, 1974), see, pp. 19, 29 – 'The underdeveloped economy is a piece of a single machine, the capitalist world economy. It occupies a particular place in this worldwide system, and fulfills definite functions in it … The theory of underdevelopment and development can only be the theory of the accumulation of capital on a world scale.'

3 I. Wallerstein, *The Modern World-System: Capitalist Agriculture and the Origins of the European World-Economy in the Sixteenth Century* (Academic Press, 1974), see especially pp. 86, 87.

4 See, for example, R. Davis, *The Rise of the Atlantic Economies* (Cornell University Press, 1973).

5 Wallerstein, *The Modern World-System*, p. 89.

6 S. Amin, 'Underdevelopment and Dependence in Black Africa – Origins and Contemporary Forms', *Journal of Modern African Studies*, 10(4), 1972.

7 P. Curtin, *The Atlantic Slave Trade: A Census* (Wisconsin University Press, 1969), p. 271.

8 J. Inikori, Working Paper on the Slave Trade, UNESCO seminar, Haiti, 1978.

9 J. Fage, *A History of West Africa* (Cambridge University Press, 1969), pp. 84–9.

10 W. Rodney, *West Africa and the Atlantic Slave Trade* (East African Publishing House, 1967); *A History of the Upper Guinea Coast, 1540-1900* (Clarendon Press,1970); *How Europe Underdeveloped Africa* (Bogle L'Ouverture Publications Tanzania Publishing House, 1972).

11 W. Rodney, 'Gold Coast', *Transactions of the Ghana Historical Society*, 10, 1969.

12 This academic position is well represented. See, for example, D. Neumark, *Foreign Trade and Economic Development in Africa: A Historical Perspective* (1964) and A.M. Kamarck, *The Economics of African Development* (1967).

13 J. Fage, *History of West Africa*, p. 89 (emphasis in original).

14 A.G. Hopkins, *An Economic History of West Africa* (Longmans, 1973).

15 Marx devoted some attention to this point when he wrote: 'The slave market maintains its supply of the commodity labour power by war, piracy, etc., and this rapine is not prompted by the process of circulation, but by the actual appropriation of the labour-power of others by direct physical compulsion.' See *Capital*, Vol. II (Progress Publishers, 1956) p. 483.

16 For a recent contribution, see J. Kombo Moyana, 'The Political Economy of the Migrant Labour System', *African Development*, 1(1), 1976.

17 C. Thomas, *Dependence and Transformation: The Economics of the Transition to Socialism*, (Monthly Review Press, 1974), p. 59.

18 On the problem of runaways in Guyana, see A. Thompson, *Some Problems Concerning Slave Desertion in Guyana, c. 1750–1814* (Cave Hill, 1976).

19 A.H. Adamson, *Sugar Without Slaves, The Political Economy of British Guiana, 1838–1904* (Yale University Press, 1972); and J.R. Mandle, *The Plantation Economy: Population and Economic Change in Guyana, 1838–1960* (Temple University Press, 1973).

20 Public Record Office, CO111, Governor's Despatch, 12 August 1902.

21 B. Hindess and P. Hirst, *Pre-Capitalist Modes of Production* (Routledge & Kagan Paul, 1975), p. 161.

22 P. Beiguelman, 'The Destruction of Modern Slavery: A Theoretical Issue', *Review*, 2(1), 1978.

23 C. Thomas, *From Foreign Plantations to State Farming: A Study of Change in the Dominant Crop of a Backward Agrarian System* (International Labour Organisation, 1979).

24 M.N. Fraginals, *The Sugarmill: The Socio-economic Complex of Sugar in Cuba* (Monthly Review Press, 1976), see especially p. 18.

25 See Adamson, *Sugar Without Slaves*; and Mandle, *The Plantation Economy*.

26 The basic work in this school of interpretation is R. Farley, 'The Rise of the Peasantry in British Guiana', *Social and Economic Studies*, 2, 1954; and his 'Aspects of Economic History of British Guiana, 1781–1852', PhD, University of London, 1956.

10. The British Colonialist School of African Historiography and the Question of African Independence

1 *Editors' note*: See M. Perham, *The Colonial Reckoning: The Reith Lectures 1961* (Fontana, 1963).

2 *Editors' note*: See A. Burns, *Colonial Civil Servant* (Allen & Unwin, 1940).

11. Education in Colonial Africa

1 The mid-1920s saw the work of the Phelps–Stokes Commission as well as other enquiries by the British and French which gave direction to what was until then an ad hoc missionary effort with marginal state participation.

2 For one of the best discussions on the Indigenous African educational systems, see A. Moumouni, *Education in Africa* (André Deutsch, 1968).

3 The perception was based on colours, patterns and shape of horns. See, for example, A.T. Bryant, *Olden Times in Zululand and Natal* (Longmans, Green & Co, 1929) pp. 573, 574. And for a broader and more modern survey of the same theme, see W. Allan, *The African Husbandman* (Oliver & Boyd, 1967).

4 See, for example, A. Richards, *Land, Labour and Diet in Northern Rhodesia: Economic Study of the Bemba Tribe* (Oxford University Press, 1939) for a comment to this effect on the Bemba.

5 Dr Kofi Busia relates how his secondary schooling at Mfantsipim in Cape Coast made him a stranger when he returned home to Asante after a few years. See K.A. Busia, *Purposeful Education for Africa* (Mouton, 1964).

6 This point is excellently brought out in J.K. Nyere, *Education for Self-Reliance* (Tanzania Government Printer, 1967).

7 See J.B. Bolibaugh, 'French Educational Strategies for Sub-Saharan Africa', (PhD dissertation, Stanford.) Therefore, the combined function of the educational policy was to secure both service and loyalty. This was specifically stated in a colonial administrative ordinance of 1899 for Madagascar; which read as follows: 'To make the young Malagasy faithful and obedient subjects of France, and to offer an education the character of which would be industrial, agricultural, and commercial so as to insure that settlers and various public services of the colony can meet their personnel requirements.' Quoted in H. Kitchen (ed.), *The Educated African: A Country-by-Country Survey of Educational Development in Africa, compiled by Ruth Sloan Associates,* (Praeger, 1962), p. 252.

8 See, for example, F. Bourret, *Ghana, The Road to Independence, 1919–1957* (Stanford University Press, 1960).

9 Bolibaugh, 'French Educational Strategies'.

10 One study that documents the blatantly inferior education in settler areas is L. James, *Racialism and Education: Aspects of Development in former British Central Africa* (Brown & Kroger, 1965).

11 This is discussed in Ghana's case by D. Austin, *The Politics of Ghana, 1946–1960* (Oxford University Press, 1964).

12 See, for example, J.S. Coleman, *Nigeria: Background to Nationalism* (University of California Press, 1958).

12. Education in Africa and Contemporary Tanzania

1 Under the rubric of 'African Education', writers almost invariably refer to Western education in colonial Africa, and ignore the African antecedents. An outstanding exception is the work of Abdou Moumini, *Education in Africa* (André Deutsch, 1968).

2 'Secret societies' and other similar confraternities in pre-colonial Africa quite consciously established goals for the society as a whole and provided instruction to that end. The Ekine dancing society of Kalabari in the Niger Delta is a case in point. Its role was to integrate newcomers into Kalabari by stimulating them to master the local (Ijo) language, customs and worldview. Consequently, although Kalabari was heterogeneous in its ethnic composition, its population had a common cultural identity. See E.J. Algoa, 'The Niger Delta States and their Neighbours, 1600–1800' in J.F.A Ajayi and M. Crowder (eds.), *History of West Africa: Volume One* (Colombia University Press, 1972) and J.F.A. Ajayi and R. Horton, 'From Fishing Village to City-State: A Social History of New Calabar', in M. Douglas and P.M. Kaberry (eds.), *Man in Africa* (Barnes & Noble, 1969).

3 J.B. Bolibaugh, *French Educational Strategies for Sub-Saharan Africa*, (University Microfilms, 1968), p. 125. Bolibaugh's study is one of the best expositions of colonial educational policy, especially since the French were prone to explain their objectives more fully than the British.

4 This passing reference to the nature of pre-colonial African societies is not intended to convey the impression of a static situation. Non-antagonistic contradictions could and did transform themselves into antagonistic ones. However, the transition took place slowly, and made itself manifest only in a few places.

5 See, for example, K.A. Busia, *Purposeful Education in Africa* (Humanities Press, 1964), p. 7: 'At the end of my first year at school ... I went home for the Christmas vacation. I had not been home for four years, and on that visit, I became painfully aware of my isolation. I understood our community far less than boys of my own age who had never been to school.'

6 A great deal of quantitative data is to be found in H. Kitchen (ed.), *The Educated African* (Praeger, 1962).

7 In December 1971, when Tanzania celebrated ten years of independence, it was their proud boast that they had achieved far more in those years than the British and German colonists had before. Several former officials of the British colonial regime were invited to test the validity of this claim. With specific reference to schooling, some data are available in J. Cameron and W.A. Dodd, *Society, Schools and Progress in Tanzania* (Pergamon, 1970).

8 A few letters, both critical and supportive of the institution, have appeared in the national press. No formal study of the National Service has been published.

9 *Mwalimu* means 'master teacher'.

10 J.K. Nyerere, *Education for Self-Reliance* (Tanzania, 1987).

11 TANU are the initials for the political party headed by President Julius Nyerere – the Tanzanian African National Union.

12 Cameron and Dodd are among those who are confused and confusing on this point. See also A.R. Thompson, 'Ideas Underlying British Colonial Education in Tanganyika', in I. Reanick (ed.), *Tanzania: Revolution by Education* (Humanities Press, 1970).

13 *Mzee* is a title of respect.

14 C.L.R. James, *A History of Pan-African Revolt* (Drum and Spear Press, 1969), p. 133.

15 P. Foster, 'Education for Self-Reliance: A Critical Evaluation', in Richard Jolly (ed.), *Education in Africa: Research and Action* (International Publication Services, 1970).

16 A transcript of Paulo Freire's discussions in Dar es Salaam in 1971 is held by the Institute of Adult Education of the University of Dar es Salaam. The same is in progress with respect to his 1972 visit. This quotation is also cited in a review of Freire's *Pedagogy of the Oppressed* by M.J. Mbilinyi, in *The African Review*, April 1972.

13. Tanzanian *Ujamaa* and Scientific Socialism

1 J.K. Nyerere, 'Ujamaa – the Basis of African Socialism', in *Freedom and Unity*, (Oxford University Press Tanzania, 1962) p. 162. The opening sentences make this point: 'Socialism, like democracy, is an attitude of mind ... The purpose of this paper is to examine that attitude. It is not intended to define the institutions which may be required to embody it in modern society.'

2 Significantly, Tanzanians or foreign observers who have been left

behind by the trend towards heightened socialist understanding seldom pay attention to more recent pronouncements of *Mwalimu* Nyerere, but consider 'Ujamaa – the Basis of African Socialism' as a final blueprint.

3 F. Engels, 'Socialism, Utopian and Scientific', in Marx and Engels, *Selected Works*, Vol. 2, (Foreign Languages Publishing House, 1962).

4 See, for example, S. Amin, *The Class Struggle in Africa* (African Research Group, 1964) and K. Nkrumah, *Class Struggle in Africa* (Panaf Publications, 1970).

5 *Editors' note:* TANU are the initials for the political party headed by President Julius Nyerere – the Tanzanian African National Union.

6 L. Senghor, *Nationhood and the African Road to Socialism* (Présence africaine, 1960), see English translation, 1962, p. 78. The most relevant passage reads as follows: 'Our plan will include three sectors: a socialised sector – agriculture; a mixed sector – public utilities and companies with mixed economy; and a free sector. The latter – banks, commerce, industry – will itself be oriented towards the objects of the Plan and, to a certain extent, controlled ... The mixed sector will preferably comprise transport and energy – within the limits of our possibilities, of course. As for agriculture, we are fortunate that it has traditionally been socialistic, because of the communal nature of Negro African Society.' Glimpses of an interesting critique of this position by the Ugandan John Kakonge are to be found in B. Onuoha, *Elements of African Socialism*, (Andre Deutsch, 1965), pp. 89–92. At that time, Kakonge espoused Marxist ideas.

7 *The Arusha Declaration and TANU's Policy on Socialism and Self-Reliance*, (TANU, 1967), p. 13.

8 J.K. Nyerere, 'Socialism and Rural Development', in *Freedom and Socialism (Uhuru Na Ujamaa): A Selection from Writings and Speeches 1965–1967* (Oxford University Press, 1969), especially pp. 342–4.

9 The one available text which juxtaposes Marx and Proudhon is unfortunately rather unenlightening. It is J.H. Jackson, *Marx, Proudhon and European Socialism* (English Universities Press, 1964), see pp. 110–11 for Proudhon's view of the petty producer.

10 See Franco Venturi, *The Roots of Revolution: a History of the Populist and Socialist Movements in Nineteenth Century Russia*, English translation, 1960. See especially the chapter on N.G. Chernyshevsky.

11 Marx and Engels, *Selected Correspondence* (Foreign Languages Publishing House, Translation of Russian edition of 1953), Engels

to Kablukova, August 1880 and Marx to Zasulich, March 1881.

12 Marx and Engels, *Selected Correspondence*, Engels to Danielson, October 1893.

13 Marx and Engels, *Selected Correspondence*, Marx to Zasulich, March 1881.

14 Marx and Engels, *Selected Correspondence*, Marx to the editorial board of the *Otechestvenniye Zapiski*, November 1877.

15 I.A. Potekhin cites an instance to the effect, which arose out of a discussion of 'African Socialism'. See W. Friedland and C.G. Rosberg (eds.), *African Socialism* (Stanford University Press, 1964). In all fairness to Leopold Senghor, it should be noted that his hostility to Scientific Socialism is seldom ill-informed, and he shows his awareness of points of clarification such as those raised in the letters cited in notes 12 and 13.

16 Marx and Engels, *Selected Correspondence*, Engels to Danielson, March 1892.

17 V.I. Lenin, *Collected Works* Vol. 3 (Foreign Languages Publishing House 1963). *The Development of Capitalism in Russia* was written in 1905 as an elaboration of one of Lenin's first analyses of political economy, entitled *New Economic Development in Peasant Life*. For this, see Vol. 1.

18 Marx and Engels, *Selected Correspondence*, Engels to Plekhanov, February 1895.

19 Marx, *Pre-capitalist Economic Formations* (ed. E. Hobsbawm), (International Publishers, 1964); and Centre d'Etudes et de Recherches Marxistes, Sur le 'Mode de Production Asiatique', (Editions Sociales, 1969).

20 C. Coquery-Vidrovitch, 'Recherches sur un Mode de Production Afriquain', *La Pensee*, April 1968; and I. Varga, 'African Mode of Production: a Research Hypothesis', Universities of East Africa Social Science Conference, Dar es Salaam, December 1970.

21 The term is best avoided, owing to the pejorative implications attached to the word 'primitive' by anthropologists of the colonial period.

22 Nyerere, 'Socialism and Rural Development', p. 339.

23 A. Cabral, 'The Weapon of Theory' (1966) in *Revolution in Guinea: Selected Texts* (Stage 1, 1969), p. 79.

24 I. Potekhin, 'On African Socialism: A Soviet View', in Friedland and Rosberg, *African Socialism*.

25 For an overview of Africa's part in the international capitalist system, see W. Rodney, *How Europe Underdeveloped Africa* (Bogle-L'Ouverture Publications, 1972.) It should be noted that if capitalism is seen as a total system, it would not even be necessary to advance an argument concerning skipping of stages.

26 Marx and Engels, *Selected Works*, Vol. 2 and *Selected Correspondence*, Engels to C. Schmidt and J. Bloch, 1890. These are two of the clear instances.

27 T. Mboya, 'African Socialism' in Friedland and Rosberg, *African Socialism*.

28 See I.G. Shivji, 'Tanzania the Silent Class Struggle', Universities of East Africa Social Science Conference, Dar es Salaam, December 1970.

29 The variety of socio-economic formations is stressed in *Socialism and Rural Development*.

30 For a brazen piece of imperialist 'academic' writing along these lines, see W.A. Nighswonger, *Rural Pacification in Vietnam* (Praeger, 1966).

31 K. Marx, *Capital*, Vol. 3, (Foreign Languages Publishing, 1962), p. 591.

32 C. Morse, 'The Economics of African Socialism', in Friedland and Rosberg, *African Socialism*.

33 In 1971, Swedish comrades reprinted 'The Silent Class Struggle' by Issa Shivji, along with comments by Saul, Rodney and Szentes. In an appended paragraph, it is stated provocatively that 'the ideology of African Socialism – be it developed by Tom Mboya, Leopold Sedar Senghor or Julius Nyerere – denies the existence of classes in African societies.' See Zenit Reprint 6, Stockholm.

34 It could be said that the formulation of 'Education for Self-Reliance' had roots in the inadequacy of the colonial education system, with particular reference to the bottleneck at the secondary school level. The coup in Uganda sparked off the *Mwongozo*, while at the time of writing, the problem of foreign exchange has led to restrictions on the importation of private cars, which politically is a curb on conspicuous consumption by the petty bourgeoisie.

35 With reference to the Russian situation, both Marx and Lenin had the highest regard for Chernyshevsky. In Cuba, José Martí falls into the same category, while Fidel Castro himself is a living example of transition from honest committed bourgeois idealism to Scientific Socialism.

14. Class Contradictions in Tanzania

1   *Editors' note:* The Tanganyika African National Union.
2   *Editors' note:* The Convention People's Party.
3   *Editors' note:* Referring to Mao's *Little Red Book*, or *Quotations from Chairman Mao Zedong*, which translated Mao's essays, texts, and polemics into aphoristic sayings. Among the most widely distributed books in history, it was ubiquitous reference point in the People's Republic, especially from the 1950s to the 1970s.

15. Transition

1   *Editors' Note:* Signed in February 1975 in Lomé, Togo, the convention was a trade and aid agreement between the then European Economic Community and seventy-one African, Caribbean and Pacific countries, particularly those who were formerly colonized by the British, Dutch, Belgian and French. It allowed for duty free agriculture and mineral exports and promised 3 billion in aid and investment from the ECC toward the ACP group countries.

16. Decolonization

1   *Editors' note:* The Afars and the Issas of Africa was the name given to the overseas territory of French Somaliland between 1966 and 1977 before it became present-day Djibouti.
2   *Editors' note:* The Liberation Front of Mozambique.
3   The committee was set up in 1963 by the Organization of African Unity (OAU); its formal name was the Coordinating Committee for the Liberation of Africa.
4   The People's Movement for the Liberation of Angola.
5   The National Union for the Total Independence of Angola.
6   The National Front for the Liberation of Angola.

Index

Walter Rodney
Foundation

Walter Rodney (1942–1980) was a historian, Africanist, professor, author and scholar-activist. Rodney challenged assumptions of Western historians about African history, provided a framework to address the underdevelopment of the African continent and its people, and proposed new standards for analyzing the history of oppressed peoples. Rodney's works provide a platform to discuss contemporary issues and are comprehensive historical resources.

The Walter Rodney Foundation (WRF) is a 501(c)(3) not-for-profit organization that was formed by the Rodney Family to share the life and works of Dr. Walter Rodney with students, scholars, researchers, activists and communities worldwide. The WRF seeks to advance Rodney's contributions to the praxis of scholarship, political activism and consciousness, and social change. Proceeds from this book support the work of The Walter Rodney Foundation.

CONTACT:

The Walter Rodney Foundation
3645 Marketplace Blvd, Suite 130-353
Atlanta, GA 30344

walterrodneyfoundation.com

Phone: 678.597.8754 | Fax : 404.601.1885
Email: walterrodneyfoundation@gmail.com
Twitter: @RodneyProject
Facebook: facebook.com/thewalterrodneyfoundation

KEY ROLES and ACTIVITIES of
THE WALTER RODNEY FOUNDATION

<u>Walter Rodney Papers</u>: In 2003, the Walter Rodney Papers were donated by the Rodney family to the Atlanta University Center Robert W. Woodruff Library (AUC RWWL) in Atlanta, Georgia. The Collection is the largest and most comprehensive collection of writings, speeches, correspondence, photographs and documents created by or about Walter Rodney anywhere in the world and are available for viewing and research. Travel Awards are available. Contact 404.978.2052 or archives@auctr.edu.

<u>Publications</u>: Rodney authored more than ten books and fifty articles, including *How Europe Underdeveloped Africa* and *A History of the Upper Guinea Coast*. An up-to-date bibliography of all books, papers, journals and articles written by and about Walter Rodney is maintained. The Foundation also publishes the peer-reviewed journal, *Groundings: Development, Pan-Africanism and Critical Theory*.

<u>Walter Rodney Legacy Projects</u>: Ongoing worldwide outreach to collect, record and preserve oral history, information and memories about Dr. Walter Rodney. All materials will become a part of the Walter Rodney Collection at the AUC RWWL.

<u>Walter Rodney Symposium</u>: Since 2004, an annual symposium is held in Atlanta, Georgia, during the week of Walter Rodney's birthday (23 March). The goal is to bring together scholars, researchers, activists, students and the community to discuss contemporary issues from a Rodney perspective and how Rodney's methodology remains relevant today.

<u>Walter Rodney Speaker Series</u>: An annual spring lecture series started in 2013, based on the life and legacy of Dr. Walter Rodney. In collaboration with Atlanta area colleges and universities, undergraduate and graduate students can register for the course component and receive credit towards their degrees.